Carlo Pedrioli's *Exploring Conflict over the Professor's Role in U.S. Legal Education: Theory v. Practice* is a thorough, well-written, and meticulously well-documented study of the American law professor from an historical and descriptive perspective. He uses communication theory to bring together both self-views from law professors and views from their consumers: students, practicing lawyers, and judges. All of these groups will find valuable insights on themselves and on legal education. This book provides a valuable extension of theory, research, and practice into legal education in general and the role of law professors specifically.

—Douglas D. McFarland, J.D., Ph.D.
PROFESSOR EMERITUS OF LAW
MITCHELL / HAMLINE SCHOOL OF LAW

In this fascinating book, Professor Pedrioli explores a core tension between the law professor as a scholar and the law professor as a practitioner. His intriguing blend of communication studies with scholarship on legal education offers an entirely novel perspective on that perennial tension within the law professoriate, which has become so entrenched that it has attracted negative attention from many in the legal community and beyond. Professor Pedrioli applies persona theory to suggest a creative path beyond that stalemate, bringing a welcome fresh perspective to a stale impasse in legal education.

—Elizabeth Mertz, Ph.D., J.D.
RESEARCH PROFESSOR
AMERICAN BAR FOUNDATION
JOHN AND RYLLA BOSSHARD PROFESSOR OF LAW EMERITA
UNIVERSITY OF WISCONSIN—MADISON LAW SCHOOL

This new book by Professor Pedrioli is a fascinating combination of rhetorical theory and law and offers a new approach to the history of American legal education. I recommend it to all those interested in the subject.

—Michael H. Hoeflich, J.D., Ph.D.
JOHN H. & JOHN M. KANE DISTINGUISHED PROFESSOR OF LAW
UNIVERSITY OF KANSAS SCHOOL OF LAW

Professor Pedrioli does an excellent job of bringing this pedagogical investigation to the attention of all those who believe our law professors should do a better job of preparing students for the practice of law. He makes a good argument that should be read and discussed widely.

—Richard D. Rieke, Ph.D.
EMERITUS PROFESSOR OF COMMUNICATION
UNIVERSITY OF UTAH

Exploring Conflict *over the* **Professor's Role** *in* **U.S. Legal Education**

Exploring Conflict *over the* **Professor's Role** *in* **U.S. Legal Education**

THEORY V. PRACTICE

Carlo A. Pedrioli

Professor of Law

Southern University Law Center

CAROLINA ACADEMIC PRESS

Durham, North Carolina

LIBRARY OF CONGRESS CATALOGING-IN-PUBLICATION DATA

Names: Pedrioli, Carlo A., author.
Title: Exploring conflict over the professor's role in U.S. legal education : theory v. practice / by Carlo A. Pedrioli.
Description: Durham, North Carolina : Carolina Academic Press, 2024. | Includes bibliographical references and index.
Identifiers: LCCN 2023058908 | ISBN 9781531027841 (paperback) | ISBN 9781531027858 (ebook)
Subjects: LCSH: Law—Study and teaching—United States. | Law—Study and teaching—United States—History. | Law teachers—United States.
Classification: LCC KF272 .P43 2024 | DDC 340.071/173—dc23/eng/20240117
LC record available at https://lccn.loc.gov/2023058908

CAROLINA ACADEMIC PRESS
700 Kent Street
Durham, North Carolina 27701
(919) 489-7486
www.cap-press.com

Printed in the United States of America

Contents

Prior Works

Prior versions of portions of this book appeared in the following papers on communication and legal education: Pedrioli, Carlo A. "Professor Kingsfield in Conflict: Rhetorical Constructions of the U.S. Law Professor Persona(e)." *Ohio Northern University Law Review*, vol. 38, 2012, pp. 701–27; Pedrioli, Carlo A. "Beyond Aristotle: Alternative Rhetorics and the Conflict over the U.S. Law Professor Persona(e)." *Ohio Northern University Law Review*, vol. 38, 2012, pp. 919–55; Pedrioli, Carlo A. "Constructing Modern-Day U.S. Legal Education with Rhetoric: Langdell, Ames, and the Scholar Model of the Law Professor Persona." *Rutgers Law Review*, vol. 66, 2013, pp. 55–80; and Pedrioli, Carlo A. "Critiquing Modern-Day U.S. Legal Education with Rhetoric: Frank's Plea and the Scholar Model of the Law Professor Persona." *Mississippi Law Journal*, vol. 83, 2014, pp. 1049–69. The author has retained copyright to the foregoing publications.

Acknowledgments

Thanks are due to various individuals who, over the years, have contributed to my understanding of legal education, my understanding of communication, my work on this book, my own related studies, or some combination of the foregoing.

I begin with professional connections. In the early 2000s, I was a law student at the University of the Pacific, McGeorge School of Law in Sacramento, California. For numerous conversations about legal education when I was trying to make sense of it, I thank Thomas Main.

During the mid-2000s, I was a graduate student in communication at the University of Utah in Salt Lake City, Utah. For introductions to new ideas about communication related, or that could be related, to law and its institutions, as well as for feedback on my own ideas, I thank David Vergobbi, Richard Rieke, Tarla Rai Peterson, Lisa Flores, Marouf Hasian, and Geoffrey Klinger. I also thank Wayne McCormack for bringing a legal perspective to discussing ideas about communication and for offering feedback on my ideas.

From 2015 to 2017, I was a visiting scholar at the American Bar Foundation at Northwestern Pritzker School of Law in Chicago, Illinois. For facilitating my visit, during which I worked on this book and other projects, I thank Jothie Rajah and Ajay Mehrotra. For various discussions about legal education, both past and present, which drew upon perspectives from anthropology and political science, I thank Elizabeth Mertz and Stephen Daniels.

Over the years, library staff members at various institutions have assisted me in locating sources. For this support, I thank librarians Patricia Brown, Louis Rosen, and Diana Botluk, as well as library assistant Caroline Devine.

I also thank anonymous library staff members who were working quietly in the backgrounds of large institutions to locate sources.

In terms of the review process, Michael Hoeflich, despite facing health challenges, offered sustained feedback on the manuscript, including recommendations for sometimes obscure, but nonetheless useful, additional sources. Stephen Sheppard added constructive criticism. I thank them for helping to strengthen the manuscript.

For interest in the manuscript and handling the technical and promotional sides of the publication process, I thank the staff at Carolina Academic Press. I hope that the partnership with Carolina Academic will be fruitful.

Moving beyond professional connections, I continue with personal connections. Although not legally trained, my parents Charles and Christine Pedrioli supported my law studies, as did my aunts Adriana and Carmen Pedrioli. Relatives often provide students with quiet background support that enables study, which is what happened in my case. For this support, as well as for that of my other educational endeavors, I am grateful.

More recently, my brother Chad Pedrioli provided copyediting of the manuscript for this book, as well as a review of the proofs. With some persistence, my friend Alina Oknianska successfully located graphic designer Rhea Mathew, whose work the cover reflects, along with that of Steve Oliva of Carolina Academic. I offer my appreciation for the support.

When I was a law student, Bobby Gabell was the husband of my classmate Paula Gabell. During my time in law school and graduate school, as well as when I was beginning my career as a professor, Bobby and I had countless conversations about numerous subjects, including higher education—and particularly law school—often while breaking bread together. Having had law school as a third party in his marriage for several years, Bobby, himself a non-traditional undergraduate student in government who managed to fit four years of higher education into twelve years of life, offered the following observation about the traditional pedagogy of U.S. legal education: "If they taught people to swim the way they teach law school, half the people would drown." For the conversations about law school, as well as the friendship, I thank Bobby.

INTRODUCTION

New Light on an Old Problem

In the wake of the collapse of the housing market and the resulting financial meltdown of 2008, the legal profession in the United States faced serious problems. Many law graduates had difficulty finding suitable employment (Palazzolo). For instance, nine months after graduation, only 55% of the class of 2011 had found full-time, long-term employment that required a law degree (Palazzolo). Numerous recent law graduates were only able to find part-time or temporary work (Bourne 658). Larger private firms were unable to hire new graduates, and some such firms even had to rescind employment offers or delay starting dates for new attorneys for up to a year (Bourne 657). Many experienced attorneys simply lost their jobs (Organ 897). Also, with the continued development of the Internet, fewer lawyers were needed for research, and some research went overseas (Bronner, "Law Schools' Applications Fall").

Although the job market for lawyers was declining, the approximately two hundred law schools accredited by the American Bar Association (ABA) continued to graduate large numbers of students ("ABA-Approved Law Schools," Henderson & Zahorsky). Over 40,000 graduates were entering the job market annually (Palazzolo). For example, in 2010, 44,258 individuals graduated from law school, an increase of over 11% from a decade earlier (Henderson & Zahorsky, Persky). In 2013, 46,766 individuals graduated from law school, while, in 2014, 43,832 individuals did so ("2014 Law Graduate Employment Data" 1).

For years, law school tuition had been on the rise. In 2001, annual public tuition had averaged $8,500, while annual private tuition had averaged $23,000 (Bronner, "Law Schools' Applications Fall"). In 2012, annual public tuition averaged $23,600, while annual private tuition averaged $40,500 (Bronner, "Law Schools' Applications Fall").

With the continued rise in law school tuition, much of which went to support law faculty salaries and research (Tamanaha 52), large amounts of debt became more and more a reality for law students (Bourne 671–72). After the financial meltdown of 2008, the average student graduated owing around $100,000 for having attended law school (Persky). In academic year 2012–13, in 2014 dollars, the average debt for public law school students was over $88,000, while the average debt for private law school students was over $127,000 (Archer et al. 31–32). These figures were calculated from the average student debt reported in the annual survey of ABA-accredited schools, not from individual student debt (Archer et al. 6, 31). From academic year 2005–06 to academic year 2012–13, student debt by school from public law school study increased by 34% in adjusted dollars, while student debt by school from private law school study increased by 25% in adjusted dollars (Archer et al. 31–32). Between 2001 and 2011, the average private law school debt jumped from $70,000 to $125,000 (Bronner, "Law Schools' Applications Fall"). In 2010, students borrowed at least $3.7 billion for law school (Henderson & Zahorsky). In one way or another, borrowing impacted most law students, as 90% of them assumed debt to pay for legal education (Bronner, "Law Schools' Applications Fall").

Given the dwindling employment prospects and the mounting cost of law school, fewer individuals took the Law School Admission Test (LSAT) and applied to law school. Between the 2009–10 school year and the 2014–15 school year, the number of LSATs administered fell from 171,896 to 102,823 ("Historical Data"). For fall 2010, 87,900 people applied to law school, but, for fall 2015, only 54,500 applied ("Archive"). For fall 2005, 95,800 people had applied ("Archive"). Indeed, the word that law school was not the safe investment that it had been in the past was getting around.

As the glow of law school began to fade, law school as an institution received criticism, often publicly in forums like *The New York Times*, for not preparing its graduates well enough to practice law. Law students continued to receive from their schools only limited hands-on training that would prepare them for the practical aspects of their future work (Segal). Instruction in legal skills was not the center of legal education and instead took a back seat to instruction in legal doctrine (Organ 890). Indeed, the lower faculty status afforded to those who provided skills instruction indicated that skills instruction was often marginalized in the law school curriculum (Organ 890).

These observations were very similar to those that the Carnegie Foundation for the Advancement of Teaching had made in a major report only a year before the 2008 financial meltdown. That particular Carnegie Foundation report had noted that law schools failed to make teaching legal skills a priority and, among other recommendations, urged law schools to make more of an effort to teach such skills in a meaningful way (Sullivan et al. 188, 191–93).

Along with the institution of law school, the law professor, "both the gatekeeper[] and molder[] of the [legal] profession" (Borthwick & Schau 193), also came under scrutiny. Critics claimed that the law professor was only remotely connected to the practice of law (Bronner, "A Call"). Indeed, a key criticism was that the law professor, increasingly the holder of a Ph.D. as well as a law degree, was spending a voluminous amount of time writing esoteric scholarship that was irrelevant to law students, the practicing bar, and the judiciary (Newton, "Preaching" 130–32, 113–25). This scholarship would appear in some of the hundreds of law journals in the United States (Segal). The critique was that such a law professor, preoccupied with scholarly interests, hardly could prepare students for the practice of law. A call went out for law faculties comprised of significant numbers of professors who possessed extensive experience in the practice of law (Newton, "Preaching" 149–50). The assumption was that members of such faculties would be less likely to produce esoteric scholarship and more likely to help future lawyers learn the actual practice of law.

While economic issues such as dwindling employment prospects, the large numbers of recent law graduates, and the increasing amount of educational debt may have been new, at least in magnitude, the issues regarding the ability of law school to teach practical skills and the role of the professor in legal education were not new. Indeed, although issues about teaching law students practical skills and the role of the law professor may have appeared new to individuals outside the legal profession, in the United States, such issues dated back at least to the nineteenth century and had lingered without productive resolution. The economic circumstances that followed the 2008 financial meltdown simply drew attention to law school and put underlying issues in the spotlight.

This book presents a study of lawyers' views of the ideal role that the law professor should perform in U.S. legal education, a matter intimately connected to the issue of teaching or not teaching practical skills. Here, the term *lawyers* refers broadly to practicing lawyers, judges, and academic lawyers. Beyond the economic circumstances of a given period in history, this study goes to the enduring heart of U.S. legal education. To pursue its goal, the study provides two research questions. First, what expectations have U.S. lawyers had regarding the ideal role for the law professor to perform as an educator? Second, if lawyers have had differing expectations regarding the ideal role of the law professor as educator, how, if at all, have lawyers reconciled such competing visions through communication?

As this study will explain, ongoing controversy has surrounded the role, or *persona*, of the U.S. law professor. Examination of legal writings since the nineteenth century will show that lawyers have been sharply divided over the persona. Indeed, lawyers have advocated two major personas for the law professor to perform. One major persona is that of the scholar, who is a full-time teacher, researcher, and sometimes public servant, but who often has limited practical experience. Another major persona is that of the practitioner, who has a substantial number of years of practice at the bar and is prepared for hands-on lawyering instruction. Some lawyers also have advocated several versions of a minor persona, the scholar/practitioner hybrid, which blends academic and practical aspects.

The research that this book will present will show that lawyers who have promoted differing expectations of the ideal law professor role have done so almost without addressing each other's underlying concerns. For instance, advocates of the scholar persona have not paid sufficient attention to the practical needs of advocates of the practitioner persona, and advocates of the practitioner persona have not given enough attention to the academic needs of advocates of the scholar persona. The various hybrid personas have had limited impact on the communication.

Although the first part of this study is descriptive, addressing the various personas and noting the very limited communication responsive to the needs of lawyers with competing expectations, the second part of this study is normative. The second part will examine how additional types of communication beyond persuasion may be fruitful in improving the communication about the law professor persona.

One final word about the nature of this book is in order. The book is not an economic study. The supply of recent law graduates, the demands of employers for such graduates, and the rising tuition and student debt associated with legal education have been important topics for study. However, the details of such matters primarily relate to economics. This book will provide a communication study of the ongoing conflict outlined above.

Works Cited in Introduction

"ABA-Approved Law Schools." *American Bar Association Section of Legal Education and Admissions to the Bar*, www.americanbar.org/groups/legal_education/resources/aba_approved_law_schools/. Accessed 28 June 2023.

Archer, Dennis W., et al. *Report of the Task Force on the Financing of Legal Education. American Bar Association*, June 2015, www.americanbar.org/content/dam/aba/administrative/legal_education_and_admissions_to_the_bar/reports/2015_june_report_of_the_aba_task_force_on_the_financing_of_legal_education.pdf. Accessed 28 June 2023.

"Archive: 2000–2015 ABA End-of-Year Summaries—Applicants, Admitted Applicants & Applications." *Law School Admission Council*, www.lsac.org/archive-2000-2015-aba-end-year-summaries-applicants-admitted-applicants-applications. Accessed 28 June 2023.

Borthwick, Robert J., and Jordan R. Schau. "Gatekeepers of the Profession: An Empirical Profile of the Nation's Law Professors." *University of Michigan Journal of Law Reform*, vol. 25, 1991, pp. 191–238.

Bourne, Richard W. "The Coming Crash in Legal Education: How We Got Here, and Where We Go Now." *Creighton Law Review*, vol. 45, 2012, pp. 651–97.

Bronner, Ethan. "A Call for Drastic Changes in Educating New Lawyers." *The New York Times*, 10 Feb. 2013, www.nytimes.com/2013/02/11/us/lawyers-call-for-drastic-change-in-educating-new-lawyers.html. Accessed 28 June 2023.

---. "Law Schools' Applications Fall as Costs Rise and Jobs Are Cut." *The New York Times*, 30 Jan. 2013, www.nytimes.com/2013/01/31/education/law-schools-applications-fall-as-costs-rise-and-jobs-are-cut.html. Accessed 28 June 2023.

Henderson, William D., and Rachel M. Zahorsky. "The Law School Bubble: How Long Will It Last If Law Grads Can't Pay Bills?" *ABA Journal*, 1 Jan. 2012, www.abajournal.com/magazine/article/the_law_school_bubble_how_long_will_it_last_if_law_grads_cant_pay_bills. Accessed 28 June 2023.

"Historical Data—LSAT Trends: Total LSATs Administered by Admin & Year." *Law School Admission Council*, report.lsac.org/TestTakers.aspx. Accessed 28 June 2023.

Newton, Brent E. "Preaching What They Don't Practice: Why Law Faculties' Preoccupation with Impractical Scholarship and Devaluation of Practical Competencies Obstruct Reform in the Legal Academy." *South Carolina Law Review*, vol. 62, 2010, pp. 105–56.

Organ, Jerome M. "Legal Education and the Legal Profession: Convergence or Divergence?" *Ohio Northern University Law Review*, vol. 38, 2012, pp. 885–909.

Palazzolo, Joe. "Law Grads Face Brutal Job Market." *The Wall Street Journal*, 25 June 2012, www.wsj.com/articles/SB10001424052702304458604577486623469958142. Accessed 28 June 2023.

Persky, Anna Stolley. "Law School? Bag It, Bloggers Say." *ABA Journal*, 1 Feb. 2011, www.abajournal.com/magazine/article/law_school_bag_it_bloggers_say. Accessed 28 June 2023.

Segal, David. "What They Don't Teach Law Students: Lawyering." *The New York Times*, 19 Nov. 2011, www.nytimes.com/2011/11/20/business/after-law-school-associates-learn-to-be-lawyers.html. Accessed 28 June 2023.

Sullivan, William M., et al. *Educating Lawyers: Preparation for the Profession of Law.* Carnegie Foundation for the Advancement of Teaching, 2007.

Tamanaha, Brian Z. *Failing Law Schools*. U of Chicago P, 2012.

"2014 Law Graduate Employment Data." *American Bar Association Section of Legal Education and Admissions to the Bar*, 28 Apr. 2015, www.americanbar.org/content/dam/aba/administrative/legal_education_and_admissions_to_the_bar/statistics/2014_law_graduate_employment_data_042915.authcheckdam.pdf. Accessed 28 June 2023.

Exploring Conflict *over the* **Professor's Role** *in* **U.S. Legal Education**

CHAPTER I

The Law Professor in the United States

The ability of law schools to teach practical skills and the role of the professor in legal education have been subjects of longstanding controversy in the United States, dating back at least to the nineteenth century. Before a detailed discussion of the communication associated with these topics is possible, some historical foundation is in order. Accordingly, this chapter will address lawyers in the United States, the rise of law professors and law schools in the United States, and existing communication research on the law professor. Finally, the chapter will offer a chapter-by-chapter description of the organization of the rest of this book.

Lawyers in the United States

For better or worse, lawyers have played very important roles in the United States. Alexis de Tocqueville, the famous French observer, made this point in the 1830s when he wrote that lawyers "are naturally called on to fill most public functions. The legislatures are full of them, and they head administrations; in this way they greatly influence both the shaping of the law and its execution" (269). Well over a century later, political scientist Donald R. Matthews identified lawyers as the "[h]igh [p]riests of American [p]olitics," noting that lawyers' skills can help individuals in gaining political offices and then in performing political duties (30–32). Shortly thereafter, echoing Tocqueville's point that "[t]here is hardly a political question in the United States which does not sooner or later turn into a judicial one" (270), U.S. Supreme Court Justice William Brennan observed "the American habit, extraordinary to other democracies, of casting social, economic, philosophical and political questions in the form of actions at law and suits in equity" (560). Naturally, lawyers are the individuals who initiate these "actions at law and suits in equity" (Brennan 560).

From the founding of the country, lawyers have been very influential. For example, twenty-five of the fifty-six signers of the Declaration of Independence, including Thomas Jefferson, its primary author, were lawyers (Alexander 631, Malone 205–07), and, of the occupations represented among the signers of the document, law was the most heavily represented occupation (Malone 96). Additionally, almost three dozen of the fifty-five Framers of the U.S. Constitution, including James Madison, the "leading spirit" of the group, were lawyers by training (Rossiter 125, 147, 155, 247). Not surprisingly, some historians have called the Constitution a "lawyer's document" (Rossiter 147).

Over the years, lawyers have continued to play important roles in the United States. For instance, lawyers have participated in social debates framed in constitutional terms to address access to racially desegregated schools, fair apportionment in voting, greater protection of the press from libel suits over criticism of the government, and freedom from government-sponsored sex-based discrimination. Law-trained individuals on the U.S. Supreme Court, such as Earl Warren and William Brennan, wrote historically consequential decisions like *Brown v. Board of Education* in 1954, *Baker v. Carr* in 1962, *New York Times Co. v. Sullivan* in 1964, and *Craig v. Boren* in 1976, which helped promote the rights just noted. In addition to serving as judges, lawyers also have played key roles in legislative bodies (Williams 397). Indeed, over the history of the United States, most members of Congress have come from the legal field (Robinson 658). When one considers, as the U.S. Supreme Court has (*Grutter v. Bollinger* 330–31), the role of lawyers in the business world, which includes offering legal advice to some of the wealthiest and most powerful people in the world and drafting the documents that shape mergers of mega-corporations, some of which effectively control the national and international media (Herman & McChesney 52–53), the importance of the profession becomes even greater.

Prospective lawyers become lawyers through training and practice. In the United States today, this process involves legal education as a graduate program within the university system. In general, after obtaining a bachelor's degree, a prospective lawyer endures three years of rigorous study to obtain a juris doctor, or doctor of jurisprudence, degree (J.D.) and then sits for a state bar examination.

The central figure in the education of prospective lawyers, "the principal actor in the [law school] classroom," is the law professor (Borthwick & Schau 195). In many cases, the law professor can represent students' first encounters with the legal field and has the opportunity to make "a positive impact" on law students (Ostrom 540). Naturally, the law professor can make a negative impact on students, too. Either way, the law professor helps shape the way law students view the legal field because, when interacting with students, "the law professor . . . convey[s] a sense of what it means to be a lawyer" (Ostrom 540).

Within the legal profession, the law professor has "a profound impact on thinking about law, procedure, and institutions" (Stevens, *Law School* xiii). Today, because "[t]he American law professor is American legal education" (McFarland, "Self-Images . . . : Rethinking the Schism" 232), he or she is "both the gatekeeper[] and molder[] of the profession" (Borthwick & Schau 193). The law professor is the one who initially socializes students for the legal profession (Mertz 21–22). In doing so, this figure introduces students to "the worldview and practices of a new profession" (Mertz 22). In 1927, Felix Frankfurter, then a law professor at Harvard University and a future justice on the U.S. Supreme Court, observed, "In the last analysis, the law is what the lawyers are. And the law and the lawyers are what the law schools make them" (Edwards, "The Growing Disjunction" 34). Given such "a tremendous influence" that the law professor has on the U.S. legal system (E. Gilmore 230), one might think of the law professor as a senior high priest among the high priests.

Despite the significance for the education of lawyers in the United States that the law professor has, as well as the "profound effect on . . . American life" more generally (Presser 6), public awareness of the specific dimensions of the law professor's role is limited. For members of the public who do not have family members or close friends in the legal profession, encounters with, and thus understandings of, the U.S. law professor are necessarily limited to media encounters. As someone who has not been to Washington, D.C., but has some familiarity with the monuments on the National Mall via media, may understand, media can function as a substitute for actual encounters that one has not had.

Thus, for most members of the U.S. public, an understanding of the law professor has to stem from media artifacts. The "archetype of the law professor" comes from the 1973 film *The Paper Chase* (Warkentine 112), "[t]he most enduring example of a Hollywood film with a law professor as teacher," which was based on a novel by John Jay Osborn, Jr. (Papke 966). In *The Paper Chase*, a young man from Minnesota named James Hart confronts Professor Charles

Kingsfield at Harvard Law School to solve the year-long mystery of Contracts, which the professor teaches. Kingsfield is the "all-knowing older White male authority figure" capable of repeatedly stumping law students (Warkentine 112), and he "stands at the center of a large amphitheater armed only with his trusted casebook," asking questions without answers (Hantzis 156). While some students in Kingsfield's classroom seek "public esteem" by trying to correctly answer Kingsfield's riddles, other students attempt, at a minimum, to avoid "public disdain" (Hantzis 156). *The Paper Chase* received reviews in high-profile forums like *The New York Times* and *Time* and was popular with the public (Austin 496, 498; Stevens, *Law School* 246).

Kingsfield is not the only media depiction of the law professor. For example, the 2001 film *Legally Blonde*, which was based on a novel by Amanda Brown, offers more recent media depictions of the law professor. In *Legally Blonde*, Elle Woods, a young woman from Southern California, attends Harvard Law School to attempt to win back her former boyfriend, who has enrolled in the famous law school. In class, Woods impresses her Criminal Law professor, Professor Callahan, and she eventually works with Callahan and several other law students on a high-profile murder case (*Legally Blonde*). To the student's surprise, Callahan takes advantage of his position and makes unwanted sexual advances on her (*Legally Blonde*). The individual who could encourage Woods to file a complaint against Callahan, but does not, is Professor Elspeth Stromwell, a senior faculty member and a female version of Kingsfield (Corcos 117–18). Although *Legally Blonde* received reviews in prominent forums such as *The New York Times* (Scott), neither Callahan nor Stromwell has surpassed Kingsfield as the dominant media image of the law professor (Chamallas 198).

Notwithstanding the now-classic media depiction of the U.S. law professor in *The Paper Chase*, the law professor is more complex than the authoritarian Kingsfield. Some background on the law professor and the law school environment will set the stage for a deeper exploration of the communication regarding the law professor in the United States.

The Rise of Law Professors and Law Schools in the United States

Perhaps not surprisingly, the role of the law professor in the United States developed alongside the role of the law school. Like many phenomena in the United States, the teaching of law can be traced to Europe and appears to date back at least to the tenth century in Lombardy, Italy (Sheppard 7). On the European continent itself before the founding of the United States, formal university education was a prerequisite for admission to the bar, although practical training was another component of admission (Currie 342). Law professors in Europe were academics who wrote commentaries on the civil law in an effort "to organize and systematize the law" (Pound, "The Achievement" 269).

To the contrary, in England, university education was not a prerequisite for admission to the bar, although many lawyers had university educations, but apprenticeship was a prerequisite (Currie 342). Teachers at the Inns of Court, which date back at least as far as the thirteenth century, and where future lawyers prepared for admission to the bar (Bovey 334), were legal practitioners (Pound, "The Achievement" 269). Although today, in the United Kingdom, an academic segment of preparation for entry into the legal field generally takes place within the parameters of an undergraduate education (Swygert 806), this was not always the case, as training for law practice used to take place exclusively in London's guilds (Coquillette & Kimball 22–26). Both lawyers and students resided at the Inns, where "students learned by observing proceedings in court and taking notes, talking to practitioners and judges, practicing in moots and, by the fifteenth and sixteen centuries, attending readings and lectures" (Boon & Webb 83).

Accordingly, while civil and canon law had been taught at Oxford and Cambridge since the Middle Ages, the teaching of common law was unknown in English universities before the time of Sir William Blackstone, the famous eighteenth-century commentator on the laws of England (Currie 346–47, Coquillette & Kimball 22). With a series of lectures at Oxford in 1753, Blackstone introduced to England the notion of teaching common law at the university (Currie 349). In his opening lecture, Blackstone lamented "the long and universal neglect" regarding the study of the common law in English universities (55). Blackstone maintained, "For I think it an undeniable position, that a competent knowledge of the laws of that society, in which we live, is the proper accomplishment of every gentleman and scholar; an highly useful, I had almost said essential, part of liberal and polite education" (54–55). The study of common law, Blackstone insisted, should be "properly and regularly academical" (67).

Although the idea did not catch on immediately, Blackstone played a key role in the development of a new English, and ultimately U.S., connection between common law and university education (Currie 349). In taking a step toward his ideal, in 1758, Blackstone became "the first professor of English law at any English University" (J. Thayer 170). Unfortunately for Blackstone, his plan for a college of law at Oxford did not materialize, and, in 1766, the professor resigned in disappointment (J. Thayer 171). Nonetheless, Blackstone set an important precedent for the university law professor within the English common law system.

In the United States, Blackstone's idea of a nexus between legal study and higher education, borrowed from continental Europe, slowly began to take hold. During the final decades of the eighteenth century, four law professorships at institutions of higher education in the States were developed, and three more such professorships were in the planning stages (Currie 350). For example, in 1779, Thomas Jefferson created, at William and Mary College, the first notable professorship of law in the United States, which George Wythe assumed (Currie 350–51). In 1794, Columbia appointed James Kent as a professor of law (Pasley 37). In his inaugural lecture, Kent noted the following:

> A lawyer in a free country, should have all the requisites of Quintilian's orator. He should be a person of irreproachable virtue and goodness. He should be well read in the whole circle of the arts and sciences. He should be fit for the administration of public affairs, and to govern the commonwealth by his councils, establish it by his laws, and correct it by his example. (338)

Kent added that the lawyer should be familiar with the Greek and Roman classics, know something of civil law, be able to reason well after having studied logic and mathematics, possess a good sense of moral philosophy, and have mastered public speaking (338–40). A notable point to be taken from Kent's lecture is that, to be well qualified to serve society, lawyers ought to have broad educations, and one source of a broad education is the university.

Although, by the late eighteenth century, the notion of the law professor had started to develop in the United States, in the late eighteenth century and the nineteenth century, most preparation for admission to the bar still took place outside of institutions of higher education (Hoeflich, Introduction 6), as it traditionally had in England (Coquillette & Kimball 22–23). Prospective lawyers would work under practicing lawyers to learn the art of lawyering (Currie 357). One key element in the study of the apprentice lawyer was the practicing lawyer's library, over which the student could pore (Rieke 56). If a student of the law were unable to study under the supervision of a practicing attorney, the student might read law independently (Rieke 58). Acquisition of the art of persuasion, if any, came from prior education, observation of lawyers in practice, or reading works of oratory (Rieke 58). This was very much a hands-on approach to learning what was then the trade of lawyering.

Nonetheless, law schools began to develop. For instance, in 1784, the Connecticut-based Litchfield Law School, although not associated with a university, opened as an extension of practical training (J. Thayer 171). Despite operating in "a small shed" that was unheated, the Litchfield Law School, which lawyer Tapping Reeve operated, attracted students from across the Union (Coquillette & Kimball 54–55). Reeve later became a judge (Warren 358). Instruction involved lecture, and the curriculum spanned fourteen months, including two holidays of a month each (Sheppard 13). Students could begin or conclude study at any time during the fourteen-month cycle (Coquillette & Kimball 56). The institution operated until 1833 (Pasley 39).

During the lifetime of the Litchfield Law School, various other independent law schools operated by legal practitioners like Reeve opened, and more such schools opened in the period after Litchfield's demise and before the Civil War (Coquillette & Kimball 59). Independent law schools contemporaneous with Litchfield operated in states such as Connecticut, Massachusetts, New York, Virginia, North Carolina, and Maryland (Coquillette & Kimball 59). Schools that came after Litchfield operated in states such as Georgia, North Carolina, Virginia, and Ohio (Coquillette & Kimball 59–60). Overall, at least two dozen or so independent law schools operated between the Revolutionary War and the Civil War, but this estimate is likely quite low (Coquillette & Kimball 59).

In 1817, two years after establishing the inaugural Royall Professorship of Law, Harvard opened its own law school (Pasley 38–39). The initial class consisted of six students, and, over the next few years, enrollment peaked at nineteen students before dropping off (Chroust 194–95). In 1829, only two or three students were enrolled (Coquillette & Kimball 60). At that point, Harvard Law School came close to closing its doors (Coquillette & Kimball 157). Various factors, including high tuition and expenses and competition from both law offices and other law schools, contributed to Harvard's struggles with operating its law school (Currie 360).

Regardless, in 1829, Joseph Story, then sitting on the U.S. Supreme Court, assumed a professorship of law at Harvard and revived that institution's law school, in part due to his "reputation as a jurist and success as a teacher" (Currie 361, 362). In his inaugural address, Story, connecting law to other fields as Blackstone and Kent had done, noted that "'law searches into and expounds the elements of morals and ethics, and the eternal law of nature, illustrated and supported by the eternal law of revelation'" (Currie 362). However, to gain new students and re-establish the law school, Story moved the law school away from other campus programs and allowed students without college degrees or even college eligibility to enter the law school (Currie 362–63). Apparently, pragmatics had to come before ideals. In his quest to revitalize Harvard Law School, Story was successful in attracting students from all over the country (Griswold 431).

Despite an early failure, Harvard Law School became "the first university school of law in any common law country" and, as "an academic professional school," stood in contrast to both "the purely academic law schools of Continental Europe and the purely professional legal education prevailing in England" (Chroust 197). Although its program drew upon existing legal education in Europe (Reimann, "A Career in Itself" 167), Harvard offered a new type of legal education that previewed the future of legal education in the United States (Chroust 197, Pasley 39).

In this antebellum period, various prominent institutions besides Harvard began to offer law schools. For instance, Columbia, Pennsylvania, and Yale all operated law schools at this time (Sheppard 16). Columbia acquired a previously independent law school in New York City, and Yale developed an earlier independent law school in New Haven into its own school (Coquillette & Kimball 59).

Throughout the portion of the nineteenth century after the Civil War and into the early part of the twentieth century, a growing group of lawyers developed U.S. law into an academic field well-established within the university. During the same time in U.S. history, other scholars were developing the social sciences into academic fields (Schlegel 319), and the university was taking root (Veysey 1–3). As research became more important, U.S. higher education became more specialized (Veysey 142–43). At Harvard Law School in 1870, Christopher Columbus Langdell assumed the deanship and, with the support of Harvard's President Charles W. Eliot, introduced the case method of instruction to his students, moving them away from conventional legal textbooks (Schlegel 314; Chase, "The Birth" 341–42). Instead of lecturing to students, professors who employed the case method that Langdell embraced would ask students questions about appellate cases (Stevens, *Law School* 52). While supporting the introduction of the case method to the law school, Eliot also supported reform in the undergraduate science curriculum and the medical school curriculum (Chase, "The Birth" 342–43).

In introducing his reforms, Langdell drew upon Blackstone's borrowed notion of law as a science, insisting that law students attempt to induce scientific principles of law through careful examination of appellate cases (Currie 350; Schlegel 314; Stevens, *Law School* 52). The idea of law as a science had come to Blackstone from the civil law tradition, which had embraced the concept at least since the Middle Ages (Reimann, "Nineteenth Century" 838). Langdell may have adopted this law-as-science perspective to please Eliot, who had a science background and had taught chemistry at Harvard (Kimball 351; Chase, "The Birth" 334). Under the resulting Langdellian paradigm, law was a system of "unitary, self-contained, value-free, and consistent... principles" for students to learn (Stevens, *Law School* 53). Langdell offered several observations about how law was a science, including the following in a speech at Harvard:

> My associates and myself, therefore, have constantly acted upon the view that law is a science, and that a well-equipped university is the true place for teaching and learning that science. Accordingly the law library has been the object of our greatest and most constant solicitude.... We have also constantly inculcated the idea that the library is the proper workshop of professors and students alike; that it is to us all what the laboratories of the university are to the chemists and physicists, the museum of natural history to the zoologists, the botanical garden to the botanists. (124)

Although U.S. lawyers could draw upon Blackstone's borrowed idea of the nexus between legal study and the university, lacking contemporary models of academic lawyers in the United Kingdom, the U.S. lawyers had to look to continental Europe, and particularly to Germany, "the citadel of legal learning," for contemporary models of academic lawyers (Reimann, "A Career in Itself" 167). During the late nineteenth and early twentieth centuries, common law lawyers thought of German legal culture as "the leader of the civil law tradition" (Reimann, "A Career in Itself" 169). In that tradition, certain lawyers had focused on scholarship and teaching since medieval times (Reimann, "A Career in Itself" 191). In light of this scholarly continental tradition, the U.S. lawyers attempted to differentiate between academic lawyers and practicing lawyers, associating the former, unlike the latter, with the university, "a powerful symbol and an increasingly powerful institution" at the end of the nineteenth century and the start of the twentieth century (Schlegel 321).

Langdell's approach to developing academic law and its role within the university in the United States was controversial but, in terms of influence and longevity, ultimately successful. During his first year of teaching, students came to know Langdell "as an 'old crank,'" and the number of students in his class fell to seven or eight (Stevens, *Law School* 66). Also, some leading lawyers like Oliver Wendell Holmes, Jr., who wrote in a book review of Langdell's casebook *Selection of Cases on the Law of Contracts* that the casebook editor was mad, disagreed with Langdell's approach to teaching law (Schlegel 322). Nonetheless, Langdell's disciples like James Barr Ames, himself appointed to a law professorship at Harvard (Borthwick & Schau 191), adopted the Langdellian approach to teaching law and helped to spread that approach throughout the legal academy. Ames himself had studied law in Germany in 1869 and 1870 and thus was familiar with Germany's well-established model for the academic lawyer (Reimann, "A Career in Itself" 173–74). Despite its many problems, such as virtually ignoring trial court records, document-drafting skills, and witness preparation (Pasley 43), Langdell's approach to teaching law seemed like "an intellectual Model T, a wholly complete, conceptually unified universe to put in the mind of the standard student" (Schlegel 323). Eventually, in 1921, after the Langdellian method had taken hold firmly, the American Bar Association (ABA) recognized the law professor's "claim to primacy in teaching law" (Schlegel 317).

As members of the university, law professors took to the production of knowledge. Traditionally, a major job of the university has been "to advance as well as transmit ordered knowledge. This is the work for which its society lets it live and gives it means" (Hurst 147). Accordingly, while the law schools had the duty of training students for practice at the bar, they also had to contribute to the larger university setting. Potential research outlets that did not last were the *Albany Law School Journal*, established in 1875, and the *Columbia Jurist*, established in 1885 (Swygert & Bruce 763–64, 766–67). One lasting outlet for legal research was the *Harvard Law Review*, established in 1887 (Currie 331). Other successful scholarly legal journals, including the *Yale Law Journal* in 1891 and the *Columbia Law Review* in 1901, followed (Stevens, *Law School* 128). In 1896, the law department at the University of Pennsylvania acquired the already-existing *American Law Register*, which dated back to 1852, as that school's law journal (Stevens, *Law School* 128; Swygert & Bruce 755–56). By 1927, forty-two law journals, or law reviews, were or had been in existence (Stevens, *Law School* 128). In general, imitation was the norm, and the law journals played "a polite little game of follow-the-leader with the *Harvard Law Review* setting the pace" (Rodell 44).

When the idea of a university legal education, complete with professors of law, as preparation for bar admission continued to develop, admissions requirements for entering law students became more rigorous. In 1874,

Columbia University required entrance examinations of potential law students, and, in 1893, Harvard announced that, in three years, all first-year law students would need bachelor's degrees or admission status to the senior class at Harvard (Currie 368–69). The Association of American Law Schools (AALS), formed in 1900, mandated that member schools admit only high school graduates, and, in 1923, the AALS required member schools to admit only students with at least one year of university studies (Currie 369). In 1925, the AALS increased its requirement to two years of university studies (Currie 369). By 1950, the American Bar Association, which had been founded in 1878 (Stevens, *Law School* 27), mandated that member schools admit only students with a minimum of three years of university work (Currie 369). The AALS soon followed the ABA's recommendation on this matter (Currie 369). Eventually, the requirement of a bachelor's degree would become the norm. Although the AALS and the ABA could not define in exact terms the nature of pre-legal education at the university level, they were becoming more insistent that entering law students have such a pre-legal education. In 1948, the Law School Admission Test (LSAT), which further restricted access to law school, was ready for general use (Stevens, *Law School* 221).

In contrast to offering a practical law office experience, university law schools were issuing academic degrees. For a long time, law schools awarded the bachelor of laws degree (LL.B.), which became the traditional standard for a law degree (Stein 315). In part because the degree generally did not require previous university work, the LL.B. was not a graduate degree (Friedman 527). However, as undergraduate prerequisites developed and the program of legal studies became more structured and rigorous, law schools eventually affirmed their status as graduate programs and issued the juris doctor, or doctor of jurisprudence, degree (J.D.), likely attempting to keep up with other fields such as medicine, chiropractic medicine, optometry, and veterinary medicine (Stevens, *Law School* 247; Power 68). Indeed, by the 1960s, the ABA and the American Law Student Association endorsed the change in degree nomenclature (Power 67). Although the J.D. dates back at least to 1902 at the University of Chicago, not until the 1960s did this degree become the national norm for what had developed into a graduate-level program in law (Stevens, *Law School* 161, 247).

While the university law school was gaining more control of access to the legal field, the practicing bar was losing some of its control. As indicated above, before the rise of the university law school, aspiring lawyers generally would study in law offices and work under lawyers to learn the practice of law. Eventually, many states began to move toward requiring law school as a means of admission to the bar and disallowed office study. In the mid-twentieth century, every jurisdiction allowed law school as a means of entering the legal field (Stevens, *Law School* 217). However, only four jurisdictions mandated apprenticeship, and fifteen jurisdictions did not allow it (Stevens, *Law School* 217). By the 1960s, "the law schools ha[d] all but eliminated other means than law school study as preparation for the practice of law" (Schoenfeld 573).

In 1895, James Bradley Thayer, himself a law professor, observed that, in developing Blackstone's borrowed notion of university legal education, complete with law professors, the United States "transplanted an English root, and nurtured and developed it, while at home [in England] it was suffered to languish and die down" (170). Thayer pointed out that "the great experiment in the University teaching of our law at Oxford" had "furnished the stimulus and the exemplar for our own early attempts at systematic legal education" (170). In short, prospective law professors in the United States had taken Blackstone's borrowed idea of the university law school, which came from continental Europe, and run with it. After the establishment of law professorships and law schools in the States, law professors developed law as an academic field, more rigorous standards for admission to law school, and eventually a more advanced degree that graduates would earn. The trade had evolved into a profession that stemmed from the university, and law professors had a crucial part to play in the preparation of future lawyers.

Based on this historical overview, one might expect that the role of the law professor stabilized as the law school, at least at nationally known universities, stabilized between 1870 and 1920, but the situation was and has been much more complex. Since the end of the nineteenth century and to the present day, great controversy has surrounded the role of the law professor in the United States. In the pages of law journals and elsewhere, two major competing perspectives have vied to assume the dominant position regarding the role of the law professor in the United States. One perspective maintains the law professor should be a scholar, whether in the traditional sense of studying only the law as an intellectual discipline or in the more recent sense of studying law as a discipline within a context that includes other disciplines (Gee & Jackson 933–34). Either way, from this perspective, the law professor is an academic. Another perspective maintains that the law professor should be a practicing lawyer of some kind, whether an activist, a clinical supervisor, or otherwise (Gee & Jackson 933–34). Under this view, the law professor is well-versed in the daily workings of law and frequently less interested in legal theory (Gee & Jackson 933–34). Essentially, the tension in this conflict is between theory and practice (McFarland, "Self-Images . . . : Rethinking the Schism" 236).

In certain cases, the conflict has become so heated that parties to the conflict have looked at each other disdainfully. For instance, some academic lawyers have scorned the work of practicing lawyers (Wellington 329), and some practicing lawyers have scorned the way in which academic lawyers teach law (Turow, Leleiko 504). With their professional futures at stake, law students are caught in the middle of this ongoing conflict (Wellington 329).

For now, one early example will suffice to illustrate how the conflict can play out. In 1873, members of the law faculty at Harvard argued over whether to hire James Barr Ames, a twenty-six-year-old graduate of Harvard Law School and a member of the bar (Borthwick & Schau 192; Seligman 37; Stevens, *Law School* 38). Because he had not practiced law extensively, Ames would come to Harvard as an academic (Stevens, *Law School* 38). Several members of the law faculty, themselves experienced practitioners, strongly objected to the appointment of Ames and even tried to block his appointment (Borthwick & Schau 192). While the effort to stop the appointment of Ames ultimately failed, this early conflict helped to set in motion the larger conflict among members of the legal profession over what role a law professor should be able to perform, whether practitioner, academic, or some combination of the two (Borthwick & Schau 192–93).

Given that today "[t]he American law professor is American legal education" (McFarland, "Self-Images...: Rethinking the Schism" 232), as well as "both the gatekeeper[] and molder[] of the profession" (Borthwick & Schau 193), this conflict should receive attention from fields with potentially valuable insights to contribute. However, to this point in time, despite having developed keen insights into understanding discourse, the field of communication has not taken up the task of studying this conflict in an effort to understand the conflict more thoroughly and then to offer some suggestions for potential improvement of the conflict. Accordingly, serious attention from communication scholars would be appropriate.

Communication Research on the Law Professor

Because of the importance of lawyers in U.S. society, communication scholars, since the early part of the twentieth century, have devoted some attention to the study of legal education in the United States. This scholarly literature is not as expansive as it might be, especially with regard to the law professor, whom communication scholars almost have ignored. Searches of the ComAbstracts, EBSCOhost, JSTOR, and ProQuest Dissertations & Theses databases, conducted using search terms such as *law school, law professor, legal education, legal training, legal profession, legal process, legal advocate,* and *legal advocacy,* found only one major prior communication study of the law professor.

Communication scholars who have studied legal education often have focused on the perceived importance of communication skills in the lawyering process (R. Smith 55, Williams 399, Underwood 109, Church 52, McBath 46, Arnold 28). Scholars have noted that law schools generally have not assumed sufficient responsibility for teaching such skills (R. Smith 55, Williams 400, Underwood 109–10, McBath 47). A lack of space in the law school curriculum has been one common reason given for this deficiency (R. Smith 55; Koegel 472; Williams 400; McBath 47; Matlon, "Bridging the Gap" 40).

Moving beyond descriptive work, communication scholars have offered several suggestions toward making "a real contribution" to "the betterment of legal education" (Williams 402). For example, Raymond H. Barnard suggested a non-credit course in public speaking for law students (41). Ronald J. Matlon proposed an undergraduate class called Communication in the Legal Process ("Teaching Communication" 399–400), while Kathleen Farrell and David Hingstman suggested advanced undergraduate seminars in legal communication (151). Matlon also proposed instruction from communication professors for the continuing legal education of lawyers ("Bridging the Gap" 49).

Joining the conversation from the sibling discipline of English, Elizabeth C. Britt urged the adoption of a client empowerment model of advocacy in law school clinics (3). Under such a model, future attorneys would assist their clients in seeing various options and prepare the clients for decision-making (Britt 3). What Britt termed "an attitude of deference" would involve drawing upon the clients' own experiences rather than what the advocates thought was best for the clients (2–4).

One notable exception to the general trend of communication research that has focused almost exclusively on the communication skills aspect of legal education was a 1983 dissertation by Douglas D. McFarland. In this study, McFarland sought to understand the images of law professors, both those images that law professors had of themselves and those images that practicing lawyers and law students had of law professors. McFarland's study, which included both rhetorical criticism and empirical components, concluded that, at least throughout the years studied, lawyers could not agree whether a law professor should be more academic or practical in nature (*Self-Images...: Rethinking Legal Education* 230–31).

The McFarland study left generous room for future communication research on the law professor. Specifically, the rhetorical criticism portion of the study addressed legal articles from the 1960s, 1970s, and early 1980s, but that portion of the study did not consider legal articles from the 1870s to the 1950s or, as a function of the time in which the study took place, from the mid-1980s to the present day (McFarland, *Self-Images…: Rethinking Legal Education* 45). Although he expressed doubt about studying the past of the conflict over the law professor, McFarland explicitly suggested as a topic for future research studying the law professor over time (*Self-Images…: Rethinking Legal Education* 237). Also, McFarland conceded that essentially "[t]he discussion in this dissertation should be read as descriptive rather than normative" (*Self-Images…: Rethinking Legal Education* 207). In other words, McFarland's study offered no suggestions for addressing the problem he identified. Hence, further communication research in this area could lead to significant new insights.

Organization of This Book

In light of the importance of the role of the U.S. law professor since the advent of the modern era of legal education in the United States in 1870 (Hoeflich, "Plus Ça Change" 862), and also because of the lack of sufficient attention from communication scholars in this area, this book develops an understanding of the ongoing communication regarding the construction of the role of the U.S. law professor. Specifically, this book maintains that, at least since the late nineteenth century, members of the legal field, having differing expectations, have contested the role of the law professor strongly.

To develop this position, the book will call upon what communication scholars call *persona theory*. As Paaige K. Turner and Patricia Ryden noted, persona theory addresses the roles, or *personas*, that communicators construct and perform in discourse, which are much like the roles writers construct and actors perform in drama (88). Although not employed in this study, persona theory also can address the roles, or personas, that audiences play in the communication process, whether the roles are idealized, marginalized, or collusive (Turner & Ryden 88, Morris 230). The theoretical approach adopted allows scholars who have identified the personas in a given discourse to understand more effectively "the rhetorical stance and operating ideologies of a specific discourse" and thus to understand more thoroughly the communicators involved (Turner & Ryden 89). Because language chosen in the process of constructing a persona helps a communicator to shape the communicator's identity (Turner & Ryden 89), the critic can learn more about how the communicator in question views the social world (McFarland, "Self-Images...: Rethinking the Schism" 234), which here is the world of legal education.

Following the present chapter's discussion of background matters, Chapter II will offer a more developed discussion of persona theory and its methodology, *persona analysis.* Then Chapters III, IV, and V will examine the various major and minor personas that lawyers have sought to construct for the law professor. The two major personas are the law professor as scholar and the law professor as practitioner. In different forms, the minor persona is the law professor as scholar/practitioner hybrid. Respectively, Chapters III, IV, and V will address how these personas have played out in the periods 1870 to 1920, 1920 to 1960, and 1960 to the present. Also, these three chapters will show how the lawyers who have constructed these personas generally have employed *Aristotelian rhetoric*, or persuasion, a process that has contributed to much discursive clash and little understanding among parties to the communication.

In addition to having a descriptive component, the book will have a normative component that offers some suggestions lawyers might consider adopting as means of helping to improve the ongoing conflict over the law professor persona. Chapter VI will embrace *invitational rhetoric*, a type of discourse that, according to Sonja K. Foss and Cindy L. Griffin, offers the audience of the communication a chance "to enter the rhetor's world and to see it as the rhetor does," but does not require a win-lose decision of the kind commonly associated with the Aristotelian rhetoric of political elections and legal trials ("Beyond Persuasion" 5). A *rhetor* is a communicator such as a speaker. The focus of invitational rhetoric is on attempting to understand the perspectives involved in a given communication (Foss & Griffin, "Beyond Persuasion" 5). The benefit of invitational rhetoric is that it addresses the dialogue that is missing from communication based largely on Aristotelian rhetoric. An application of invitational rhetoric to the conflict over the construction of the law professor persona will follow in Chapter VII. Of note, this application of invitational rhetoric will be about a beneficial communication process, as opposed to a specific content. Because a prescribed content would violate the invitational spirit of invitational rhetoric, the exact content of the rhetoric will remain up to the invitational communicators.

While invitational rhetoric offers the much-needed dialogic component to the communication among lawyers involved in the ongoing conflict over the law professor persona, invitational rhetoric is only one key component in the final suggested approach. Generally, invitational rhetoric is not effective for decision-making, something which lawyers involved in this conflict eventually will need to embrace if they seek to find a substantive resolution to the conflict. Chapter VIII will offer *cooperative rhetoric*, which is a dialectical fusion of Aristotelian rhetoric and invitational rhetoric. Gregg B. Walker and Steven E. Daniels observed that cooperative rhetoric allows for an attempt at understanding the views of other parties, but it also allows for argumentation about the merits of those views (140–41). Ultimately, lawyers can employ cooperative rhetoric to balance the legal field's need for advocacy of personal expectations with a much needed understanding of competing expectations. Seen as an important ingredient in cooperative rhetoric, invitational rhetoric can help develop cooperative rhetoric. From this perspective, invitational rhetoric can assist in expanding cooperative rhetoric as a theory.

Cooperative rhetoric is quite similar to *collaborative law*, a legal alternative to litigation that employs both argumentation and dialogue to improve inter-party communication and thus open new doors to dealing with conflict. Attorney Stu Webb noted that collaborative law focuses on "offering 'kinder and gentler' ways of helping parties resolve their differences" (315). The use of collaborative law in the legal system suggests that cooperative rhetoric can work within the legal field. Ideally, the result of employing cooperative rhetoric will be a more-informed decision-making process regarding the law professor persona.

Finally, a conclusion will address some of the major implications of this research. The conclusion also will suggest possibilities for future research.

In closing, this first chapter offers several words from James Bradley Thayer, himself a law professor. In 1895, Thayer declared, "This, then, is our American distinction, to have accepted and carried... into practice the doctrine that English law should be taught systematically at schools and at the Universities" (173). Thayer added "that our law must be studied and taught as other great sciences are studied and taught at the Universities, as deeply, by like methods, and with as thorough a concentration and life-long devotion of all the powers of a learned and studious faculty" (173). The ensuing conflict over the construction of the role that faculty members who teach law within the university system should perform has continued ever since.

Works Cited in Chapter I

Alexander, Jay F. "Legal Careers in Eighteenth Century America." *Duquesne Law Review*, vol. 23, 1985, pp. 631–58.

Arnold, William E. "Debate and the Lawyer." *Journal of the American Forensic Association*, vol. 3, 1966, pp. 26–28.

Austin, Arthur D. "The Waste Land of Law School Fiction." *Duke Law Journal*, vol. 1989, 1989, pp. 495–509.

Baker v. Carr. 369 U.S. 186 (1962). *Library of Congress*, tile.loc.gov/storage-services/service/ll/usrep/usrep369/usrep369186/usrep369186.pdf. Accessed 28 June 2023.

Barnard, Raymond H. "A Non-Credit Course in Business and Professional Speaking." *Speech Teacher*, vol. 2, 1953, pp. 41–45.

Blackstone, William. "A Discourse on the Study of the Law." *The Gladsome Light of Jurisprudence: Learning the Law in England and the United States in the 18*th *and 19*th *Centuries*, edited by Michael H. Hoeflich, Greenwood Press, 1988, pp. 53–73.

Boon, Andrew, and Julian Webb. "Legal Education and Training in England and Wales: Back to the Future?" *Journal of Legal Education*, vol. 58, 2008, pp. 79–121.

Borthwick, Robert J., and Jordan R. Schau. "Gatekeepers of the Profession: An Empirical Profile of the Nation's Law Professors." *University of Michigan Journal of Law Reform*, vol. 25, 1991, pp. 191–238.

Bovey, Wilfrid. "The Control Exercised by the Inns of Court over Admission to the Bar in England." *American Law School Review*, vol. 3, 1913, pp. 334–38.

Brennan, William J. "Constitutional Adjudication." *Notre Dame Lawyer*, vol. 40, 1965, pp. 559–69.

Britt, Elizabeth C. *Reimagining Advocacy: Rhetorical Education in the Legal Clinic.* Pennsylvania State UP, 2018.

Brown v. Board of Education. 347 U.S. 483 (1954). *Library of Congress,* tile.loc.gov/storage-services/service/ll/usrep/usrep347/usrep347483/usrep347483.pdf. Accessed 28 June 2023.

Chamallas, Martha. "The Shadow of Professor Kingsfield: Contemporary Dilemmas Facing Women Law Professors." *William and Mary Journal of Women and the Law*, vol. 11, 2005, pp. 195–208.

Chase, Anthony. "The Birth of the Modern Law School." *American Journal of Legal History*, vol. 2, 1979, pp. 329–48.

Chroust, Anton-Hermann. *The Rise of the Legal Profession in America*. Vol. 2. U of Oklahoma P, 1965.

Church, Russell Taylor. "The Educational Value of Oral Communication Courses and Intercollegiate Forensics: An Opinion Survey of College Prelegal Advisors and Law School Deans." *Journal of the American Forensic Association*, vol. 12, 1975, pp. 49–55.

Coquillette, Daniel R., and Bruce A. Kimball. *On the Battlefield of Merit: Harvard Law School, the First Century*. Harvard UP, 2015.

Corcos, Christine A. "Growing Up with Popular Culture in the Time of Title IX." *Louisiana Law Review*, vol. 83, 2022, pp. 59–128.

Craig v. Boren. 429 U.S. 190 (1976). *Library of Congress*, tile.loc.gov/storage-services/service/ll/usrep/usrep429/usrep429190/usrep429190.pdf. Accessed 28 June 2023.

Currie, Brainerd. "The Materials of Law Study." *Journal of Legal Education*, vol. 3, 1951, pp. 331–83.

Edwards, Harry T. "The Growing Disjunction between Legal Education and the Legal Profession." *Michigan Law Review*, vol. 91, 1992, pp. 34–78.

Farrell, Kathleen, and David Hingstman. "Teaching Advanced Seminars in Legal and Business Argument: Sharpening the Critical Edge." *Argumentation and Advocacy*, vol. 36, 2000, pp. 151–60.

Foss, Sonja K., and Cindy L. Griffin. "Beyond Persuasion: A Proposal for an Invitational Rhetoric." *Communication Monographs*, vol. 62, 1995, pp. 2–18.

Friedman, Lawrence M. *A History of American Law*. Touchstone, 1973.

Gee, E. Gordon, and Donald W. Jackson. "Bridging the Gap: Legal Education and Lawyer Competency." *Brigham Young University Law Review*, vol. 1977, 1977, pp. 695–990.

Gilmore, Eugene A. "Some Criticisms of Legal Education." *American Bar Association Journal*, vol. 7, 1921, pp. 227–30.

Griswold, Erwin N. "English and American Legal Education." *Journal of Legal Education*, vol. 10, 1958, pp. 429–35.

Grutter v. Bollinger. 539 U.S. 306 (2003). *Library of Congress*, tile.loc.gov/storage-services/service/ll/usrep/usrep539/usrep539306/usrep539306.pdf. Accessed 28 June 2023.

Hantzis, Catharine W. "Kingsfield and Kennedy: Reappraising the Male Models of Law School Teaching." *Journal of Legal Education*, vol. 38, 1988, pp. 155–64.

Herman, Edward S., and Robert W. McChesney. *The Global Media: The New Missionaries of Corporate Capitalism*. Cassell, 1997.

Hoeflich, M. H. "Plus Ça Change, Plus C'est la Même Chose: The Integration of Theory and Practice in Legal Education." *The History of Legal Education in the United States*, edited by Steve Sheppard, vol. 2, Salem Press, 1999, pp. 861–75.

Hoeflich, Michael H. Introduction. *The Gladsome Light of Jurisprudence: Learning the Law in England and the United States in the 18th and 19th Centuries*, edited by Hoeflich, Greenwood Press, 1988, pp. 1–14.

Hurst, James Willard. "Research Responsibilities of University Law Schools." *Journal of Legal Education*, vol. 10, 1957, pp. 147–61.

Kent, James. "An Introductory Lecture to a Course of Law Lectures." *Columbia Law Review*, vol. 3, 1903, pp. 330–43.

Kimball, Bruce A. *The Inception of Modern Professional Education: C. C. Langdell, 1826–1906*. U of North Carolina P, 2009.

Koegel, Otto E. "Speech and the Legal Profession." *Quarterly Journal of Speech*, vol. 37, 1951, pp. 471–72.

Langdell, C. C. "Teaching Law as a Science." *American Law Review*, vol. 21, 1887, pp. 123–25.

Legally Blonde. Directed by Robert Luketic, performances by Reese Witherspoon, Luke Wilson, Selma Blair, Matthew Davis, Victor Garber, and Jennifer Coolidge, Metro-Goldwyn-Mayer Pictures, 2001.

Leleiko, Steven H. "Legal Education—Some Crucial Frontiers." *Journal of Legal Education*, vol. 23, 1971, pp. 502–27.

Malone, Dumas. *The Story of the Declaration of Independence*. Oxford UP, 1954.

Matlon, Ronald J. "Bridging the Gap between Communication Education and Legal Education." *Communication Education*, vol. 31, 1982, pp. 39–53.

---. "Teaching Communication in the Legal Process." *Communication Education*, vol. 30, 1981, pp. 399–409.

Matthews, Donald R. *The Social Background of Political Decision-Makers*. Doubleday, 1954.

McBath, James H. "Speech and the Legal Profession." *Speech Teacher*, vol. 10, 1961, pp. 44–47.

McFarland, Douglas D. "Self-Images of Law Professors: Rethinking the Schism in Legal Education." *Journal of Legal Education*, vol. 35, 1985, pp. 232–60.

McFarland, Douglas Dale. *Self-Images of Law Professors: Rethinking Legal Education*. 1983. University of Minnesota, Ph.D. dissertation.

Mertz, Elizabeth. *The Language of Law School: Learning to "Think like a Lawyer."* Oxford UP, 2007.

Morris, Charles E. "Pink Herring & the Fourth Persona: J. Edgar Hoover's Sex Crime Panic." *Quarterly Journal of Speech*, vol. 88, 2002, pp. 228–44.

New York Times Co. v. Sullivan. 376 U.S. 254 (1964). *Library of Congress*, tile.loc.gov/storage-services/service/ll/usrep/usrep376/usrep376254/usrep376254.pdf. Accessed 28 June 2023.

Ostrom, Jason. "The Competing Roles of Law Professors." *South Texas Law Review*, vol. 42, 2001, pp. 539–44.

The Paper Chase. Directed by James Bridges, performances by Timothy Bottoms, Lindsay Wagner, and John Houseman, 20th Century Fox, 1973.

Papke, David Ray. "Crusading Hero, Devoted Teacher, and Sympathetic Failure: The Self-Image of the Law Professor in Hollywood Cinema and in Real Life, Too." *Vermont Law Review*, vol. 28, 2004, pp. 957–73.

Pasley, Robert S. "The Position of the Law School in the University." *Catholic University Law Review*, vol. 16, 1966, pp. 34–52.

Pound, Roscoe. "The Achievement of the American Law School." *Dicta*, vol. 38, 1961, pp. 269–75.

Power, Garrett. "In Defense of the J.D." *Journal of Legal Education*, vol. 20, 1967, pp. 67–70.

Presser, Stephen B. *Law Professors: Three Centuries of Shaping American Law*. West Academic, 2017.

Reimann, Mathias. "A Career in Itself: The German Professoriate as a Model for American Legal Academica." *The Reception of Continental Ideas in the Common Law World: 1820–1920*, edited by Reimann, Duncker & Humblot, 1993, pp. 165–202.

---. "Nineteenth Century German Legal Science." *Boston College Law Review*, vol. 31, 1990, pp. 837–97.

Rieke, Richard Davis. *Rhetorical Theory in American Legal Practice*. 1964. Ohio State University, Ph.D. dissertation.

Robinson, Nick. "The Decline of the Lawyer-Politician." *Buffalo Law Review*, vol. 65, 2017, pp. 657–737.

Rodell, Fred. "Goodbye to Law Reviews." *Virginia Law Review*, vol. 23, 1936, pp. 38–45.

Rossiter, Clinton. *1787: The Grand Convention*. Macmillan, 1966.

Schlegel, John Henry. "Between the Harvard Founders and the American Legal Realists: The Professionalization of the American Law Professor." *Journal of Legal Education*, vol. 35, 1985, pp. 311–25.

Schoenfeld, Marcus. "J.D. or LL.B. as the Basic Law Degree?" *Cleveland-Marshall Law Review*, vol. 12, 1963, pp. 573–79.

Scott, A. O. "A Rich Ditz Has Both Brains and the Last Laugh." *The New York Times*, 13 July 2001, www.nytimes.com/2001/07/13/movies/film-review-a-rich-ditz-has-both-brains-and-the-last-laugh.html. Accessed 28 June 2023.

Seligman, Joel. *The High Citadel: The Influence of Harvard Law School*. Houghton, 1978.

Sheppard, Steve. "An Introductory History of Law in the Lecture Hall." *The History of Legal Education in the United States*, edited by Sheppard, vol. 1, Salem Press, 1999, pp. 7–71.

Smith, Ralph. "The Teaching of Public Speaking in Law Schools." *Quarterly Journal of Speech Education*, vol. 11, 1925, pp. 54–57.

Stein, Jay W. "The Juris Doctor." *Journal of Legal Education*, vol. 15, 1963, pp. 315–20.

Stevens, Robert. *Law School: Legal Education in America from the 1850s to the 1980s*. U of North Carolina P, 1983.

Swygert, Michael I. "Striving to Make Great Lawyers—Citizenship and Moral Responsibility: A Jurisprudence for Law Teaching." *Boston College Law Review*, vol. 30, 1989, pp. 803–20.

Swygert, Michael I., and Jon W. Bruce. "The Historical Origins, Founding, and Early Development of Student-Edited Law Reviews." *Hastings Law Journal*, vol. 36, 1985, pp. 739–91.

Thayer, James Bradley. "The Teaching of English Law at Universities." *Harvard Law Review*, vol. 9, 1895, pp. 169–84.

Tocqueville, Alexis de. *Democracy in America*. Translated by George Lawrence and edited by J. P. Mayer, HarperCollins, 2000.

Turner, Paaige K., and Patricia Ryden. "How George Bush Silenced Anita Hill: A Derridian View of the Third Persona in Public Argument." *Argumentation and Advocacy*, vol. 37, 2000, pp. 86–97.

Turow, Scott. "Law School v. Reality." *The New York Times Magazine*, 18 Sept. 1988, www.nytimes.com/1988/09/18/magazine/law-school-v-reality.html. Accessed 28 June 2023.

Underwood, Willard A. "A Survey of Lawyers' Training in and Attitudes toward Speech in Illinois." *Journal of the American Forensic Association*, vol. 6, 1969, pp. 108–10.

Veysey, Laurence R. *The Emergence of the American University*. U of Chicago P, 1965.

Walker, Gregg B., and Steven E. Daniels. "Dialogue and Deliberation in Environmental Conflict: Enacting Civic Science." *Environmental Communication Yearbook*, edited by Susan L. Senecah, Lawrence Erlbaum, 2004, pp. 135–52.

Warkentine, Edith R. "Kingsfield Doesn't Teach My Contracts Class: Using Contracts to Teach Contracts." *Journal of Legal Education*, vol. 50, 2000, pp. 112–33.

Warren, Charles. *A History of the American Bar*. Little, Brown, 1911.

Webb, Stu. "Collaborative Law Introduction." *Pepperdine Dispute Resolution Law Journal*, vol. 4, 2004, p. 315.

Wellington, Harry H. "Challenges to Legal Education: The 'Two Cultures' Phenomenon." *Journal of Legal Education*, vol. 37, 1987, pp. 327–30.

Williams, Donald E. "Group Discussion and Argumentation in Legal Education." *Quarterly Journal of Speech*, vol. 41, 1955, pp. 397–402.

CHAPTER II

Persona Theory

Persona theory can assist in gaining a better idea of lawyers' expectations of the ideal role of the law professor and, in turn, the implications of these expectations. This chapter will offer a discussion of persona theory to set up the analyses in the next three chapters of the book. In turn, the chapter will address the personas, methodology, and value of persona theory.

The Personas of Persona Theory

As communication scholars Paaige K. Turner and Patricia Ryden explained, *persona theory* addresses the roles, or *personas*, that speakers employ in their communication (88). While typically human, speakers also can be corporate (Paliewicz 75–76). Scholars have enumerated several types of personas that can be present in communication. More than one persona can be present in the same discourse (Kendall 63, Aden et al. 611). In such cases, two or more personas can work together to strengthen the persuasiveness of discourse (Doss & Jensen 485, 500); alternatively, the personas can work against each other to undermine the credibility of the speaker (Pedrioli, "Judicial Neutrality" 216–17). To provide some theoretical landscape, this section of the chapter will discuss four enumerated personas. Given the focus of this book on the first type of persona, specifically as it relates to the U.S. law professor since 1870, this section will concentrate on that persona. Although roles can be constructed nonverbally (Cali 43), such as with images (Doss), the roles in the case of the law professor have been constructed verbally.

Turner and Ryden described the first type of persona, or the *first persona*, as "the constructed speaker/writer or 'I'" in communication (88). Paul Newell

Campbell observed that this role is "'the created personality put forth in the act of communicating'" (394), while Walter G. Kirkpatrick commented that this role allows the communicator to identify with the audience (12). In literature, according to Emory B. Elliott (49) and Paul Newell Campbell (391), this role is the speaker or character a writer constructs in writing such as poetry or fiction. In a way, this role is a mask that the speaker chooses to wear while performing, and, because the role at issue is a mask, the role is not necessarily the same as the speaker (Sloan 14, 26). In some cases, the speaker's choice of masks may be limited (Cloud 200).

Several examples of first personas that speakers have adopted will help illustrate these principles. Communication scholars B. L. Ware and Wil A. Linkugel noted that, in 1916, Marcus Garvey, the then-unknown leader of the new Universal Negro Improvement Association, faced the problem of leading members of an outsider racial group against social injustice (52–53). In part, Garvey met the challenge by assuming a Black Moses persona (Ware & Linkugel 61). Specifically, in his communication, Garvey relied upon subjects like election, captivity, and liberation, calling to mind Moses and the Jewish experiences from Scripture (Ware & Linkugel 56–61). While Garvey was not actually Moses, Garvey did assume the Moses persona. A more recent speaker who adopted the Moses persona, among other roles, was Louis Farrakhan. In his Million Man March speech, delivered on October 16, 1995, in Washington, D.C., Farrakhan attempted to enhance his image, which had suffered due to Farrakhan's prior inflammatory racial rhetoric, by assuming a prophetic persona, specifically that of Moses (Pauley 522–23). In a related example, Martin Luther King, Jr., assumed, in his communication against civil rights violations, the general persona of a prophet (P. Campbell 394).

The prophetic persona is a contribution to Western communication that comes from the Hebrew tradition (Zulick 126–28). Often, those who most effectively assume prophet personas speak from outsider perspectives (Woodyard, "Depatriarchalizing" 38–39). By adopting one version or another of the prophet persona, and, as African Americans, speaking from outsider perspectives, Garvey, Farrakhan, and King employed

> discourse grounded in the sacred, rooted in a community experience that offer[ed] a critique of existing communities and traditions by charging and challenging society to live to the ideals they espoused, while offering celebration, encouragement and hope for a brighter future. (A. E. Johnson 270–71)

Regardless of which first persona a speaker performs, the idea of this role comes from Greek and Roman theater and in Latin refers to the idea of a "mask" or a "false face" (Ware & Linkugel 50). In this theatrical context, the actor would put on a mask and assume the persona of the mask (Ware & Linkugel 50). Such a historical understanding suggests that a given role is pre-existing, and the actor only needs to select that role from a menu of cultural archetypes, or original models or prototypes, and assume the role (Ware & Linkugel 50).

Although with exceptions (e.g. Jensen et al. 4–5, Brooks 513–14), communication research on the first persona often has focused on the performance of personas that speakers select (e.g. Ware & Linkugel 61; Japp 337, 339–43; Pauley 522–23; Ofulue 50; Lawrence 42; Gibson & Heyse 253; A. E. Johnson 268; Houck & Brooks 36–37; Pedrioli, "Judicial Neutrality" 201–05; McDonald 88). As illustrated above, the Judeo-Christian prophet is a classic communication object of study. Along this line, scholars, frequently having focused on the performance of roles, have not sufficiently explored the idea that speakers construct, via their communication, roles for future use.

Because some speakers may create their own roles (Kirkpatrick 22), not all roles must be pre-existing. For instance, in drafting the U.S. Constitution, the Framers refused to allow the chief executive to be a king, instead opting to have a president as chief executive (U.S. Const. art. II, § 1, cl. 1). After the ratification of the Constitution, George Washington assumed, and indeed developed, the non-monarchical chief executive role, which, in evolved form, remains today. At the time of the Constitutional Convention in the summer of 1787, none of the delegates assumed the role of a national president, yet, through their communication and ultimately Article II of the Constitution, which details the chief executive's position, the delegates created the role of a national president. Thus, noting that some speakers can create their own roles, which then can become part of an available menu of options from which other speakers can select, is important.

While, in certain cases, the performance and construction of the first persona can function together, distinguishing between two major subtypes of the first persona is necessary. On one hand, a speaker can select and assume a role in communication. The focus of study in this situation is on performance, so thinking of this type of persona as the *first persona performed* (FPP) is appropriate. On the other hand, a speaker might construct the role, which the speaker or a different speaker can employ in subsequent communication. The purpose is the construction of a communication tool for later implementation. This type of first persona is the *first persona constructed* (FPC). The theoretical distinction allows critics to focus either on performance or construction of roles. While another study might consider how a speaker constructs a persona in one communication and then performs the persona in a later communication, this study will focus on the construction of a role.

In addition to helping to explain the roles that speakers can adopt for themselves, persona theory also addresses the roles, as speakers constitute them, that audiences play in the communication process (Turner & Ryden 88). Although this book will employ persona theory as it relates to the first persona, a general understanding of the broad theoretical landscape of persona theory can afford a better understanding of the first persona. Accordingly, an overview of three additional enumerated personas is now appropriate.

Discussion of audience-centered roles begins with the second type of persona, or the *second persona.* As Edwin Black pointed out, communication scholars can identify ideological appeals and in turn locate an "implied auditor" who is supposed to respond to the given appeals (112). In this sense, *ideology* refers to "the network of interconnected convictions that functions in a man epistemically and that shapes his identity by determining how he views the world" (Black 112). The implied auditor is not necessarily the actual audience (Kor 62–63). This implied auditor is the "'you' of a discourse who is ideologically positioned" (Turner & Ryden 89). Thus, by identifying the ideological appeals of the speaker, a scholar "can see in the auditor implied by a discourse a model of what the rhetor would have his real auditor become" (Black 113). A *rhetor* is a communicator such as a speaker. Black argued that this manner of reading discourse can make moral judgment of the discourse feasible (113), although some research has cautioned that the critic who studies the discourse should not ignore the context of the communication by focusing solely on the communication itself (Kurtz 280).

An example illustrates how the second persona can play out in discourse. One possible reading of some of Ronald Reagan's 1980 election speeches suggests that, at times, Reagan's communication was morally suspect. For instance, Reagan spoke at Stone Mountain, Georgia, where the Ku Klux Klan historically had burned crosses, and declared that Jefferson Davis was one of his heroes ("Historians Discuss"). Also, Reagan spoke in Philadelphia, Mississippi, where three civil rights workers had been killed in 1964, and expressed his belief in states' rights ("Historians Discuss"). In this case, the ideological appeals, implicit as well as explicit, of segregation, the Confederacy, and states' rights would sit well with demographics in the South that were hostile to civil rights. Hence, an analysis of the artifacts, including the symbolic contexts of the remarks (Kurtz 280), would reveal a suspect ideology and a suspect implied audience, leaving the discourse itself suspect.

Communication scholar Philip Wander observed that the second persona "may be an invitation turned down; it may even be an offensive invitation; but it is an invitation which can be heard and responded to here and now" (209). This second persona is "an invitation to act" (Wander 209), and, when the actual audience of the communication takes on this role, serious consequences can result. For instance, voting for a candidate with a subtly racist ideology can help lead to racially insensitive government policies. On a more positive note, accepting a pastor's invitation to agree to disagree civilly with members of one's religious community over a controversial theological subject can provide for a more loving community (Katz 440–41).

In addition to the second persona, another potential aspect of the speaker's view of audience upon which persona theory can shed light is the *third persona*. While the first persona is the assumed "I" and the second persona is the assumed "you," the third persona is "the 'it' that is not present, that is objectified in a way 'you' and 'I' are not" (Wander 209). This persona captures the experience of negation (Wander 210). Various communicators have constructed members of traditionally marginalized groups as third personas. In some cases, other communicators may use discourse to come to the aid of those who have been constructed as third personas (Pedrioli, "Pope Francis" 392).

The creation of the U.S. Constitution in the summer of 1787 offers one example of how communicators have constructed members of traditionally marginalized groups as third personas. All fifty-five individuals who met in Philadelphia and crafted the Constitution were prosperous men (Monk 10, 12; Levy xxxiv). Moreover, most of the Framers had enjoyed training in the law and accordingly held an associated degree of social privilege (Rossiter 147). The Framers were able to voice their perspectives in the creation of the Constitution, but no women or racial minorities were present to voice their own perspectives. Also, men without property lacked a voice. These marginalizations became part of the Constitution, which, for example, originally did not allow women and African Americans to vote (Monk 12–13). In drafting the Constitution, the Framers crafted a host of third personas: women, racial minorities like African Americans and Native Americans, and men from the lower classes.

A more recent example comes from President George H. W. Bush's handling of his controversial 1991 U.S. Supreme Court nomination of Judge Clarence Thomas, in which Bush framed Professor Anita Hill as the third persona. During the confirmation hearings in the Senate, Hill, who was African

American as well as female, accused Thomas, who also was African American, of having sexually harassed her in the workplace. In his press conferences in the midst of the controversy, Bush employed several tactics to support his nominee: "choosing to discuss Thomas and his virtues rather than Hill and her accusations, ... marginalizing Hill's supporters, and ... focusing on the inappropriateness of the topic, rather than the act of the sexual harassment" (Turner & Ryden 95). In doing so, Bush constructed a role for Hill that was "irrelevant, unimportant, [and] incredible," but Bush never explicitly said anything bad about Hill herself (Turner & Ryden 95). In this situation, Bush communicatively crafted Hill into the third persona.

The final enumerated audience-centered persona that this chapter will address is the *fourth persona*. Charles E. Morris described this persona as "a collusive audience constituted by the textual wink" (230). Like the second persona, the fourth persona is an implied auditor of a given ideological position, but a key distinction between these two personas is that the communication that creates the fourth persona operates at two levels: the level of those in the know and the level of those who do not understand the double entendre (Morris 230). Like the third persona, the fourth persona pertains to "partial constitution by silence," but, with the fourth persona, the difference is that the silence works in a constructive manner rather than in a marginalizing manner (Morris 230).

While this dynamic of winking "to an in-the-know audience" can play out in other types of communication (Gibbons 52–55), the fourth persona is particularly useful in addressing sexual minority communication. For example, the behavior of Director J. Edgar Hoover of the Federal Bureau of Investigation during the 1930s, including his close relationship with Clyde Tolson, another bachelor, has lent itself to a gay reading (Morris 231). This reading maintains that Hoover, having felt the pressure to be heterosexual from a society that feared and persecuted sexual minorities, used the pink herring of persecuting sexual minorities to distract the public from his arguably gay performances (Morris 231, 234–35). This pink herring, which, in sexual minority communication, functions like the better-known red herring in traditional argumentation, afforded Hoover the opportunity to avoid detection by the public (Morris 241). Nonetheless, a sexual minority audience, the persona represented in Hoover's communication, would have been able to read between the lines of the famous F.B.I. leader's discourse (Morris 231, 241). In Hoover's case, the role proved menacing rather than comforting (Morris 241).

As this section of Chapter II has noted, a speaker can employ various personas in communication. A speaker can select or construct a persona, which the speaker then assumes. A speaker may construct a persona for later use, as has been the case when lawyers have constructed personas for the law professor in the United States. Also, through discourse, the speaker can employ at least three audience-centered personas, which respectively tend to be idealized, marginalized, and collusive in nature. Environment, particularly that of the media, can complicate the employment of personas (Waisanen & Becker 259–61, 265).

The Methodology of Persona Theory

Not all communication scholars have employed persona theory from the perspective described in the prior section of this chapter (Hacker et al. 232–35), but this book will call upon persona theory from such a perspective, specifically to analyze lawyers' writings on the ideal role of the law professor. Communication scholars have provided discussion of the methodology of persona theory, which some scholars like Craig R. Smith (64) and Turner and Ryden (90) have labeled *persona analysis.*

In terms of the first persona, at least two types of analysis are possible. One type of analysis considers roles that speakers perform in communication, while the other type of analysis considers the construction of roles that speakers might perform in the future. Although a focus on performance often has been the traditional approach that communication scholars have taken, a focus on construction, which this book seeks to develop, is more appropriate for this study. Here, the interest is in the expectations that lawyers have had for the ideal role of the law professor. Still, contrasting these two types of analysis will afford a better understanding of the study of construction of roles, so this section of the chapter initially will review how one can conduct a study of performance before the section then reviews how one can conduct a study of construction.

Regarding studying the performance of roles, B. L. Ware and Wil A. Linkugel argued that the scholar who performs the analysis should identify a speaker who "represents or symbolizes an historic period, a movement, or world-view" (62). In other words, the speaker studied should be significant in one way or another. An example would be a politician or social activist. After identifying the speaker, the critic consults relevant texts that become the objects for study (Turner & Ryden 90). Relevant texts might be the diary entries, speeches, and other discursive performances of a communicator.

After selecting the artifacts, the scholar can consult a variety of sources, including "the aesthetic realm of literature or myth, or ... an analogous historical episode," for authority on the persona the speaker in question arguably adopts (Ware & Linkugel 62). Often, the adopted persona is a cultural archetype, which is an original model or prototype (Ware & Linkugel 50). These sources offer the critic a selection of possibilities for potential roles, which the critic uses in arguing that the speaker employed a particular role in the text. For instance, in their study of African American activist Marcus Garvey, Ware and Linkugel consulted the *Book of Exodus* for an understanding of the Moses prophet persona, which they then argued Garvey had assumed (54). If the scholar is concerned with the response of the specific audience in question, the scholar may need to determine whether the audience would ascribe to the speaker the qualities of the given persona (Ware & Linkugel 62). This inquiry could be whether an African American audience of the early twentieth century would be likely to link a social activist with a prophetic persona like that of Moses.

Regardless of whether a scholar is concerned with an audience's ascribing to a speaker the particulars of a persona, the scholar still needs to explain how the speaker called upon the persona, which addresses the strategy at hand (Ware & Linkugel 62). In their study of Garvey, Ware and Linkugel made numerous comparisons between Garvey's circumstances and communication and the circumstances and communication of Moses in *Exodus*, including calls to leadership, signs of leadership like drawing large audiences, characterizations of people as divinely chosen, and experiences of liberation from captivity (55, 58, 59–61). Ideally, the critic will complete the analysis with an explanation of how the assumed persona could impact the communication situation. For example, Ware and Linkugel noted that Garvey's communication was a factor that helped him assume a position of leadership in the movement for African American equality in the United States during the early twentieth century (52–53). This was historically important because the death of Booker T. Washington in 1915 had left a void in leadership in the African American community (Ware & Linkugel 53).

Regarding studying the construction of roles, which will be the tool in the present study, a slightly different approach is suitable. In this case, conducting such an analysis involves consideration of articles and other legal writings about lawyers' expectations of the ideal law professor role produced since 1870, the beginning of the modern era of legal education in the United States (Hoeflich, "Plus Ça Change" 862). More details on the selection of texts will follow shortly.

Such consideration involves identification of the various traits for which lawyers have argued in their writings on the ideal law professor role and organization of such traits into various categories. For instance, such traits include participating in full-time teaching and research, as well as having extensive practical experience in lawyering. These traits may be more scholarly or more pragmatic in nature. When considered together, the characteristics within artifacts offer an outline of a law professor persona that speakers have put forth. Unlike an analysis of the performance of a role, an analysis of the construction of a role may not give the scholar the opportunity to rely upon various precedents for the role because the role is new or substantially new.

Unfortunately, research for this book located few examples of studies of the construction of roles (e.g. Jensen et al. 4–5, Brooks 513–14). As noted above, communication scholars often have focused their energies on studying the performance of roles (e.g. Ware & Linkugel 61; Japp 337, 339–43; Pauley 522–23; Ofulue 50; Lawrence 42; Gibson & Heyse 253; A. E. Johnson 268; Houck & Brooks 36–37; Pedrioli, "Judicial Neutrality" 201–05; McDonald 88). Nonetheless, roles have to come from somewhere, so, at some point in time, they must have been constructed. Accordingly, this book will offer a study of the construction of roles.

The selection of texts for this book comes from a search of HeinOnline, an electronic database that contains legal articles that date back to the nineteenth century. For example, the database contains the first issue of the *American Law Register*, which debuted in 1852 and later became the *University of Pennsylvania Law Review*. The *American Law Register* made its first appearance decades before the well-known *Harvard Law Review* debuted in 1887. HeinOnline contains hundreds of law journals, or law reviews, including those at both more-elite and less-elite law schools. Also, a key advantage of the database is that, unlike databases such as Westlaw and LexisNexis, HeinOnline contains, across the board, articles that date from the beginning of the conflict over which role the law professor should assume. Hence, because it contains so many older articles, as well as newer articles, HeinOnline proved to be a suitable database for this study.

The search in HeinOnline identified any legal article since 1870 that contained the terms *law* and *professor* in the title. Clearly, many such articles, although not all, would be likely to address the subject of this book, but, by itself, such a sample of articles might miss some insights found in articles not primarily focused on the law professor. To increase the number of articles identified, the search included locating relevant articles cited in the footnotes of the articles that resulted from the HeinOnline search. Accordingly, while the texts located for this study are by no means all those relevant to the topic, they are both broad in their historical origins and not necessarily limited to articles that focused primarily on the law professor.

Another point relevant to the selection of the texts considered for this book is that a review of the articles suggested that the search successfully located various key positions in the conflict over the construction of the ideal law professor role. When an attorney is attempting to determine where the law stands on a particular matter, the attorney conducts research until the same main points of law continue to recur within the body of research. Then the attorney can be reasonably confident that the relevant law on a given matter is in hand. In the same way, this search identified several recurring perspectives in the communication on the ideal law professor role. As the ensuing three chapters will show, the perspectives include the law professor as scholar, the law professor as practitioner, and the law professor as some sort of hybrid of the first two perspectives. These next three chapters will demonstrate how these perspectives have played out in the conflict, but, at this point, it is important to note that the recurrence of such perspectives suggests that the search successfully focused in on a common nucleus of operative views in the conflict, even if different advocates may have presented the views in slightly different ways.

Several final thoughts about the nature of the selection of texts are in order. As may become apparent from a reading of the ensuing three chapters, other matters besides the professional background of the law professor role are at play in, or lurking behind, the texts studied.

One relevant matter is sex. For instance, the names of the lawyers cited in Chapter III are male. Clearly, women were not seriously included in the conflict from 1870 to 1920. While more women were able to attend law school in the 1870s and 1880s than in prior decades, women who pursued legal education faced "the lonely, often hostile environment of the male-run law schools" (Drachman 37–38, 41). By the 1920s, most U.S. law schools had admitted women, but female law students remained "a small, isolated minority among an overwhelming majority of male classmates" (Drachman 145–46). Before World War II, women comprised only three percent of law students nationwide (Kay 2–3). At that time, women comprised slightly more than two percent of the national bar (Kay 2–3). This proved to be a greater presence than at the end of the Civil War in 1865, when no women had been known to be practicing law in the United States (Kay 2).

Additionally, as one would expect from the low numbers of female law students and attorneys, female law professors were in very short supply. Prior to 1960, only fourteen women served as faculty members at American Bar Association-accredited schools that were members of the Association of American Law Schools (Kay 1). In 1919, Barbara Nachtrieb Armstrong become the first female law faculty member, accepting a lecturer position at the University of California, Berkeley, where she became an assistant professor four years later (Kay 1, 5).

This general absence should not be surprising because, as communication scholar Karlyn Kohrs Campbell noted, nineteenth-century U.S. culture viewed "femininity and rhetorical action... as mutually exclusive" (9). Indeed, the culture at that time had "'separate spheres' for men and women" (Woodyard, "'If by Martyrdom'" 282). Lingering well into the twentieth century, this gendering helped to explain why U.S. society did not allow women access to civic participation for a long time. For example, women were only allowed to vote nationwide in 1920 (Kelly et al. 2: 428).

Even many decades later, as the 1970s film *The Paper Chase* showed, law schools retained norms that were male in nature, something which, according to legal academics Martha Chamallas (197–99) and Christine Haight Farley (343), has been a challenge for women in law teaching. One challenge has been that professors who teach legal writing generally have had lower status within the law school (Cook 65–67), and women primarily have populated such legal writing positions (Liemer & Temple 385, 398–99). A 1996 report by the American Bar Association's Commission on Women in the Profession and legal scholarship that followed the report called this phenomenon the "pink ghetto" (Durako 563–65).

Race is another relevant matter. Given that Chapter III covers a conflict among lawyers in the United States from 1870 through 1920, the participants in the conflict inevitably were mostly White. With the passage of the Thirteenth, Fourteenth, and Fifteenth Amendments to the U.S. Constitution in the years after the Civil War, African Americans had received legal rights on paper, but, in general, those rights did not play out in practice (Kelly et al. 1: 361). Likewise, the status of members of other racial minority groups was far from ideal. By 1920, U.S. society had not come close to fulfilling the promises of the post-Civil War Amendments.

Even after racial minorities were able to enter law teaching in greater numbers during the late 1960s and early 1970s, major challenges remained (Delgado & Bell 349). Often, racial minorities did their jobs "without the presumption of competence enjoyed by [their] white colleagues" (Delgado & Bell 349). In many cases, such racial minorities were "overworked, excluded from informal information networks and describe[d] their work environment as hostile, unsupportive, or openly or subtly racist" (Delgado & Bell 369). Decades later, in the 2010s, racial minorities, including those who were female, held disproportionately few law school leadership positions (Deo 465–66).

Additionally, class, although perhaps less apparent than sex and race (Gordon 153), is yet another relevant matter. This has been so at least since the origin of modern legal education at Harvard in the nineteenth century (Weisbrod 1660). Law professors in the United States are primarily the graduates of elite university law schools (Fossum 507, Borthwick & Schau 226–27, Redding 599–600, Gordon 149–50). Since higher socio-economic status facilitates much greater access to elite institutions of higher education (Jerrim 8, 11; Reardon et al. 6–7; Markovic 827), and "graduation from an elite [law] school may be the most important criteri[on] used in law school hiring" (Borthwick & Schau 230), the law school hiring system regularly denies individuals from lower socio-economic backgrounds access to positions in legal academia (Gordon 153). As such, "a group of law professors who are the product of wealth-based education control the hiring of more law professors who are also the product of wealth-based education" (Gordon 149). This dynamic is especially present at the most elite law schools, although it is by no means limited to them (Segall & Feldman 618).

Cognizant of the above and similar matters that can be at play in, or lurking behind, the texts examined, the present study considers the broad outline of the ideal law professor role. The study pays particular attention to the professional background of the role.

The Value of Persona Theory

For multiple reasons, persona theory can offer a variety of benefits, both in the context of the present study and beyond that context. First, persona theory allows individuals to understand more effectively "the rhetorical stance and operating ideologies of a specific discourse" and thus to understand more thoroughly the communicator involved (Turner & Ryden 89). Because language chosen in the process of constructing a role helps a speaker to shape the speaker's identity (Turner & Ryden 89), the scholar can learn more about how the speaker in question views the social world (McFarland, "Self-Images...: Rethinking the Schism" 234). Statements made or not made toward varying audiences can provide additional insight into a speaker's ideology.

In terms of lawyers' visions of the ideal law professor role, persona theory can shed light on the ideologies behind the communication in this conflict. For instance, some lawyers may want the law professor to operate as a teacher of hands-on lawyering. This type of preference might be indicative of ideologies that prefer the world of legal practice to the world of legal academics. Conversely, other lawyers may want the law professor to operate as an individual who encourages students to think about the law in a critical, reflective manner. This type of preference might be indicative of ideologies that prefer the world of legal academics to the world of legal practice. Still other lawyers may want some of both qualities in their ideal law professor role. Regardless, persona theory can help lawyers understand more deeply the ideologies behind the discourse.

Second, and on a related note, persona theory can open the door to potential change. Persona theory can shed light on possible problems within the legal community. If lawyers have argued for law professor roles inconsistent with the goals of legal education, the legal field would do well to alter its expectations for the law professor roles. On the other hand, if lawyers have argued for law professor roles consistent with the goals of legal education, presumably less need for educational change would be present. Either way, persona theory can help the legal field examine its educational assumptions for potential need for change.

Third, persona theory also allows speakers to have a better understanding of themselves. While a speaker may assume a particular persona, the choice may not always be intentional. However, since communication employed and identity are very difficult, if not impossible, to separate (Turner & Ryden 96), a better understanding of the persona in question can lead to a better understanding of the constructed public self of a speaker.

This observation applies aptly to the conflict over the construction of the ideal law professor role. Studying the texts that lawyers have produced can shed light on the qualities, such as practical abilities or scholarly abilities, that lawyers want in their ideal law professor personas. If lawyers are not happy with the roles identified in this book, they have a chance to modify their communication to comport with different roles. In effect, the research can help lawyers reflect upon their communication.

Fourth, persona theory can help check the influence of very powerful social institutions. As it pertains to the conflict over the ideal law professor role, persona theory can give lawyers a means of monitoring the influence of the social institution of legal education. Legal education is a well-established institution, and modifications tend to come slowly (Hoeflich, "Craft of the Law" 500). Indeed, in the 1930s, Karl N. Llewellyn, himself a law professor, colorfully observed the following about legal education and tradition:

> But, cries the Devil's Advocate, we cannot junk tradition, we need stability, we need continuity, tradition provides the skeleton, we must continue. Right, Sir. Precisely right, Sir. We *cannot* junk tradition. "Continuity with the past is not a duty; *it is only a necessity*." There are a hundred odd men in American legal education who for some ten years have been striving to see new needed things, and do them. They stick in tradition as a body sticks in muck. They are tied hand, foot, and eyes. Five years of struggle gets one hand free, to wave for help. This is why freaks are not a danger: they are very few, they are so little freakish, they are so tradition-ridden in what freakishness they have. (652)

Although change tends to come very slowly, it may be necessary so that legal education uses its social influence more responsibly. For example, new law graduates might not be leaving law school adequately prepared for the practice of law, and the law professor role may be part of the problem. In potentially functioning as an instrument to critique the powerful citadel of legal education, persona theory can be of great value to lawyers.

Conclusion

This chapter has offered an understanding of persona theory, including the personas, methodology, and value of the theory. Because communication scholars often have focused their attention on the performance of first personas, of special importance has been the suggestion that such scholars pay additional attention to the construction of first personas. The concept of a first persona constructed will be helpful in the ensuing discussion of the conflict over the ideal U.S. law professor role. As the next three chapters will demonstrate, lawyers have constructed two main roles that have vied for pride of place in the realm of legal education.

Works Cited in Chapter II

Aden, Roger C., et al. "Doubling Down: President Barack Obama's Doubled Persona after the Zimmerman Verdict." *Communication Studies*, vol. 67, 2016, pp. 605–22.

Black, Edwin. "The Second Persona." *Quarterly Journal of Speech*, vol. 56, 1970, pp. 109–19.

Borthwick, Robert J., and Jordan R. Schau. "Gatekeepers of the Profession: An Empirical Profile of the Nation's Law Professors." *University of Michigan Journal of Law Reform*, vol. 25, 1991, pp. 191–238.

Brooks, Maegan Parker. "Oppositional Ethos: Fannie Lou Hamer and the Vernacular Persona." *Rhetoric & Public Affairs*, vol. 14, 2011, pp. 511–48.

Cali, Dennis D. "'Persona' in the 2012 Presidential Campaign." *Studies of Communication in the 2012 Presidential Campaign*, edited by Robert E. Denton, Lexington Books, 2014, pp. 41–70.

Campbell, Karlyn Kohrs. *Man Cannot Speak for Her: A Critical Study of Early Feminist Rhetoric*. Vol. 1, Praeger, 1989.

Campbell, Paul Newell. "The *Personae* of Scientific Discourse." *Quarterly Journal of Speech*, vol. 61, 1975, pp. 391–405.

Chamallas, Martha. "The Shadow of Professor Kingsfield: Contemporary Dilemmas Facing Women Law Professors." *William and Mary Journal of Women and the Law*, vol. 11, 2005, pp. 195–208.

Cloud, Dana L. "The Null Persona: Race and the Rhetoric of Silence in the Uprising of '34." *Rhetoric and Public Affairs*, vol. 2, 1999, pp. 177–209.

Cook, John. "Taking a Shot at the (Unmodified) Title: The Value of the Title 'Professor of Law' for Improving the Status of Legal Writing Faculty and ALWD/LWI Survey Trends." *The Journal of the Legal Writing Institute*, vol. 24, 2020, pp. 65–70.

Delgado, Richard, and Derrick Bell. "Minority Law Professors' Lives: The Bell-Delgado Survey." *Harvard Civil Rights-Civil Liberties Law Review*, vol. 24, 1989, pp. 349–75.

Deo, Meera E. "Trajectory of a Law Professor." *Michigan Journal of Race and Law*, vol. 20, 2015, pp. 441–84.

Doss, Erin F. "Indie Dyers, Instagram, and the Visual Persona." *The Electronic Journal of Communication/La Revue Électronique de Communication*, vol. 29, 2019, www.cios.org/getfile/029126_EJC. Accessed 28 June 2023.

Doss, Erin F., and Robin E. Jensen. "Balancing Mystery and Identification: Dolores Huerta's Shifting Transcendent Persona." *Quarterly Journal of Speech*, vol. 99, 2013, pp. 481–506.

Drachman, Virginia G. *Sisters in Law: Women Lawyers in Modern American History.* Harvard UP, 1998.

Durako, Jo Anne. "Second-Class Citizens in the Pink Ghetto: Gender Bias in Legal Writing." *Journal of Legal Education*, vol. 50, 2000, pp. 562–86.

Elliott, Emory B. "*Persona* and Parody in Donne's *The Anniversaries.*" *Quarterly Journal of Speech*, vol. 58, 1972, pp. 48–57.

Farley, Christine Haight. "Confronting Expectations: Women in the Legal Academy." *Yale Journal of Law and Feminism*, vol. 8, 1996, pp. 333–58.

Fossum, Donna. "Law Professors: A Profile of the Teaching Branch of the Legal Profession." *American Bar Foundation Research Journal*, vol. 1980, 1980, pp. 501–54.

Gibbons, Michelle G. "Persona 4.0." *Quarterly Journal of Speech*, vol. 107, 2021, pp. 49–72.

Gibson, Katie L., and Amy L. Heyse. "'The Difference between a Hockey Mom and a Pit Bull': Sarah Palin's Faux Maternal Persona and Performance of Hegemonic Masculinity at the 2008 Republican National Convention." *Communication Quarterly*, vol. 58, 2010, pp. 235–56.

Gordon, Daniel. "Hiring Law Professors: Breaking the Back of an American Plutocratic Oligarchy." *Widener Law Journal*, vol. 19, 2009, pp. 137–58.

Hacker, Kenneth L., et al. "Components of Candidate Images: Statistical Analysis of the Issue-Persona Dichotomy in the Presidential Campaign of 1996." *Communication Monographs*, vol. 67, 2000, pp. 227–38.

"Historians Discuss Reagan's Legacy." *PBS Newshour*, 7 June 2004, www.pbs.org/newshour/show/historians-discuss-reagans-legacy. Accessed 28 June 2023.

Hoeflich, M. H. "The Craft of the Law: An Essay after Forty Years as a Law Teacher." *Kansas Law Review*, vol. 70, 2022, pp. 483–503.

---. "Plus Ça Change, Plus C'est la Même Chose: The Integration of Theory and Practice in Legal Education." *The History of Legal Education in the United States*, edited by Steve Sheppard, vol. 2, Salem Press, 1999, pp. 861–75.

Houck, Davis W., and Maegan Parker Brooks. "Fannie Lou Hamer, 'We're on Our Way' (September 1964)." *Voices of Democracy*, vol. 6, 2011, pp. 21–43.

Japp, Phyllis M. "Esther or Isaiah? The Abolitionist-Feminist Rhetoric of Angelina Grimké." *Quarterly Journal of Speech*, vol. 71, 1985, pp. 335–48.

Jensen, Robin E., et al. "Theorizing the Transcendent Persona: Amelia Earhart's Vision in *The Fun of It*." *Communication Theory*, vol. 20, 2010, pp. 1–20.

Jerrim, John. "Family Background and Access to 'High Status' Universities." *Sutton Trust*, 13 Nov. 2013, www.suttontrust.com/our-research/family-background-access-high-status-universities/. Accessed 28 June 2023.

Johnson, Andre E. "The Prophetic Persona of James Cone and the Rhetorical Theology of Black Theology." *Black Theology: An International Journal*, vol. 8, 2010, pp. 266–85.

Katz, Taylor. "The Second Persona and the Third Way: Danny Cortez's Ideological Rhetoric." *Western Journal of Communication*, vol. 87, 2023, pp. 432–50.

Kay, Herma Hill. *Paving the Way: The First American Women Law Professors*, edited by Patricia A. Cain, U of California P, 2021.

Kelly, Alfred H., et al. *The American Constitution: Its Origins and Development*. 7th ed., Norton, 1991. 2 vols.

Kendall, Brenden E. "Personae and Natural Capitalism: Negotiating Politics and Constituencies in a Rhetoric of Sustainability." *Environmental Communication*, vol. 2, 2008, pp. 59–77.

Kirkpatrick, Walter G. "Bolingbroke and the Opposition to Sir Robert Walpole: The Role of a Fictitious *Persona* in Creating an Audience." *Central States Speech Journal*, vol. 32, 1981, pp. 12–23.

Kor, Ryan. "The Commenting Persona: Reception Theory and the Digital Rhetorical Audience." *Journal of Media Research*, vol. 11, 2018, pp. 55–70.

Kurtz, Jeffrey B. "Condemning Webster: Judgment and Audience in Emerson's 'Fugitive Slave Law.'" *Quarterly Journal of Speech*, vol. 87, 2001, pp. 278–90.

Lawrence, Windy Y. "A Crisis in Civil Rights Leadership: The Prophetic Persona in Lyndon B. Johnson's Howard University Address." *Texas Speech Communication Journal*, vol. 31, 2007, pp. 35–43.

Levy, Leonard W. "Introduction: The Making of the Constitution, 1776–1789." *Essays on the Making of the Constitution*, edited by Levy, 7th ed., Oxford UP, 1987, pp. ix–xl.

Liemer, Susan P., and Hollee S. Temple. "Did Your Legal Writing Professor Go to Harvard? The Credentials of Legal Writing Faculty at Hiring Time." *University of Louisville Law Review*, vol. 46, 2008, pp. 383–436.

Llewellyn, K. N. "On What Is Wrong with So-Called Legal Education." *Columbia Law Review*, vol. 35, 1935, pp. 651–78.

Markovic, Milan. "The Law Professor Pipeline." *Temple Law Review*, vol. 92, 2020, pp. 813–35.

McDonald, Nicole D. "The Persona of the Humble Teacher: A Rhetorical Theory to Engage in Dialogue about Sexuality in the Church." *Journal of Communication and Religion*, vol. 45, 2022, pp. 86–96.

McFarland, Douglas D. "Self-Images of Law Professors: Rethinking the Schism in Legal Education." *Journal of Legal Education*, vol. 35, 1985, pp. 232–60.

Monk, Linda R. *The Words We Live By: Your Annotated Guide to the Constitution*. Hyperion, 2003.

Morris, Charles E. "Pink Herring & the Fourth Persona: J. Edgar Hoover's Sex Crime Panic." *Quarterly Journal of Speech*, vol. 88, 2002, pp. 228–44.

Ofulue, Nneka Ifeoma. "President Clinton and the White House Prayer Breakfast." *Journal of Communication and Religion*, vol. 25, 2002, pp. 49–63.

Paliewicz, Nicholas S. "Industrial Pioneerism in the Beehive State: Rio Tinto and the Corporate Persona." *Western Journal of Communication*, vol. 86, 2022, pp. 60–82.

Pauley, John L. "Reshaping Public Persona and the Prophetic *Ethos*: Louis Farrakhan at the Million Man March." *Western Journal of Communication*, vol. 62, 1998, pp. 512–36.

Pedrioli, Carlo A. "Judicial Neutrality Awash with Ideology: Justice Scalia, Sexual Orientation, and Rhetorical Personae." *Texas Journal on Civil Liberties & Civil Rights*, vol. 21, 2016, pp. 183–217.

---. "Pope Francis, Poverty, and the Third Persona." *Iowa Journal of Gender, Race & Justice*, vol. 21, 2018, pp. 367–93.

Reardon, Sean F., et al. "Race, Income, and Enrollment Patterns in Highly Selective Colleges, 1982–2004." *Stanford University Center for Education Policy Analysis*, 3 Aug. 2012, cepa.stanford.edu/sites/default/files/race%20income%20%26%20selective%20college%20enrollment%20august%203%202012.pdf. Accessed 28 June 2023.

Redding, Richard E. "'Where Did You Go to Law School?' Gatekeeping for the Professoriate and Its Implications for Legal Education." *Journal of Legal Education*, vol. 53, 2003, pp. 594–614.

Rossiter, Clinton. *1787: The Grand Convention*. Macmillan, 1966.

Segall, Eric J., and Adam Feldman. "The Elite Teaching the Elite: Who Gets Hired by the Top Law Schools?" *Journal of Legal Education*, vol. 68, 2019, pp. 614–22.

Sloan, Thomas O. "The Persona as Rhetor: An Interpretation of Donne's *Satyre III*." *Quarterly Journal of Speech*, vol. 51, 1965, pp. 14–27.

Smith, Craig R. "The Persona of Jesus in the Gospel according to St. Matthew." *Journal of Communication and Religion*, vol. 14, 1991, pp. 57–69.

Turner, Paaige K., and Patricia Ryden. "How George Bush Silenced Anita Hill: A Derridian View of the Third Persona in Public Argument." *Argumentation and Advocacy*, vol. 37, 2000, pp. 86–97.

U.S. Const. art. II, § 1, cl. 1. *Constitution Annotated*, constitution.congress.gov/browse/article-2/section-1/. Accessed 28 June 2023.

Waisanen, Don J., and Amy B. Becker. "The Problem with Being Joe Biden: Political Comedy and Circulating Personae." *Critical Studies in Media Communication*, vol. 32, 2015, pp. 256–71.

Wander, Philip. "The Third Persona: An Ideological Turn in Rhetorical Theory." *Central States Speech Journal*, vol. 35, 1984, pp. 197–216.

Ware, B. L., and Wil A. Linkugel. "The Rhetorical *Persona*: Marcus Garvey as Black Moses." *Communication Monographs*, vol. 49, 1982, pp. 50–62.

Weisbrod, Carol. "Brahmin Connections: A Note on the Vocation of the Law Professor." *Connecticut Law Review*, vol. 52, 2021, pp. 1653–82.

Woodyard, Kerith M. "Depatriarchalizing in Rhetorical Theory: Toward a Feminist Prophetic Tradition." *Ohio Communication Journal*, vol. 48, 2010, pp. 27–42.

---. "'If by Martyrdom I Can Advance My Race One Step, I Am Ready for It': Prophetic *Ethos* and the Reception of Elizabeth Cady Stanton's *The Woman's Bible*." *Journal of Communication and Religion*, vol. 31, 2008, pp. 272–326.

Zulick, Margaret D. "The Agon of Jeremiah: On the Dialogic Invention of Prophetic Ethos." *Quarterly Journal of Speech*, vol. 78, 1992, pp. 125–48.

CHAPTER III

1870–1920
The Conflict over the Construction of the Ideal Law Professor Persona in the Early Days of a New Paradigm in U.S. Legal Education

As Chapter I noted, in the antebellum period, various independent law schools operated, as did law schools at several elite institutions of higher education. Nonetheless, during the nineteenth century, apprenticeship flourished as the primary means of preparation for law practice, and academics did not play a part in the apprenticeship system (Coquillette & Kimball 50). This situation would change. In the 1870s, the modern system of legal education began to develop (Hoeflich, "Plus Ça Change" 862). Harvard Law School, which Justice Joseph Story had helped to save decades earlier, led the way (W. Johnson xii). At a time when the social sciences were developing into professionalized disciplines, key lawyers at Harvard were developing law into another professionalized discipline (Schlegel 313–14).

During this period, lawyers who supported the law school approach to legal education faced the challenge of justifying their non-mainstream approach (Schlegel 320). These lawyers needed to distinguish their product from the much more traditional product of law office study. To do so, they attempted to differentiate between academic lawyers and practicing lawyers and chose to associate the former, unlike the latter, with the university, "a powerful symbol and an increasingly powerful institution" at the end of the nineteenth century and the start of the twentieth century (Schlegel 321). From this perspective, the lawyer with a law school education could claim the benefit of having studied law under university legal scholars. As the nineteenth century drew to a close, university law school attendance became increasingly more important (Epstein 27), and this trend toward professionalization continued until, in the early 1920s, the American Bar Association recognized the law professor's "claim to primacy in teaching law" (Schlegel 317). The law schools were taking over, and the law professor was a key player in the drama.

In associating legal education with the university, lawyers who supported the academic study of law attempted to raise standards for law school admission, legal study, and bar admission. The raised standards included the requirements of some university education prior to law school and more time spent in the study of law (Bartholomew 388). For example, at Harvard Law School, students without undergraduate degrees had to pass entrance examinations comprised of subjects such as William Blackstone's *Commentaries* and Latin or French (Friedman 530–31). Also, the faculty at Harvard increased the program of study from under two years to two full years in 1871, and from two years to three years in 1876, although then the third year did not have to be in residence (Friedman 531). By 1899, Harvard required all three years of study to be in residence (Friedman 531). The elevated standards for university law schools precluded many immigrants and children of immigrants from attending law school at universities, which may have pleased some of the lawyers at the law schools that sought more "respectability" (Bartholomew 388).

As Chapter II explained, the first persona is "the constructed speaker/writer or 'I' of discourse" (Turner & Ryden 88). The present chapter traces the portion of the conflict over the ideal first persona of the law professor between 1870 and 1920. During this time, advocates of change were making their case to the legal field, and the law schools were vying to assume control of access to the legal profession. A resulting dominant persona that was constructed would manifest itself in the law school classroom for years to come, thus significantly impacting the education of future lawyers and U.S. society. To trace that conflict, the chapter will consider the various roles that emerged in the conflict, including the law professor as scholar, the law professor as practitioner, and the law professor as scholar/practitioner hybrid. Each section also will address the type of rhetoric that lawyers employed.

The Law Professor as Scholar

Beginning in the late nineteenth century, key players at Harvard Law School and other elite law schools energetically advocated a new law professor persona, much as, in creating the U.S. Constitution, the Framers opted to create a new chief executive persona, that of a non-monarch (U.S. Const. art. II, § 1, cl. 1). James Barr Ames, first a professor and later a dean at Harvard Law School, maintained that the law professorship would be "a new career in the legal profession" (136). William R. Vance, a professor at Yale Law School, referred to this persona as that which "the new class of lawyers just emerging into group consciousness" would adopt (7). As communication scholar Craig Smith suggested is possible (59–63), this law professor persona involved multiple dimensions, specifically at least four key dimensions, including an almost exclusive professional commitment, teaching duties, research, and a public function.

In constructing this persona, lawyers called upon *Aristotelian rhetoric* because the lawyers were making and supporting claims to advance their position, as well as occasionally refuting the other major position in the conflict, that of the pro-practitioner camp. Aristotelian rhetoric has the goal of persuasion (Leff 6), whereas *invitational rhetoric*, another type of rhetoric, has the goal of developing understanding of other perspectives (Foss & Griffin, "Beyond Persuasion" 5). In adopting the former type of rhetoric, the lawyers advanced four main claims. First, the law professor persona should involve devoting almost all professional time to the university. Second, the law professor persona should include a teaching dimension. Third, the law professor persona should have a research dimension. Fourth, the law professor persona should include a public function dimension. To support these major claims that comprised the scholar persona, lawyers offered various types of evidence. This discussion examines the arguments that fleshed out this scholar persona.

First, under this new position, pro-scholar advocates argued that the law professor should devote almost all professional time to the university (Ames 137). Ames noted that "[t]he work of a law professor is strenuous enough to tax the energies of the most vigorous and demands an undivided allegiance" (137). To support his vision for this dimension of the law professor persona, Ames claimed that, at various law schools like Harvard, Columbia, Virginia, Washington and Lee, Cornell, and Stanford, a professional devotion had become the norm for law professors (137). Vance agreed with Ames (4). James Bradley Thayer of Harvard offered essentially the same position on this point that the law professor should devote a career to the university, specifically noting that law belonged in the university setting and adding that a "studious faculty" should guide the study of law (173). Professors "shall give, substantially, their whole time and strength to the work," Thayer urged (183).

In advancing this argument and also, in part, refuting the claim that opponents of this position made regarding the need for practical experience, another Thayer at Harvard, Ezra Ripley Thayer, explained what might happen if a law professor had substantial duties outside of the university. If a law professor had to practice law, the uncertainties of legal practice, especially the timing of trials, could conflict with the law professor's teaching (E. Thayer 269). Indeed, "the impossibility of combining a trial practice with proper teaching" was a problem (E. Thayer 269). Ezra Ripley Thayer suggested that, if the number of treatises law professors had produced had declined, this was due to the lack of time for production of such research (272–73). In short, law professors were not to spend much time in the practice of law; rather, the university deserved their almost undivided attention.

Second, advocates of the scholar persona argued that the law professor persona should include a teaching dimension. The law professor who had mastered an area of law had to find ways to teach that area of law to students (Ames 138). Ames endorsed the Langdellian inductive method of legal studies, by which students would ascertain legal principles from appellate cases and discern where the law stood on a given matter (139). The professor would lead classroom debates on a subject, and ideally the debates would continue outside the classroom so that the students would have vigorously engaged the course materials (Ames 140). H. B. Hutchins of the University of Michigan also noted the importance of teaching as one dimension of the law professor persona (371), as did Felix Frankfurter (539), who eventually taught at Harvard Law School and later sat on the U.S. Supreme Court. Suggesting that the law professor had to place "before his students and make[] beautiful to their eyes those great principles of right and justice that either do underlie, or should underlie, all of our rules of law," Vance went so far as to compare a law professor's teaching in the classroom to the teaching of Jesus in the New Testament (7–8).

On this note, as James Bradley Thayer observed, professors had to devote a substantial amount of time to teaching (183). According to this Thayer, "when the work is fitly performed, [it] calls for an amount of time, thought and attention bestowed on the personal side of a man's relation to his students which instructors now can seldom give" (183). Ezra Ripley Thayer contended that "[t]he mere preparation for [the law professor's] class-room work will itself be a large matter" (271). From this perspective, the law professor would need to spend time considering how to make sense out of what the professor's own law professors had taught the professor (E. Thayer 271). Once the law professor had formulated a personal understanding of the law, the professor would discuss that understanding with students not only in class but also outside class (E. Thayer 271).

While some experience with legal practice might be present, such experience was not the main feature behind the teaching dimension of the law professor persona (Hutchins 368). Indeed, the practitioner was the law professor of the past. Under the old regime, the law professor might have been someone who was "a lawyer in full practice and a teacher only as his professional engagements [would] permit" or perhaps "a judge upon the bench and a teacher incidentally" (Hutchins 362). However, the law professor of the present was "a lawyer withdrawn from practice and its emoluments" (Vance 5), who had learned law "by scholarly research" (McGovney 19).

Christopher Columbus Langdell, dean at Harvard Law School, argued the following about the new law professor, in part refuting the claim that opponents of the scholar persona made about the need for practical experience:

> What qualifies a person ... to teach law, is not experience in the work of a lawyer's office, not experience in dealing with men, not experience in the trial or argument of causes, not experience, in short, in using law, but experience in learning law, not the experience of the Roman advocate, or of the Roman praetor, still less of the Roman procurator, but the experience of the Roman jurisconsult. (124)

Indeed, for Langdell and the lawyers who agreed with his position, a law professor was one who was more familiar with the path of learning the law than the path of practicing the law. As unorthodox as this may have been at the time, the new law professor persona was not oriented toward having a dimension related to legal practice (McGovney 18).

Third, advocates of the scholar persona argued that the persona also should have a research dimension (Ames 141). Calling upon the continental European tradition of legal education, Ames asserted that, in Germany, "we find a large body of legal literature, of a high quality, the best and the greater part of which is the work of professors" (141). Identifying several law professors as "the lights of the legal profession in Germany," Ames took care to note that "[t]he influence of their opinions in the courts is as great or even greater than that of judicial precedents" (141). Ames lamented his perception that legal literature in the United States lagged behind that of Europe, and he desired that law professors in the United States would begin to develop "treatises on all the important branches of the law, exhibiting the historical development of the subject and containing sound conclusions based upon scientific analysis" (141, 142). The advantage of this was that the judge, who was not an expert in all areas of the law, would "have the benefit of the conclusions of specialists or professors" (Ames 143).

Other lawyers besides Ames argued for the importance of the production of research as a dimension of the law professor persona. For instance, James Bradley Thayer justified the research dimension of the law professor persona by claiming that the law professor had "much formidable labor [to do] in exploring the history and chronological development of our law in all its parts" (183). Also, Hutchins viewed scholarship as "[a] first requisite of effective law teaching" (368), a requisite that would inform one's teaching. By the term *scholarship*, Hutchins did not refer to "the scholarship of the practitioner who investigates from time to time parts of subjects to meet immediate professional demands"; instead, Hutchins referred to "the scholarship that comes from scientific and systematic study in a rather limited field of our jurisprudence" (368). The law professor's research would point out "not only what the law within a given field has been and is, but also what it should be" (Hutchins 370). Vance cited examples of research on the law such as John Henry Wigmore's work in evidence and John Chipman Gray's work in property, particularly regarding the rule against perpetuities, which aims to limit control of property by the deceased (8). Hutchins maintained that the ideal law professor persona of the future would be free of distractions that would detract from "the field of research and legal authorship" (371).

Such research that was an important part of the new law professor persona would be specialized in nature. The law professor, Hutchins argued, should not have "to become a master of half a dozen disconnected subjects in the law and to speak and write in regard to them with authority" (368). Rather, the law professor was to become an expert in one, two, or perhaps three areas of the law and publish in these areas (Hutchins 369). Accordingly, the specialist law professor might produce "treatises of the highest class" (E. Thayer 270).

Fourth, and on a note related to research, pro-scholar lawyers argued that the law professor persona should include a public function dimension (Hutchins 371). This public function could play out in several ways. For instance, as suggested above, the law professor could conduct research that would benefit the judiciary. Also, the law professor's research could provide advice for legislators (Ames 145). Further, the law professor might participate in the drafting of legislation, perhaps joining judges and practicing lawyers in the preparation of such legislation (Ames 145). One example of this might be the re-drafting of criminal statutes (Vance 8).

Beyond the production of research for the judiciary and legislature and the drafting of legislation, such a public function included advancing the standards for admission to study law (Hutchins 371). Such standards might include an increased number of years of preparation for the study of law. Noting, in 1908, that four years of high school were the general requirement for law school admission, Hutchins predicted that more schools would adopt the requirement of a year of university work, which some law schools already required, and that, in the future, multiple years of university work could become the prerequisite for law school admission (372). Regardless of the particulars, the law professor would be the one to work on standards, especially because the law professor was in touch with the needs of the students who were already studying law (Hutchins 372).

From a pragmatic perspective, Felix Frankfurter explained why the law professor persona should include a public function dimension. Frankfurter noted that, unlike the members of the judiciary and the practicing bar, who were "overworked," law professors, who were "free... from the absorption of practice," could use some of their time for developing the law (537–38). Operating under the law-as-science paradigm, Frankfurter suggested that law professors might develop legal hypotheses that practicing lawyers and judges would test (538). Frankfurter used Joseph Story's work on developing a restatement of the English common law as an example to further this particular point (538). In this manner, Frankfurter refuted the pro-practitioners' call for the law professor to practice and teach simultaneously.

As just laid out, the scholar version of the law professor persona included four main dimensions for which lawyers offered support: an almost exclusive professional commitment, teaching duties, the production of research, and a public function. While one might have expected that the law professor persona would contain a teaching dimension, although perhaps not one often devoid of practical experience, the almost exclusive time commitment, production of research, and public function dimensions came together to help construct a new persona, that of a full-time member of the academy whose work could benefit the outside world. Although this persona consisted of several dimensions, these dimensions formed one unified scholar persona. In the United

States, then, this was the new professor-as-scholar persona that key lawyers at Harvard and various other elite law schools constructed and energetically disseminated through their rhetoric.

In presenting their ideal law professor persona, lawyers who adopted the pro-scholar position employed Aristotelian rhetoric. This rhetoric involved the advancing and supporting of claims, as well as some limited response to the other major position in the conflict, that of the pro-practitioner camp. The texts studied here did not suggest any consideration on the part of the pro-scholar advocates of competing positions for the purpose of understanding those positions, with the exception of understanding for the purpose of refuting, as several examples above suggested. Thus, the lawyers were not calling upon invitational rhetoric.

The Law Professor as Practitioner

While lawyers like Langdell and Ames were attempting to construct the law professor persona as scholarly in nature, other lawyers, often at less-elite institutions, were trying to construct the law professor persona as more practical in nature. This latter understanding of the law professor was much less revolutionary than that of Langdell and Ames, but, in light of the spirited advocacy of these Harvard lawyers, the latter position required vigorous advancement.

In constructing their ideal persona, lawyers called upon Aristotelian rhetoric because the lawyers were making and supporting claims to advance their position, as well as refuting the pro-scholar position, the other major position in the conflict. Through Aristotelian rhetoric, these lawyers offered two major claims. First, law was a practical subject that called for practical training. Second, only an individual with a practical background could be well-suited for assuming the law professor persona. To support these major claims that comprised the practitioner persona, lawyers offered various types of evidence. This discussion examines the arguments that fleshed out the practitioner persona.

First, as noted, lawyers who supported the practitioner persona for the law professor argued that law was a practical subject that called for practical training. For example, Paul L. Martin, dean of the Creighton University Law School, argued that a lawyer's academic training alone was insufficient because it would "fail to fit the law graduate for that immediate service which he aspires to render" (237). Instead, "a sufficient training in practice" was vital (Martin 237). Relying upon a medical analogy, Martin pointed out that medical students would spend the majority of their final two years in hospitals and clinics in which the students would "learn to apply practically what they have gleaned from the books" (238). Martin extended the significance of this analogy by noting that dental, pharmacy, and engineering students also had practical components to their respective educations (238). Claiming that law schools could give law students "more than mere theory," Philip T. Van Zile, dean of the Detroit College of Law, agreed that law students should gain substantial practical experience (73). Van Zile maintained that law schools could not pay too much attention to the teaching of legal practice because the idea was to give law students as much experience as possible, not only in the realm of litigation, but also in other branches of practice (74).

David Werner Amram of the University of Pennsylvania, who concurred with the positions of lawyers like Martin and Van Zile, further argued for the importance of practical subjects. To help justify more practical work in U.S. law schools, Amram considered the processes for entering the legal fields in other countries. For instance, law graduates in Germany had three years of apprenticeship before practicing law, including one year in public administration, one-and-a-half years in lower court practice, and a half year in higher court practice; law graduates in Canada had to spend several years as clerks in solicitors' offices (440–41). While the German and Canadian systems were not perfect, the U.S. system, Amram argued, lagged behind in preparing lawyers to practice. Amram proposed that the following practical subjects appear in the curriculum at U.S. law schools: practice and procedure, preparation of litigation papers, inspection of courts, preparation of non-contentious papers, law office management, use of the law library, and brief preparation (441–44). Thinking that students would learn trial conduct more effectively in actual courts, Amram left that subject off his list of recommended practical subjects (446–49).

While lawyers were the principal participants in this conflict, they were not the only participants. For example, Walter K. Towers, a law student at the University of Michigan, joined the cause to promote the practitioner model. Towers conveyed the story of a colleague "who finished a year's study of the law with excellent marks, yet did not know what '34 Michigan, 254,' meant" (557). This was a reference to the form for citing legal cases. Towers pointed out that, because law students often entered a new and unfamiliar world when they commenced studying law, one could not assume "that the ordinary law student has, or can secure for himself, any practical details that are not taught as part of or involved in the regular school work" (556).

Second, as this rhetoric would suggest, individuals who adopted this practice-oriented position argued that only an individual with a practical background was well-suited for assuming the law professor persona. J. Newton Fiero, dean of the Albany Law School, claimed that only the practitioner had "a true perspective" as to the various topics at law school and that the practitioner's illustrations from actual practice would impress the student (559). As Van Zile noted, law professors "should be something more than school teachers" (74). Instead,

> [t]hey should be men who have had practice in the profession, in the law office, and in the courts; men of experience in all the work of the profession, as well as men of learning, who are able to teach the law and apply it, who are not confined to books alone, but who can draw from the wellsprings of legal lore gathered from an actual and successful practice. (Van Zile 74)

Pro-practitioner lawyers argued, then, that a law professor who assumed a scholar persona was not well equipped for the job. Refuting the argumentation of the advocates of the scholar model, Fiero contended that a law professor who took up the persona of a scholar without substantive practical experience was very much like an individual who took up the persona of an engineer and then attempted to offer an explanation "of the functions and possibilities of a steam engine, without instruction as to the method of its operation" (559). Extending the analogy, Fiero suggested that

> [i]t would scarcely be deemed wise to place in charge of a passenger train a locomotive engineer whose knowledge of his engine was derived solely from books explaining its construction, and who had no instruction as to which lever should be used in going ahead, and which one for stopping or backing his train. (559)

In short, a lack of practical experience at the bar was a serious handicap for law professors (Fiero 560).

In advancing his position, Fiero responded to the pro-scholar position of Langdell, Ames, and others. Fiero maintained that his rhetorical opponents had "overlooked the fact that there were able lawyers in the days before law schools, when the only place for study was in the office of the practicing lawyer" (559). By calling on a more traditional approach to learning law, Fiero attempted to deny the need for the new Harvard approach.

Thus, despite the rhetoric designed to construct the law professor persona as that of a scholar, vigorous opposing rhetoric appeared in an effort to present a different law professor persona. Some lawyers simply did not accept the scholar persona and made their case for the practitioner persona.

In putting forth their ideal law professor persona as a practitioner, lawyers who adopted this position employed Aristotelian rhetoric. This rhetoric included advancing and supporting claims, as well as a great amount of responding to the scholar position, the other major position in the conflict. As with the texts from the pro-scholar lawyers, the texts studied here did not suggest any consideration of other perspectives for the purpose of understanding, except understanding for the purpose of refuting. Accordingly, the pro-practitioner lawyers were not calling upon invitational rhetoric.

The Law Professor as Scholar/Practitioner Hybrid

Amid this ongoing conflict over the construction of the ideal law professor persona, several hybrid options emerged. Although they may have leaned in one direction or the other, the hybrid options were not almost exclusively focused on either the scholar persona or the practitioner persona. Instead, advocates of the hybrid options claimed that a compromise was appropriate. This point is consistent with Craig Smith's suggestion that a multidimensional first persona is possible (59–63).

In constructing versions of this hybrid persona, lawyers called upon a blend of Aristotelian rhetoric and invitational rhetoric because, as well as making and supporting claims to advance a position, the lawyers employed rhetoric that demonstrated thorough consideration of competing interests in the conflict, which neither of the above-noted camps did. This part of the chapter examines the arguments and considerations that helped to flesh out the hybrid personas.

One position for working out some sort of a compromise came from Albert M. Kales of Northwestern University Law School, who argued for a restricted amount of practical experience for the law professor ("Should the Law Teacher" 255). Drawing a distinction between taking care of clients and taking care of cases, Kales viewed client care as more business than law and something that took a large amount of a lawyer's time ("Should the Law Teacher" 254). Kales believed that a law professor should handle cases, not clients, and, to those cases, the law professor would bring expertise in a given area ("Should the Law Teacher" 255). The reason Kales offered for allowing the law professor limited practice was that, in the course of litigation, the law professor could test various "speculations" of former law professors ("Should the Law Teacher" 259, "Discussion" 10). By testing such speculations, or, under the law-as-science paradigm, hypotheses, in court, the law professor would have a better understanding of the legal world (Kales, "Should the Law Teacher" 259). Additionally, the law professor would be able to draw upon that developed understanding of the legal world and become a better teacher (Kales, "Should the Law Teacher" 260). As such, the law professor would not do well to procrastinate in testing important principles, in effect leaving the next generation of lawyers to test those principles (Kales, "Discussion" 10).

Kales replied to the objection that the law professor lacked time to practice law ("Should the Law Teacher" 265). In response to Ames and other like-minded lawyers, Kales suggested that the new law professor should dedicate time exclusively to studying and teaching law and that, later in a career, when the law professor had developed an area of expertise, the professor should handle some cases ("Should the Law Teacher" 266). At least by the later stages of one's career, this approach would balance both scholarly and practical dimensions of a law professor persona, although not necessarily before that point in time.

Another hybrid persona came from Harlan F. Stone, the dean at Columbia University Law School and later both Attorney General and Chief Justice of the United States. Noting that there was "nothing peculiar about the art of law teaching, as distinguished from other kinds of professional training, which should render practical experience a detriment to successful teaching," Stone argued that a law professor should be both a scholar and one who has practiced law ("The Importance" 206). Logical and practical considerations were both part of practicing law, and a law professor should be familiar with both types of considerations (Stone, "The Importance" 207). For example, practical wisdom might prove helpful in addressing the details of motion papers in a court (Stone, "The Importance" 208). Stone contended the following:

> [T]he man who would become a law teacher, and who possesses the talent for stimulating intellectual activity in others, will, as a law teacher, possess greater power, exert a wider influence, and render a more useful service to his students and to his profession, if he has had experience in practice, and there is always the danger that, if he takes up his teaching without such experience, he will lack the intellectual balance which should come from a practical knowledge of his profession, and he will inevitably be a stranger to its sentiments and traditions. ("The Importance" 207)

To this message, Stone added, "The law teacher has indeed missed his calling who has nothing to offer his students but the solution of the purely intellectual problems of the law" ("The Importance" 208). Like Kales, Stone appreciated the idea of law professors who still practiced ("The Function" 13–14), and Stone was also open to having some essentially full-time practitioners on the law faculty ("The Function" 14). Nonetheless, the law professor should have learned something about legal scholarship as well (Stone, "The Function" 15). In short, Stone wanted the law professor persona to be that of "a well-rounded lawyer" ("The Importance" 210).

While the advocates of various hybrid personas did not reject the practitioner persona, they did not reject the scholar persona either. Instead, as the above examples demonstrate, the advocates of the hybrid personas sought to merge, in a functional manner, the two poles of the conflict over the construction of the ideal law professor persona. Because, in addition to arguing for their positions, the advocates of these hybrid personas looked to and addressed various considerations from different camps, the lawyers offered a blend of Aristotelian rhetoric and invitational rhetoric. Chapter VIII will explain that one term for this type of blended rhetoric is *cooperative rhetoric.*

Conclusion

This chapter has illustrated how, in the portion of the conflict over the ideal law professor persona between 1870 and 1920, three personas appeared. These personas were the law professor as scholar, the law professor as practitioner, and the law professor as scholar/practitioner hybrid.

Importantly, the lawyers in the sample of texts studied for this period tended to employ Aristotelian rhetoric as opposed to other types of rhetoric because, as suggested above, the lawyers were making and supporting claims to advance positions. Because lawyers receive training in advocacy, this focus on Aristotelian rhetoric should not be a surprise.

Such a focus on Aristotelian rhetoric led to notable communication problems during this period. While some lawyers supported one model and critiqued another model, including the pro-scholar lawyers who argued that a practitioner would not have time to teach and the pro-practitioner lawyers who argued that a scholar would not have sufficient practical experience, other lawyers in this period were often non-responsive to the concerns of lawyers with a different position. For instance, many of the lawyers who argued for the scholar model developed their arguments without addressing competing arguments from the pro-practitioner camp. These non-responsive advocates simply talked past their discursive opponents, ignoring underlying concerns.

This point demonstrates an apparent lack of understanding of or interest in other positions in the conflict. One exception to this generally problematic communication was that lawyers like Kales and Stone, who advocated hybrid personas, were balancing competing concerns about academic and practical needs, which suggests that these lawyers had given some consideration to differing positions. Regardless, based on the sample of texts studied for the period between 1870 and 1920, the rhetorical approach of lawyers like Kales and Stone was not a typical one because most lawyers were either critiquing competing positions or generally ignoring those competing positions.

The largely Aristotelian-rhetoric-based conflict during this period was one aspect of the larger conflict over whether law was a profession, often described by some at the time as a type of science (Langdell 124), or a trade. The *Report of the President of the Carnegie Foundation for the Advancement of Teaching for 1913* noted that the issue of whether law was then a profession or a trade was very much alive ("The Study of Legal Education" 450). While engaged in this conflict, the legal field lagged behind other fields in professionalizing. For example, in medicine at that time, a physician would have earned a doctor of medicine degree (M.D.), which would provide evidence of medical training ("The Study of Legal Education" 450). In law, however, an attorney would not necessarily even have earned a bachelor of laws degree (LL.B.), the law degree of the day; often passing a bar examination was the only requirement ("The Study of Legal Education" 450). Clearly, the credentials were not the same.

Rhetoric, specifically Aristotelian rhetoric, was one tool for improving the status of the legal field. As such, Langdell, Ames, and their allies, generally at elite institutions, argued for a professor-as-scholar model that met the standards for membership on a university faculty. In addition to the dimension of full-time devotion to the job, such a persona included teaching, research, and service dimensions (Vance 7). Because the new model was that of a scholar, not of a practitioner, this new model looked much like the one that prospers in the university of the present day, which, as McFarland noted, includes "teaching, writing, and service" (*Self-Images . . . : Rethinking Legal Education* 222). Since key lawyers at Harvard and their allies viewed law as a science (Langdell 124), the law professor persona they rhetorically constructed logically would be professional in nature (Richards 9).

In 1900, Ames declared, "I have the faith to believe that at no distant day there will be at each of the leading university law schools, a body of law professors of distinguished ability, of national and international influence" (146). The professors would be "men teaching in the grand manner, and adding lustre by their writings to the University and to the legal profession" (Ames 146).

Eventually, Ames would get his way. As the law school gained control of much of the access to the legal field, the law professor would assume the persona of a scholar and ultimately become the gatekeeper to the profession (Fossum 547). No longer someone with a trade, the law professor, like the practicing lawyer, would be someone with a profession.

Works Cited in Chapter III

Ames, James Barr. "The Vocation of the Law Professor." *American Law Register*, vol. 48, 1900, pp. 129–46.

Amram, David Werner. "Law School Instruction in Practice." *American Law School Review*, vol. 3, 1914, pp. 439–49.

Bartholomew, Mark. "Legal Separation: The Relationship between the Law School and the Central University in the Late Nineteenth Century." *Journal of Legal Education*, vol. 53, 2003, pp. 368–403.

Coquillette, Daniel R., and Bruce A. Kimball. *On the Battlefield of Merit: Harvard Law School, the First Century*. Harvard UP, 2015.

Epstein, Sandra P. *Law at Berkeley: The History of Boalt Hall*. U of California, Institute of Governmental Studies P, 1997.

Fiero, J. Newton. "Teaching Law without Experience at the Bar." *American Law School Review*, vol. 3, 1914, pp. 558–60.

Foss, Sonja K., and Cindy L. Griffin. "Beyond Persuasion: A Proposal for an Invitational Rhetoric." *Communication Monographs*, vol. 62, 1995, pp. 2–18.

Fossum, Donna. "Law Professors: A Profile of the Teaching Branch of the Legal Profession." *American Bar Foundation Research Journal*, vol. 1980, 1980, pp. 501–54.

Frankfurter, Felix. "The Law and the Law Schools." *American Bar Association Journal*, vol. 1, 1915, pp. 532–40.

Friedman, Lawrence M. *A History of American Law*. Touchstone, 1973.

Hoeflich, M. H. "Plus Ça Change, Plus C'est la Même Chose: The Integration of Theory and Practice in Legal Education." *The History of Legal Education in the United States*, edited by Steve Sheppard, vol. 2, Salem Press, 1999, pp. 861–75.

Hutchins, H. B. "The Law Teacher: His Functions and Responsibilities." *Columbia Law Review*, vol. 8, 1908, pp. 362–74.

Johnson, William R. *Schooled Lawyers: A Study in the Clash of Professional Cultures*. New York UP, 1978.

Kales, Albert M. "Discussion: The Ultimate Function of the Teacher of Law." *American Law School Review*, vol. 3, 1911, pp. 9–11.

---. "Should the Law Teacher Practice Law?" *Harvard Law Review*, vol. 25, 1912, pp. 253–69.

Langdell, C. C. "Teaching Law as a Science." *American Law Review*, vol. 21, 1887, pp. 123–25.

Leff, Michael. "The Habitation of Rhetoric." *Argument and Critical Practices: Proceedings of the Fifth SCA/AFA Conference on Argumentation*, edited by Joseph W. Wenzel, Speech Communication Association, 1987, pp. 1–8.

Martin, Paul L. "Practical Legal Education." *American Law School Review*, vol. 3, 1913, pp. 237–40.

McFarland, Douglas Dale. *Self-Images of Law Professors: Rethinking Legal Education*. 1983. University of Minnesota, Ph.D. dissertation.

McGovney, Dudley O. "The Function of the American University Law School." *American Law School Review*, vol. 3, 1911, pp. 17–19.

Richards, H. S. "Discussion: The Ultimate Function of the Teacher of Law." *American Law School Review*, vol. 3, 1911, pp. 8–9.

Schlegel, John Henry. "Between the Harvard Founders and the American Legal Realists: The Professionalization of the American Law Professor." *Journal of Legal Education*, vol. 35, 1985, pp. 311–25.

Smith, Craig R. "The Persona of Jesus in the Gospel according to St. Matthew." *Journal of Communication and Religion*, vol. 14, 1991, pp. 57–69.

Stone, Harlan F. "The Function of the American University Law School." *American Law School Review*, vol. 3, 1911, pp. 11–17.

---. "The Importance of Actual Experience at the Bar as a Preparation for Teaching Law." *American Law School Review*, vol. 3, 1912, pp. 205–11.

"The Study of Legal Education." *American Law School Review*, vol. 3, 1914, pp. 450–54.

Thayer, Ezra Ripley. "Note." *Harvard Law Review*, vol. 25, 1912, pp. 269–73.

Thayer, James Bradley. "The Teaching of English Law at Universities." *Harvard Law Review*, vol. 9, 1895, pp. 169–84.

Towers, Walter K. "A Student's Opinion of Practical Law School Instruction." *American Law School Review*, vol. 2, 1911, pp. 556–58.

Turner, Paaige K., and Patricia Ryden. "How George Bush Silenced Anita Hill: A Derridian View of the Third Persona in Public Argument." *Argumentation and Advocacy*, vol. 37, 2000, pp. 86–97.

U.S. Const. art. II, § 1, cl. 1. *Constitution Annotated*, constitution.congress.gov/browse/article-2/section-1/. Accessed 28 June 2023.

Vance, William R. "The Ultimate Function of the Teacher of Law." *American Law School Review*, vol. 3, 1911, pp. 2–8.

Van Zile, Philip T. "Practice Work in the Law Colleges." *American Law School Review*, vol. 2, 1907, pp. 71–76.

CHAPTER IV

1920–1960
The Conflict over the Construction of the Ideal Law Professor Persona in the Days of a More Established Paradigm in U.S. Legal Education

By the early 1920s, law school was establishing itself as the main portal of entry into the legal field in the United States. Despite this change in the legal education scene, some observers, including U.S. Attorney General Harlan F. Stone ("The Future" 233), were concerned that, while law school was more the norm for prospective lawyers, not all schools had high standards. This was "the development in the United States of two distinct types of law school" (Stone, "The Future" 233). Stone suggested that one type of law school, the university law school, had "high entrance requirements and exacting educational standards," while another type, often the night or part-time school, had "low admission requirements, low educational standards and on the whole low professional ideals" ("The Future" 233).

The American Bar Association, which itself had expressed concern for "'creat[ing] conditions which [would] tend to strengthen the character and improve the efficiency of those admitted to the practice of law'" ("Conference on Legal Education" 637), spoke to Stone's concern by addressing standards for legal education in the United States. In 1921, the ABA's Section of Legal Education and Admissions to the Bar recommended, and the ABA then accepted, that every candidate for bar admission should have graduated from a law school that had the following standards: two years of university as a prerequisite, three years for full-time law study or longer for part-time law study, an adequate library available for law students, and a large enough number of faculty members who would devote their full attention to the law school ("Conference on Legal Education" 637–38). This action by the ABA effectively recognized the law professor's "claim to primacy in teaching" law because the ABA was helping the law school to take over legal education, and the law professor was a key player within the law school (Schlegel 317). Additionally, the ABA recommended that, after graduation from an appropriate law school, a candidate should have to take "an examination by public authority" before joining the bar ("Conference on Legal Education" 638).

In light of this ongoing evolution of U.S. legal education from law office study toward university law school study, this chapter traces the contours of the portion of the conflict over the construction of the ideal law professor persona from 1920 to 1960, the period in the United States during which law school education as preparation for legal practice had become much more the norm than the exception. The chapter draws the line at 1960 because, as the next chapter will address in more detail, during the 1960s, the field of law eventually entered a new era by discursively maturing into the professional graduate program of study it is today. To trace the contours of the portion of the conflict over the construction of the appropriate law professor persona between 1920 and 1960, the chapter will consider two major personas that emerged in the conflict, including the law professor as scholar and the law professor as practitioner. Ultimately, the apparent lack of significance of the law professor as scholar/practitioner hybrid during this period compared with the period between 1870 and 1920 will receive brief consideration as well. As relevant, each section also will address the type of rhetoric that lawyers employed in this ongoing conflict.

The Law Professor as Scholar

The law professor as scholar model that Langdell, Ames, and others had promoted between 1870 and 1920 remained crucially important between 1920 and 1960. Various lawyers argued in favor of the merits of this law professor persona, including how the law professor persona was quite different from that of the judge or practicing attorney, but controversy still remained. For the most part, this rhetoric sounded much as it had in previous decades because the law professor persona had major dimensions that included a full-time dedication to the job, teaching duties, production of research, and a public function. As in the period from 1870 to 1920, this scholar version of the law professor persona was multidimensional, which communication scholar Craig Smith suggested is one possibility for a persona (59–63).

In promoting this persona, lawyers called upon Aristotelian rhetoric because the lawyers were making and supporting claims. The lawyers advanced four main claims: (1) the law professor persona should involve devoting almost all professional time to the university, (2) the law professor persona should include a teaching dimension, (3) the law professor persona should have a research dimension, and (4) the law professor persona should include a public function dimension. To support these major claims that outlined the scholar persona, lawyers offered various types of evidence. The ensuing discussion examines the arguments that fleshed out this scholar persona.

First, pro-scholar lawyers argued that the law professor persona should include full-time university work. For instance, Chief Justice William Howard Taft of the U.S. Supreme Court pointed out that the law professor should be a full-time individual (555). Judge Learned Hand of the U.S. Court of Appeals for the Second Circuit advanced the very same position (466), as did Karl N. Llewellyn of Columbia University Law School (658). Taft justified the position that he, Hand, Llewellyn, and others took by claiming that full-time work in the practice of law while one held employment in a law school would prove to be a large distraction from one's scholarly duties (556). From the position of having been an associate dean at a practitioner-taught law school, Carl C. Wheaton of the St. Louis University Law School argued that the active practitioner had "almost no time to prepare lectures" for class (344). Although time was so short for the legal practitioner, the law professor had to be available full-time for teaching law students and assuming other duties. Accordingly, the law professor persona should be that of a full-time individual.

Second, advocates of the scholar persona argued that the law professor persona should include a teaching dimension. Roscoe Pound, at that time at the University of California, Los Angeles, Law School, stated, "If one's main interest is in anything but his teaching he will be no teacher" ("Some Comments" 532). According to Pound, some of the ideal qualities in teachers were "a sense of their high calling as lawyers and as teachers of law, devotion to duty, and putting forth of their powers to the utmost in the work of the law school and the service of the students" ("Some Comments" 530). By comparison, Hand suggested that members of the bench and bar were "not competent as teachers," so the teaching dimension of the law professor was special (466). This approach clearly assigned teaching to the persona of the law professor rather than to the personas of other members of the legal field, and, in doing so, the approach omitted many, although not all, of the practical aspects of law that experienced judges and lawyers might bring to the classroom.

Third, pro-scholar advocates claimed that, because teaching was not enough, the law professor persona should have a research dimension. Noting, in 1926, that "reports during the last quarter century are proof enough of... an increasing tendency to accept as authoritative the conclusions of the great writers" on the law, Hand described the research dimension of the law professor persona as having "preeminence" (468). William Prosser, dean at the University of California, Berkeley, Law School, recalled many applicants for law professorships who had never written much, if anything, scholarly in nature (511). Prosser noted that individuals who were interested in teaching law but not interested in writing about law had "the wrong approach" to entering the legal academy, and Prosser, as well as probably many law school deans, would not have been likely to hire such candidates (511–12).

Several other points about this research-oriented dimension of the law professor persona are of note. For example, Harold Gill Reuschlein of Georgetown University added that a legal researcher should be well "grounded in the law and other disciplines" (69–70). Also, good research involved a professor's ability to make contributions to the academic legal literature; this would not necessarily involve quantity but instead quality (Reuschlein 71–72; Pound, "Some Comments" 532). Observing a relationship between the research and teaching dimensions of the law professor persona, Pound maintained that research would be a source of inspiration for teaching ("Some Comments" 532). Research, then, would inform and improve a professor's work in the classroom.

James Willard Hurst of the University of Wisconsin Law School offered a noteworthy justification for the need for research to be a key dimension of the law professor persona. Writing in the late 1950s, Hurst conceded that law schools were supposed to produce law graduates who would be able to practice law, but he also pointed out that the law school, by then well-established within the university system, had a duty to contribute to one of the main functions of the university, which involved advancing and transmitting knowledge (147). In light of this point, Hurst called for renewed vigor in university law school research that would contribute to the university's aim of enhancing humankind's knowledge of the world, including the legal world (161).

Fourth, pro-scholar advocates argued that the law professor persona should include a public function dimension. Hand argued that the law professor would provide guidance to the bench and bar for a clear statement of "a doctrine, with a complete knowledge of its origin, its authority and its meaning" (468). Hand even went so far as to state that, because the law professor assumed a persona that was "less prone" to align itself with "the side of wealth," the law professor might be better suited "to solve new questions" of doctrine (471). In Hand's opinion, the law professor assumed a persona that was more interested in doctrinal matters than financial matters. Also in terms of the public function dimension, a law professor had to help bring "about better requirements for admission to the bar" (Pound, "Some Comments" 519). One might assume that such improvements would aid both the legal profession and the public.

For purposes of comparison, while the law professor persona was that of "the scholar," the persona of someone on the bench or at the bar was that of "the man of affairs" (Hand 482). Members of the bench and bar heard cases and practiced law, respectively, but they did not assume the roles of scholars. Rather, members of the bench and bar would handle the cases that might "stimulate an excessive fertility of invention" in the minds of legal scholars (Hand 472). Again, although the personas of the professor, the judge, and the practicing lawyer all might work toward a "common enterprise of keeping and advancing the law" (Hand 480), each individual had a different persona to assume.

This rhetoric during the 1920s, 1930s, 1940s, and 1950s of a law professor persona with the dimensions of full-time dedication to the job, teaching duties, production of research, and a public function sounded much like the rhetoric of Langdell, Ames, and their colleagues from the fifty-year period before 1920, but one minor modification began to appear in the law professor as scholar model. Some limited practical experience became more acceptable in the background of the law professor persona. For instance, Taft admitted that some practical experience might be of value to the law professor persona (555). Prosser observed that, for various courses, law schools were looking "for some practice before teaching, some experience of some kind in the field" (513). As an estimate, Prosser indicated that three years of practical experience would be "about right" for the future law professor (513). Wheaton felt that, in some cases, fewer than five years might be appropriate (345). Suggesting that only a poor law faculty would have absolutely no professors with practical experience, Reuschlein agreed that some legal experience was beneficial (72–73). Indeed, the professor ought to "become familiar with at least the ordinary problems that arise in practice" (Wheaton 346). Consequently, a limited amount of practice prior to a professorship had begun to become more acceptable.

Despite the nod to the practitioner and hybrid models of the law professor noted in Chapter III, this nod was limited in nature. The hybrid models were not embraced. For example, the position that law professors ought to continue practicing while teaching and thus be able to test legal hypotheses, an idea which Kales had suggested years earlier ("Should the Law Teacher" 259), did not appear in the texts studied for this chapter, nor did Stone's notion of having full-time practitioners on the faculty ("The Function" 14). Should one think that the emerging acceptance of some limited practical experience in the background of the law professor persona was a major addition to the scholar model, consideration of a response from Prosser would be appropriate. Prosser quite sharply pointed out the following: "One thing on which all law schools are in agreement is that too many years of practice hardens the arteries, stunts the intellect, and ossifies the ideas, so that few lawyers over the age of fifty are ever much of a success when they retire and enter teaching" (513).

The acceptance of a few years of practical legal experience proved to be a small concession to the lawyers who had been advocating the practitioner and hybrid models of the law professor persona. Indeed, the essential model of the law professor persona as that of a scholar remained. Langdell, Ames, and their allies presumably would have been pleased with this perpetuation of their own model of the law professor.

In presenting their ideal law professor persona as the scholar, lawyers who adopted this position in the period from 1920 to 1960 generally employed Aristotelian rhetoric, as had the pro-scholar lawyers in the period from 1870 to 1920. The rhetoric between 1920 and 1960 involved the advancing and supporting of claims. The texts studied here did not suggest consideration on the part of the pro-scholar advocates of competing positions for the purpose of understanding those positions, with the one minor exception of understanding that a few years of practical experience may be of some limited value. Thus, for the most part, the rhetoric was Aristotelian in nature.

The Law Professor as Practitioner

Regardless of this general affirmation of the law professor persona as essentially that of a scholar, resistance to that position remained. One of the strongest voices, although not the only voice, against the law professor as scholar model came from Judge Jerome Frank, a federal appellate judge who took more than one opportunity to speak his mind on this matter. Frank was a member of the legal realist school of jurisprudence, which questioned the supposedly decisive role of doctrine in legal decision-making and instead considered the contexts of law (Barzun 1139–44). In 1947, Frank observed that he had been calling for a different type of legal education, which included an alternative law professor persona, for the past fifteen years ("A Plea" 1303).

In constructing this alternative persona, Frank and his colleagues called upon Aristotelian rhetoric because these lawyers were making and supporting claims to advance their position, which included a vigorous refutation of the pro-scholar position. Through Aristotelian rhetoric, these lawyers provided two major claims: (1) the scholar model generally did not address the needs of legal education adequately and (2) the practitioner model was much better suited for legal education. To support these major claims, the pro-practitioner lawyers offered various types of evidence. The following discussion examines the arguments that developed the practitioner persona.

In making the argument that the scholar persona was inadequate, Frank placed legal education within its historical context as he saw it. Going back to the days of Langdell, whom Frank called "a brilliant neurotic" ("A Plea" 1303), Frank maintained that, "[d]ue to Langdell's idiosyncrasies, *law school came to mean 'library-law'*" ("Why Not" 908). Langdell's teaching method "was the expression of the strange character of a cloistered, retiring bookish man" (Frank, "Why Not" 908). Under the Langdellian paradigm of legal education, the law professor would become one who "had little or no contacts with or a positive distaste for the rough-and-tumble activities of the average lawyer's life" (Frank, "Why Not" 908). Indeed, this approach to teaching law was akin to teaching future horticulturists through the use of cut flowers or future physicians with individuals "who had seldom seen a patient or diagnosed the ailments of flesh-and-blood human beings" (Frank, "Why Not" 912, 915). One might also compare the Langdellian approach to teaching law with teaching "toe-dancing, swimming, automobile-driving, hair-cutting, or cooking wild ducks" by merely talking about them and having students read about them (Frank, "A Plea" 1311). Thus, to Frank's chagrin, practical legal experience was not an important component of the scholar persona ("Why Not" 909).

Frank and other lawyers who generally agreed with his position further critiqued the scholar model. For instance, Frank suggested that a law school which adopted the scholar model forced law professors who had substantial practical experience to capitulate "to an atmosphere in which the memories of practice became shadowy and unreal" ("A Plea" 1304). In class, the professor with legal experience had "to belittle his experience at the bar" (Frank, "A Plea" 1304). Irving M. Mehler of the Colorado Bar and the New York Bar asked, "How can a teacher deem himself competent to project in a live and compelling way, if he himself has never been confronted with not one or a few, but with many live legal problems?" (234). To this, Arch M. Cantrall of the West Virginia Bar added that often the idealized scholarly professor of the day was "just fresh from the doors of some law school" ("Law Schools and the Layman" 910), and Albert K. Orschel of the Illinois Bar suggested that producing scholarship did not necessarily help students learn the practice of law (123–24). Naturally, critics of the scholar persona saw that phenomenon as problematic because the students would lose out on the practical experience of a professor.

Taking a different angle on legal education, Frank and his colleagues offered a position in sharp contrast to that of Langdell and his followers. Rather than favoring "experience in learning law" (Langdell 124), Frank favored looking beyond "rules and principles" of cases and toward two main tasks of the lawyer, which included predicting future court decisions in particular lawsuits and trying to persuade courts in given cases to render decisions favorable to one's clients ("Why Not" 910–11). Mehler reminded the legal field that "the primary purpose of a law school [was] to train lawyers" (231). Upon leaving law school, lawyers had to be ready for the experiences of the "first year or two of practice," as Cantrall noted ("Practical Skills" 319). Indeed, if new lawyers learned law while beginning to practice, clients would have to pay the price (Cantrall, "Practical Skills" 321). This understanding of law school and legal practice helped explain why the law student needed to observe what transpired in law offices and in court (Frank, "Why Not" 911).

Accordingly, Frank and other lawyers constructed a different version of the law professor persona, which one might call that of "a 'live' lawyer" (Mehler 232). First and foremost, Frank maintained, the law professor should assume a persona endowed with practical experience, and by that he meant "*not less than five to ten years of varied experience in the actual practice of law*" ("Why Not" 914). Mehler suggested that at least seven years of practical experience might suffice (231). This practical experience would come from "the trial courts, appellate courts, in office work, in dealing with clients, [and] in negotiation" (Frank, "Why Not" 914). Such experience would be that of individuals

> who ha[d] drafted contracts,...tried and defended tort actions,...drafted wills and trusts,...handled corporate matters,...foreclosed mortgages,...quieted titles,...defended those accused of crime,...had experience in trial and appellate practice, and...counseled clients regarding ordinary and difficult legal problems. (Mehler 232)

The law schools should make "[e]xtensive use of practitioners in every law school course" (Cantrall, "Practical Skills" 322).

Such practical experience incorporated into the law professor persona would help the professor enhance personal ethos, or credibility, with law students and thus enhance the learning experience of the students (Mehler 232). Mehler argued that, when a teacher is lacking in "the practical touch," students have less regard for the professor and in turn lose interest in the professor's subject (232). However, when "the practical touch" is present in the learning environment, "the subject glows, the respect and admiration for the instructor is heightened, and even a supposedly 'dead' subject becomes very much alive" (Mehler 232). Since ethos can have a relationship with persona (Cherry 402), the practitioner persona of the law professor likely would enhance the ethos of the individual who assumed that persona, and the benefit would be a better learning environment for the students.

Lawyers who accepted this position maintained that the law professor who assumed the practitioner persona ought to teach students the practical aspects of law. One such venue for this teaching was the legal clinic (Frank, "Why Not" 917). To illustrate the benefits of the practitioner persona, Frank listed several insights that law students would gain from clinical instruction. These insights included learning about how juries decide cases, the uncertain nature of facts, the nature of how witnesses impact parties' legal rights, influences on judicial decision-making, negotiations and settlements, and drafting (Frank, "Why Not" 918–20). While learning appellate law was an aspect of learning law, it was not the most significant aspect because "upper courts... are relatively unimportant for most clients" (Frank, "A Plea" 1306). Frank pointed out that "the overwhelming majority of lawsuits are never appealed, and, in most of the small minority which are appealed, the appellate courts accept the facts as 'found' by the trial court" ("A Plea" 1306). Frank added, "In most suits, no disagreement arises about the rules, and the disputes relate solely to the facts" ("A Plea" 1310). Also, Frank claimed, "Intelligent men can learn [criticism of appellate cases] in about six months" ("A Plea" 1318).

Mehler extended Frank's argument by explaining how law students would learn from more realistic experiences in the classroom as well as in the clinic. For instance, a professor who had assumed a practitioner persona might bring to class a set of articles of incorporation, documentation used to establish a corporation, that the professor had drafted and thus with which the professor was familiar (Mehler 233). Other examples would involve documents for matters that related to "wills, contracts, partnership, property, and many other courses" (Mehler 233). Under this approach, the student would be able to engage actual legal drafting and benefit from a "touch of realism" (Mehler 233). In the end, "the student [would] have had a taste of real law" (Mehler 233).

In addition, Frank added that the law professor could draw from other fields in order to enhance the education of future legal practitioners. As a good legal realist, Frank proposed that the law professor call upon the social sciences and other allied fields to instruct law students in "the inter-actions of the conduct of society and the work of the courts and lawyers" ("Why Not" 921–22). Frank explained that "the vaguest recollections of [one's] pre-legal work" provided for "an insufficient feeling of the inter-relation between law and the phenomena of daily living, and an artificial attitude towards 'Law' as something totally distinct and apart from the facts" ("Why Not" 922).

Critics of the scholar persona did concede that their approach would allow some law professors to assume an exclusively scholarly persona (Frank, "Why Not" 914; Orschel 122). Nonetheless, law schools should not primarily focus on developing academics; the schools ought to focus on developing practitioners (Frank, "Why Not" 915). As such, "the 'library-law' teacher should cease to dominate the schools" (Frank, "Why Not" 915), and the law schools should back away from "Langdell's morbid repudiation of actual legal practice" (Frank, "A Plea" 1313).

While very much invested in the hands-on aspect of the practitioner persona of the law professor, various lawyers who supported this position were careful to clarify that their vision of the law professor was not one that necessarily called for a trade school approach to legal education. Rather, the law professor would assume the practitioner persona in a context that would blend "[k]nowledge of what courts and lawyers do" and "visual demonstration of the possible values of a rich and well-rounded culture in the practice of law" (Frank, "Why Not" 923). Indeed, some scholarship could be appropriate in the law school, too (Mehler 231). This was a view of what Frank called "a realistic lawyer-school" ("Why Not" 923). However, although Frank and his colleagues were willing to allow some academic influence to brush against their preferred law professor persona, their focus was on the practical aspects of the persona. Based on the above rhetoric, one can conclude that these lawyers wanted students to emerge from law school, even if it were not a trade school, as practice-ready graduates.

Interestingly enough, in 1947, Frank noted that essentially no one had listened to his call for reform in legal education, which included significantly altering the nature of the Harvard version of the ideal law professor persona ("A Plea" 1303). Those few individuals who may have listened to Frank and his allies refused to allow practicality to be at the center of legal education or at the core of the law professor persona (Frank, "A Plea" 1327). This suggests that the understanding of the law professor persona as that of a practitioner was out of touch with the prevailing understanding of the law professor persona.

As shown above, in developing their ideal law professor persona as a practitioner, lawyers who adopted this position employed Aristotelian rhetoric. This rhetoric consisted of advancing and supporting claims, including a vigorous refutation of the scholar model. As with the texts from the pro-scholar lawyers from this period, the texts from the pro-practitioner lawyers did not suggest sustained consideration of other positions for the purpose of understanding, although Frank did concede that a few professors at a law school might adopt the scholar model. At this point in history, Frank simply may have realized that the scholar model was assuming a position of prominence in legal education. Accordingly, the pro-practitioner lawyers were employing Aristotelian rhetoric.

The Law Professor as Scholar/Practitioner Hybrid

Other than the odd fragment like a comment by Frank that the law professor might continue to practice law while teaching ("Why Not" 921), this particular study did not locate rhetoric from the period between 1920 and 1960 that suggested hybrid models of the law professor. Such a finding is not to say that these models had disappeared completely. However, compromise models like the ones Albert M. Kales ("Should the Law Teacher" 259) and Harlan F. Stone ("The Function" 14) respectively advocated, both of which Chapter III discussed, did not appear in any notable detail in the texts studied for the period between 1920 and 1960.

Conclusion

As this chapter has illustrated, in the sample of texts from the portion of the conflict over the construction of the ideal law professor persona between 1920 and 1960, two major personas appeared. These were the law professor as scholar persona and the law professor as practitioner persona. The law professor as scholar/practitioner hybrid persona did not appear in notable form in this sample of texts. Essentially, the scholar model, which Frank conceded was dominant ("A Plea" 1303), remained largely unchanged from the period between 1870 and 1920, except that advocates of this model made the minor concession that some limited practice before a lawyer assumed a professorship may have been acceptable for the scholar persona. Meanwhile, the practitioner model, complete with its focus on helping to foster practice-ready law graduates, remained much the same as it had between 1870 and 1920, but the advocates of this model did make a slight nod to the university context of the law school, admitting that law school was more than only training for legal practice. Nonetheless, Frank maintained, "Our law schools must learn from our medical schools," which had strong practical components ("A Plea" 1315).

Much like the lawyers in the previous chapter, the lawyers in the present chapter tended to employ Aristotelian rhetoric as opposed to other types of rhetoric because the focus was on argumentation instead of understanding. Indeed, the lawyers were advancing and supporting claims that represented their ideal law professor personas.

Like the focus on Aristotelian rhetoric in the period from 1870 to 1920, the focus on Aristotelian rhetoric in the period from 1920 to 1960 led to communication problems. Some of the lawyers in this period, especially those in favor of the scholar model, presented and supported their own model and were largely non-responsive to the lawyers who supported another model. This point demonstrates an apparent lack of understanding of or interest in different views in the conflict. Other lawyers, including Frank and some of his colleagues in favor of the practitioner model, did respond quite directly to a competing model, especially when Frank made fun of Langdell's law professor as one who "had little or no contacts with or a positive distaste for the rough-and-tumble activities of the average lawyer's life" ("Why Not" 908). Nonetheless, Frank and his colleagues did not give serious consideration to the underlying concerns of lawyers who favored the scholar model. Consequently, lawyers during this period either largely ignored or attacked competing visions. Several minor concessions noted above, including the point that limited practice in the law professor's background might be acceptable and that law schools had become institutionalized within the university, did not suggest more than a superficial understanding of competing views.

These minor concessions aside, clearly the dividing line between advocates of the scholar model and advocates of the practitioner model was the background of the persona of the law professor. From one perspective, the law professor should assume a scholarly persona and fit comfortably within the university setting, yet, from another perspective, the law professor should assume a practitioner persona and work to help develop students into legal practitioners. This tension between the values of intellectualism and practicality remained during the period from 1920 to 1960, but the law school was now firmly tied to the university system (Hurst 147). In light of a strong scholarly impulse, perhaps all that remained for the U.S. system of legal education to turn further in the direction of the continental European system of legal education was for U.S. law professors to have earned doctorates instead of what rhetorically seemed like undergraduate degrees.

Works Cited in Chapter IV

Barzun, Charles L. "Jerome Frank and the Modern Mind." *Buffalo Law Review*, vol. 58, 2010, pp. 1127–74.

Cantrall, Arch M. "Law Schools and the Layman: Is Legal Education Doing Its Job?" *American Bar Association Journal*, vol. 38, 1952, pp. 907–10, 972.

---. "Practical Skills Can and Must Be Taught in Law Schools." *Journal of Legal Education*, vol. 6, 1954, pp. 316–23.

Cherry, Roger D. "Ethos versus Persona: Self-Representation in Written Discourse." *Written Communication*, vol. 15, 1998, pp. 384–410.

"Conference on Legal Education." *American Bar Association Journal*, vol. 7, 1921, pp. 637–38.

Frank, Jerome. "A Plea for Lawyer-Schools." *Yale Law Journal*, vol. 56, 1947, pp. 1303–44.

---. "Why Not a Clinical Lawyer-School?" *University of Pennsylvania Law Review*, vol. 81, 1933, pp. 907–23.

Hand, Learned. "Have the Bench and Bar Anything to Contribute to the Teaching of Law?" *Michigan Law Review*, vol. 24, 1926, pp. 466–82.

Hurst, James Willard. "Research Responsibilities of University Law Schools." *Journal of Legal Education*, vol. 10, 1957, pp. 147–61.

Kales, Albert M. "Should the Law Teacher Practice Law?" *Harvard Law Review*, vol. 25, 1912, pp. 253–69.

Langdell, C. C. "Teaching Law as a Science." *American Law Review*, vol. 21, 1887, pp. 123–25.

Llewellyn, K. N. "On What Is Wrong with So-Called Legal Education." *Columbia Law Review*, vol. 35, 1935, pp. 651–78.

Mehler, Irving M. "In Defense of Practitioners as Teachers." *Journal of Legal Education*, vol. 9, 1956, pp. 231–34.

Orschel, Albert K. "Is Legal Education Doing Its Job? Brief of *Amicus Curiae*." *American Bar Association Journal*, vol. 40, 1954, pp. 121–24, 166–69.

Pound, Roscoe. "Some Comments on Law Teachers and Law Teaching." *Journal of Legal Education*, vol. 3, 1951, pp. 519–32.

Prosser, William L. "Advice to the Lovelorn." *Journal of Legal Education*, vol. 3, 1951, pp. 505–14.

Reuschlein, Harold Gill. "Law Professor—Post-War." *Minnesota Law Review*, vol. 30, 1946, pp. 68–77.

Schlegel, John Henry. "Between the Harvard Founders and the American Legal Realists: The Professionalization of the American Law Professor." *Journal of Legal Education*, vol. 35, 1985, pp. 311–25.

Smith, Craig R. "The Persona of Jesus in the Gospel according to St. Matthew." *Journal of Communication and Religion*, vol. 14, 1991, pp. 57–69.

Stone, Harlan F. "The Function of the American University Law School." *American Law School Review*, vol. 3, 1911, pp. 11–17.

---. "The Future of Legal Education." *American Bar Association Journal*, vol. 10, 1924, pp. 233–35.

Taft, William Howard. "Legal Education and the University Law School." *Minnesota Law Review*, vol. 10, 1926, pp. 554–56.

Wheaton, Carl C. "Law Teaching and Pragmatism." *Georgetown Law Journal*, vol. 25, 1937, pp. 338–50.

CHAPTER V

1960–Present

The Conflict over the Construction of the Ideal Law Professor Persona in an Era of Graduate Law Study

By the 1960s, if not before, the law school was thinking of itself as a graduate program within the university system (Bergin 649). The evidence supported this perception because, to enter law school by that time in history, a prospective law student generally needed to have completed an undergraduate degree and taken a standardized admissions examination. Having the status of a university graduate program has allowed the law school to tap into the ethos of the university and use such ethos to enhance the ethos of the law school, establishing a form of what communication scholars Richard D. Rieke et al. called *secondary credibility* (168–69). This relationship has been mutually beneficial because the law school has helped the university enhance its prestige, too (A. M. Johnson 1235). For instance, one would have a hard time thinking "of Harvard, Yale, Stanford, the University of Virginia, or the University of Southern California without a law school" (A. M. Johnson 1235).

However, while an upgrade in the status of the law school within the university might have been beneficial for law schools in general, another part of the legal field has become less pleased with the implications of this approach. At least since the 1960s, what Harry H. Wellington of Yale University described as the "'two cultures' phenomenon" has become apparent within the legal field (327). Wellington's description alluded to scientist C. P. Snow's *The Two Cultures and the Scientific Revolution*, which, in the middle of the twentieth century, argued that "a gulf of mutual incomprehension" and "hostility and dislike" had developed between science and the humanities (4–6). On one hand, some lawyers, usually those within the university, have become more academically-oriented, and, on the other hand, other lawyers, usually those in legal practice or sitting on the bench, have become more pragmatically-oriented. Problems arise when these two groups begin to talk differently from each other (Wellington 327). In a way, the field of law has developed into at least two different legal professions (Stevens, "American Legal Scholarship" 445), and the gap between these two groups is growing (Edwards, "The Role" 291). Not surprisingly, practitioners and academics have experienced tension because of this situation (Allen 131).

Within such a context, this chapter traces the contours of the portion of the conflict over the construction of the ideal law professor persona from 1960 to the present. The chapter draws the line at 1960 because, as suggested above, during the 1960s, the field of law finally entered a new era by maturing into the graduate program of study it is today. To illustrate the contours of the conflict, this chapter will commence with a consideration of the 1960s controversy over the nature of the law degree, a controversy that had implications for both the status of law school as a graduate program and the status of the law professor as a fully-fledged member of the academy. Then the chapter will address the two major personas that have emerged in the conflict, including the law professor as scholar and the law professor as practitioner. Also, the chapter will trace the limited appearance of the law professor as scholar/practitioner hybrid persona during this period. As appropriate, each section of the chapter also will address the type of rhetoric that lawyers employed. A concluding section will synthesize some of the communication problems that have emerged in this ongoing conflict, not only during the period from 1960 to present, but also during the two previous historical periods studied, often due in part to a heavy reliance on Aristotelian rhetoric as a communication strategy.

Conflict over the Doctorate

One significant event during the 1960s that had implications for the construction of the law professor in the United States, especially with regard to the research and teaching dimensions of the scholar persona, which will receive further consideration later in this chapter, was the conflict over the nature of the law degree that U.S. universities issued. This conflict ultimately spoke to the ethos of the law professor. Thus, at this point, the chapter will address a conflict that helped to launch the contemporary period in U.S. legal education.

Until the 1960s, most law schools in the United States issued the bachelor of laws degree (LL.B.). However, in the 1960s, some legal educators began to question seriously the propriety of issuing a second bachelor's degree to the law graduate who already had earned at least a bachelor's degree such as a B.A. or B.S. at university before attending law school. Additionally, much confusion resulted from the issuance of the LL.B. Some law schools thought of the degree as an undergraduate degree, while others thought of it as a professional or graduate degree (Stein 318). For reference, in most countries of the world, law primarily has been taught at the undergraduate level (Moliterno 276). As one might imagine, this divergence of views in the U.S. complicated law school graduations. Some universities hooded law graduates with doctoral hoods, and others did not (Stein 318). The proposed solution was the juris doctor, or doctor of jurisprudence, degree (J.D.). Although the J.D. dated back at least to 1902 at the University of Chicago, few law schools had adopted it before the 1960s (Stevens, *Law School* 161, 247).

The Latin background of the term *doctor* and related terms will help in understanding the debate over the doctorate in law. Of note, the Latin nouns *doctor*, which refers to a male, and *doctrix*, which refers to a female, mean "teacher, instructor" ("Doctor," *A Latin-English Dictionary* 605; "Doctrix" 605). Another expression of the meaning is "teacher, instructor, professor" ("Doctor," *Follett World-Wide Latin Dictionary* 125). Meanwhile, the Latin infinitive *docēre* signifies "[t]o tell, inform"; "[t]o instruct"; "[t]o demonstrate, show"; and "[t]o teach…, instruct in" ("Doceō" 568). Of interest to those who work in or follow the law and are familiar with legal doctrine, the Latin noun *doctrīna* means "teaching, instruction" ("Doctrīna" 605). As such, the English word *doctor*, borrowed from Latin and related to various other Latin words, has implications for the instructional process, including in higher education.

As the following pages will show, this side conflict, like most of the discourse addressed elsewhere in this chapter and in the two previous chapters, unfolded in an Aristotelian manner. Participants in the conflict advanced a series of claims regarding the merits of their positions and attempted to back those claims with evidence. The participants also clashed through repeated refutation of each other's claims.

Various lawyers made the case for adoption of the J.D., but John G. Hervey, dean at Oklahoma City University School of Law and an advisor to the American Bar Association's Council of the Section of Legal Education and Admissions to the Bar, became one of the principal advocates of the J.D. One author eventually credited Hervey with "almost single handedly br[inging] the legal profession to the threshold of revolution" on this issue (Power 67).

In advancing his case, Hervey described the J.D. as a professional doctorate akin to the doctor of medicine degree (M.D.) and the doctor of dental surgery degree (D.D.S.) ("Law School Graduates" 5). Hervey pointed out that, although the LL.B. involved more work than a master's degree and as much work as a Ph.D., many circles still considered the LL.B. akin to a second bachelor's degree ("Law School Graduates" 6). To develop the significance of this observation, Hervey claimed that this perception would "impair the image of the legal profession" and of law school, suggesting they were inferior to other professions and programs ("Law School Graduates" 7). While the LL.B. might have been appropriate for 1900, when an undergraduate degree was not a uniform requirement for admission to law school, by the 1960s, law school admission standards generally had come to require an undergraduate education as a prerequisite for the study of law (Hervey, "Law School Graduates" 6). Times had changed, and the law degree should change with them.

In terms of employment, Hervey argued that having the LL.B. rather than the J.D. had hurt lawyers in governmental work. Hervey offered the example of an LL.B. holder who had applied for a business law position at a public school in Minnesota ("Law School Graduates" 7). The school would not hire the lawyer as an assistant professor because the school recognized the LL.B. as being, at best, the equivalent of a master's degree but inferior to a doctorate; instead, the school hired the lawyer as an instructor and paid him less money (Hervey, "Law School Graduates" 7). According to the dean of the business school in question, "'The College looks upon the J.D. as being equivalent to a Ph.D., D.B.A., or Ed.D.... I realize that this is unjust but there is not a great deal we can do about it at the present time'" (Hervey, "Law School Graduates" 7). Beyond this example, Hervey pointed out that the U.S. Air Force considered an LL.B. the equivalent of a master's degree and clearly inferior to a doctorate ("Law School Graduates" 8). Naturally, this classification would have had implications for rank and salary. Extending his military discussion, Hervey observed that military lawyers who served overseas received the title *esquire*, while their European legal counterparts received the title *doctor*, a source of embarrassment for U.S. military lawyers ("Law School Graduates" 8). In the

1960s, when most law professors were men, one could have said the same about law professors who received the title *mister* rather than *doctor* (Power 70).

Garrett Power of the University of Maryland Law School developed Hervey's argument about the term *doctor.* Power noted that, in U.S. culture, the term is an honorific (68). Indeed, the term *doctor* is a highly valued term akin to terms like *progress, science,* and *American* because all these terms and others like them rank as culturally dominant above other terms (Weaver 212, 215, 218). To provide an example of the term *doctor* as an honorific, Power pointed out that, in the late eighteenth and early nineteenth centuries, some medical schools in the United States changed the bachelor of medicine degree (M.B.) to the doctor of medicine degree (M.D.) in order to incorporate the term *doctor* in the degree they issued (68). For good measure, Power added that, as far back as circa 75 A.D., lawyers in the Western world had used the term *doctor* to refer to themselves (69).

In light of his critique of the LL.B., Hervey called for adoption of the J.D. as the new standard for the law degree. Thinking as lawyers are apt to think, he pointed out that law schools would need precedent for the change. Hervey noted that Midwestern schools like Northwestern University and the University of Chicago, mavericks of legal education, had issued the J.D. for decades ("Law School Graduates" 27). Also, in 1906, the American Bar Association's Committee on Legal Education had recommended issuance of the J.D. to law school graduates who already had completed undergraduate degrees (Hervey, "Law School Graduates" 27). While most law schools were not yet where Hervey wanted them to be, the dean did offer some key precedents for his proposal.

Hervey was involved in a conflict with other lawyers, so consideration of the opposing side in that conflict is now appropriate. One key opponent of Hervey and his allies was George P. Smith of the University of Michigan Law School, who offered several arguments in response to Hervey's arguments. For example, Smith suggested that legal educators should spend their time improving the content of legal education rather than the label they placed on the degree that resulted from that education (8). Also, Smith submitted that Hervey had generalized too hastily in his governmental examples of the prospective assistant professor and members of the military, and Smith maintained that governmental entities were not hostile toward holders of the LL.B. (8–9). Indeed, in 1965, most of the approximately 1,075 lawyers in the U.S. Department of Justice and approximately 205 lawyers in the U.S. Department of Labor did not hold J.D.s, and the booklet *Federal Government Job Opportu-*

nities for Young Attorneys essentially ignored discussion of the J.D. (G. Smith 9). As such, "the J.D. holders [were] not so highly venerated as Dean Hervey would suggest" (G. Smith 9). Smith added that the harms of less professional prestige Hervey had identified were mere assertions without factual documentation (9).

Smith added several other arguments to develop his position. For instance, Smith pointed out that many of the law schools that were advocating a move to the J.D. were non-members of the Association of American Law Schools, an influential legal education organization in the United States (10). Also, schools like Harvard, which was "generally regarded as the number one law school in the country," were advocating continuing the issuance of the LL.B. (G. Smith 10, 26). Here, Smith suggested that lawyers follow the Harvard status quo approach to resolving the conflict. The quality and prestige of the law school, not the label on the degree, mattered (G. Smith 26). Additionally, Smith quoted Dean Leon H. Wallace of Indiana University School of Law, who had said, "'In thirteen years of active practice I never had a client ask me what kind of a law degree I had or even indicate any interest in it. Even though I have had my diploma framed on the wall of my office, I doubt whether it would have generated much client curiosity'" (26). From Smith's vantage point, the J.D. was overrated.

In response to Smith's position, Hervey presented several arguments. Hervey addressed Smith's Harvard argument by noting that, on more than one occasion, the *Harvard Law Review* had called for change ("Juris Doctor Degree" 12). Over sixty years before Hervey was writing in 1966, the board of the *Harvard Law Review*, which then had included future U.S. Supreme Court Justice Felix Frankfurter, had called for the J.D. to replace the LL.B. because law students at Harvard, although not at most other law schools at that time, already had earned undergraduate degrees (Hervey, "Juris Doctor Degree" 12). Hervey noted that, more recently, the board of the *Harvard Law Review* had argued, "'It is time for the Harvard Law School to get out of its conservative rut and switch to the J.D.'" ("Juris Doctor Degree" 12). The year before Hervey wrote his reply to Smith, the editorial board of the *Harvard Law Review* had pointed out that "'the LL.B. is little more than an unfortunate anachronism'" (Hervey, "Juris Doctor Degree" 12). In short, the administration at the Harvard Law School was behind the times.

Moreover, Hervey suggested that law schools needed to take the initiative and move to the J.D. regardless of whether elite schools like Harvard did so ("Juris Doctor Degree" 12–13). The accomplishments of less-high-profile schools deserved recognition rather than critique (Hervey, "Juris Doctor Degree" 13). Hervey quoted from *The Summation*, a publication of the Student Bar Association of the University of Utah, which proclaimed the following: "'Let us lead! Don't allow our graduates to go without the advantages (of the J.D. degree) because we lack confidence in ourselves'" ("Juris Doctor Degree" 13). Indeed, the obstacles to change were "the ivy-covered institutions of the East which [were] too marinated in the vintage brine of tradition to appreciate the innovation" (Power 67). Other schools, however, were making changes.

The dean of Oklahoma City University School of Law offered several other arguments of note. For example, Hervey maintained that, although clients might not care about the nature of the law degree, lawyers might care ("Juris Doctor Degree" 13). Just as the physician might prefer to have an M.D. rather than a B.S.Med., so might the lawyer prefer to have a J.D. rather than an LL.B. (Hervey, "Juris Doctor Degree" 13). In terms of the quality of the schools that adopted the J.D., Hervey urged a close look at each school rather than sweeping generalizations about membership in the Association of American Law Schools ("Juris Doctor Degree" 28). In passing, Hervey also added that the J.D. would function well as an analogue to some foreign legal doctorates because, like the J.D., such foreign degrees did not require bachelor's or master's degrees in law before the doctorate ("Juris Doctor Degree" 28–29).

As tradition gave way to a change in legal education, Hervey and his supporters ultimately prevailed in this conflict over the characterization of the law degree in the United States. During the 1960s, the American Bar Association and the American Law Student Association endorsed the change in degree nomenclature (Power 67). While, in 1960–61, only 5.9% of law graduates received the J.D. rather than the LL.B., by 1966–67, 43% of law graduates received the J.D. rather than the LL.B. ("Juris Doctor Information" 24). As the trend continued throughout the 1960s, the J.D. became the standard for the law degree (Stevens, *Law School* 247), even if not everyone in the legal world would be satisfied with the J.D. over the next few decades (Manley 393). Some schools that recently had adopted the J.D. even allowed their alums to trade LL.B.s for J.D.s ("Minnesota Adopts" 24).

This conflict over the nature of the law degree, which finally resulted in the systematic promulgation of a professional doctorate known as the J.D., had implications for the conflict over the construction of the ideal law professor persona in the United States. As previous chapters noted and as this chapter will note, the teaching and research dimensions of the scholar persona were and have continued to be important for advocates of that model. Professors in U.S. universities, as well as those in universities in other countries, usually need to hold doctorates to secure tenure-line positions. Among other duties, these professorships entail teaching and research duties. Normally, a university does not allow an individual with only a bachelor's degree to teach and research at the university. In that sense, an LL.B. was problematic for advocates of the scholar model of the law professor because the scholar's signature degree is a doctorate. In short, while some may have thought that the movement toward the J.D. was "much ado about nothing" (G. Smith 8), the movement spoke to legitimizing the U.S. law professor as a fully-fledged member of the university community. Regardless of whether lawyers in the world of practice cared about the nature of the law degree, lawyers in the world of the university needed to care because part of their professorial ethos was on the line (Bergin 638). Therefore, when, in the 1960s, the legal field recognized its main degree as comparable to the M.D., the Ph.D., and other doctorates, the implications for the law professor persona were significant.

The Law Professor as Scholar

In light of the prominence of the J.D., the law professor as scholar model has remained the dominant understanding of the law professor persona in the period since 1960. Because the rhetoric of lawyers who have supported this model has sounded much as it had in previous decades, the law professor persona has continued to have dimensions that include a full-time dedication to the job, teaching duties, production of research, and a public function. Although the appropriate weight for each dimension may have been somewhat ambiguous (E. Wald 997–98), the overall model has been clear.

In fine-tuning the construction of this persona, lawyers have called upon Aristotelian rhetoric because the lawyers have been making and supporting claims to advance their position. In adopting Aristotelian rhetoric, the lawyers have continued to advance the four main claims from earlier periods: (1) the law professor persona should involve devoting almost all professional time to the university, (2) the law professor persona should include a teaching dimension, (3) the law professor persona should have a research dimension, and (4) the law professor persona should include a public function dimension. To develop these major claims that have outlined the scholar persona, lawyers have offered various types of evidence. The following discussion examines the arguments that have continued to flesh out this scholar persona.

To begin with, as in the previous period from 1920 to 1960 (Stevens, "Legal Education" 482), advocates of the law professor as scholar model have maintained that full-time dedication to the job should continue to be an important dimension of the law professor persona. Various aspects of this dimension come from the fact that the law professor is a member of the university after perhaps only a short tenure in legal practice, if that at all. As Robert A. Leflar noted, following two to five years of private practice or government experience, the law professor focuses on full-time work in the academy, although some outside work may take place on the side, provided that work does not "interfere with [the law professor's] day-to-day performance" of working in the university (23). Robert L. Bard of the University of Connecticut suggested that the law professor has the status that comes with ready access to various individuals such as secretaries and research assistants (736). Often, ready access to these people is an indication of full-time employment within an organization. Meanwhile, Robert M. Jarvis of the Nova University Center for the Study of Law noted that the law professor has a good amount of available time, and much of that time is open for conducting research (76). This available time is designed to keep the law professor away from "the greater financial rewards offered by private practice" of law (Jarvis 70–71). Bard concurred with that point (736). In making the point, Jarvis was suggesting largely separate spheres for lawyers in the academy and for those in the world of practice. In short, because the law school is situated in the university (Crabb 329), the law professor tends to be a regular member of the university faculty and does not hold other major positions.

In addition to full-time devotion to career, since 1960, advocates of the law professor as scholar model have argued that teaching duties should remain an important aspect of the law professor's persona, and various examples help demonstrate this point. For instance, lawyers have discussed the purposes and methods of law teaching. Anthony D'Amato of Northwestern University argued that teaching law should be about teaching law students to cope with legal problems (493). Unlike traditional undergraduate lectures that tend to do nothing to change a student's "mental pathways," the process of "[t]eaching [law] is an attempt to change the student's mind" (D'Amato 462). In this sense, the law professor has a duty to try to do more than teach the memorization of legal rules, instead needing to enhance the student's thinking skills because not endeavoring to do so would have the impact of indirectly harming "the poor future client who discovers too late that her lawyer is part of her problem and not part of her solution" (D'Amato 494).

As such, law professors often employ what they describe as the Socratic method of questioning students regarding the materials for classes (D'Amato 466). D'Amato argued that the questions a professor asks while employing the Socratic method should not suggest specific answers; instead, the questions should encourage students to develop new ways of thinking (466). Also, the Socratic method should help students to learn to work with ambiguity (Binford 550–51).

Lawyers have made various other points about law teaching. Jarvis maintained that the law professor should instruct students specifically in legal policy (77), while Roger C. Cramton of Cornell Law School noted that, because the law professor spends so much time teaching large classes of students, teaching is a key part of the law professor persona (8). Due to law school economics, such large courses may include one hundred to one hundred fifty students each (Christie 315). Regardless, law professors are still supposed to make the classroom experience valuable for students. Getting students to learn actively through writing exercises, visual aids, and other means can be helpful (Boyle 3–7, 19–25). Of course, some teaching, such as coaching moot court, involves working with smaller groups of students (Case 368, 381–82).

More specifically, lawyers have staked out ground on issues relevant to the new law professor. One such lawyer was Susan J. Becker of Cleveland State University, who noted that two of these issues include deciding which law courses to teach and learning how to teach (433, 434). Becker explained that the specifics of law teaching consist of items such as self-presentation in front of students, choosing course materials, preparation of a syllabus, handling the first day of class, and interacting with students (434–42).

In terms of interacting with students, Becker reflected in the following manner:

> In my brief career, I have faced students who repeatedly arrived ten minutes late for class (usually with steaming cup of coffee in hand); talked audibly while I or a fellow student had the floor; raised their hands in a Pavlovian response every time a question or comment danced into their heads; continued to wave the raised hand like a first-grader in need of a bathroom pass until I called on them; yawned as if they had never been so bored in their entire lives; asked questions that had been asked and answered at least twice in the previous five minutes; coughed so loudly during class that I could not speak over the noise; fell asleep (sitting straight up, no less); exhibited the dreaded

> "So what are you going to do about it?" sneer while informing me that they weren't prepared to discuss the assigned material; and even passed a case brief to a student I had called on who obviously hadn't read the assignment. (440)

In response to such behaviors, Becker advocated responses like commenting on the offending behavior (440–41). Thus, in reply to the yawning student, the professor might comment, "'I'm sorry if we're boring you; I'll try to move on to something more exciting as soon as possible'" (Becker 441). In part because lawyers like Becker have reflected on their teaching in this manner, teaching has remained an important dimension of the law professor as scholar persona.

Not only have lawyers embraced the continuing importance of the law professor's relatively traditional teaching duties, but some lawyers have advanced alternative ways to teach, especially those ways which outsider philosophies have informed. For instance, in critiquing the domineering Charles Kingsfield model from the 1973 film *The Paper Chase*, Catharine W. Hantzis of the University of Southern California offered a feminist perspective on law teaching, suggesting that such teaching would benefit from the professor's spending time with students, showing students that the professor cares, and finding new experiences for the professor's students (156–57, 162–63). Respectively, these suggestions might manifest themselves in a law professor's having lunch with a colleague in the student cafeteria so that the professor is available for informal student interaction, providing students with written exercises, and perhaps even requiring students in a class on disability law to maneuver around the campus in a wheelchair for a few hours (Hantzis 162–63). One goal of such a feminist approach to teaching is for the professor to be "both practical and student centered" (Hantzis 162).

Along similar lines, Robert P. Schuwerk of the University of Houston advocated for an approach to teaching that involved collaborative learning. Rather than calling on individual students in a large class, Schuwerk proposed calling on pairs of students or small groups of students no larger than four people (790–91). Among other things, Schuwerk maintained that this approach would reduce the tension between a professor and students, facilitate mutual support in learning, and improve the quality of class discussion (793).

Also moving away from the Kingsfield model, some lawyers have stressed the importance of bringing personal experience to the classroom. For instance, to facilitate an environment supportive of diversity, a professor might bring her lesbianism to a Decedents' Estates discussion of a state constitutional amendment that had aimed to prohibit same-sex marriage (A. Gilmore 94–101). To model cultural competence, a professor could bring her experience with being Native American to a classroom mainly populated by non-Native Americans (EagleWoman 269). To support students who are struggling with mental health issues, a professor might bring to class his own experience of struggling with depression and anxiety (Clarke 410–14).

Of note, sharing personal experience can risk rejection by the power structure in legal education (Arriola 484, 491). Accordingly, the professor may try not to bring to class some aspects of her own personal experience, such as the impact of living in a culture with a "barrage of images of unarmed Blacks being killed, racist attacks, and the growth of white supremacy" (Rutledge 233).

As well as bringing personal experience to the classroom, the professor should be mindful of the personal considerations that students might bring to class. Heidi K. Brown of New York Law School stressed the importance of understanding the many student-related factors at play in one's classroom. For instance, the students in a given class may learn via visual, auditory, kinesthetic, and other means (Brown 303). Certain students may be introverted, while their classmates are extroverted (Brown 303). Various students might fear speaking in public (Brown 303), or, as Susan Greene of Brooklyn Law School added, they may have stress and anxiety about law school in general (751–52). Some students may have dyslexia (Brown 303). Others might be non-native English speakers (Coleman & Albertson 2–3), while still others could have responsibilities for children or parents (Brown 303). Sean Darling-Hammond of the U.S. District Court for the District of Maryland and Kristen Holmquist of U.C. Berkeley observed that various students may be members of underrepresented or stereotyped groups or lack prior exposure to the law (4). Some such students may desire the freedom in class not to speak about given topics that especially implicate them (Rutledge 234). For example, some racial minority students may not wish to discuss race (Rutledge 234). Under extraordinary circumstances, such as those that arose in March 2020, students may need distraction from a global pandemic (Tamer & Shultz), particularly because of anxiety about the international public health crisis and the loss of loved ones (Ahmad 21, 30). Brown maintained that, in teaching, a professor should aim to be aware of these types of concerns and may need to make students feel safe about sharing their own learning-related concerns with the professor (303).

While full-time dedication to the job and teaching have continued to function as notable dimensions of the professor as scholar model, since 1960, advocates of this model also have argued that research should be a major focus of the scholar persona. Such research is typically conducted on a solo basis rather than with other individuals (Meyerson 563–64). Attention given to multiple aspects of research, including its justifications, illustrates the point about the importance of research. For example, Anthony Chase of the Nova University Center for the Study of Law argued that law professors have had to produce legal scholarship because, at one time, the legal profession chose "to utilize universities to control the supply of lawyers in the United States" ("The Legal Scholar" 65). In essence, scholarship constitutes the dues that law professors owe to the universities in exchange for the universities' granting "the socially and economically useful premises and auspices of the American university" to the legal field (Chase, "The Legal Scholar" 67). As members and beneficiaries of the university system, then, law professors have had to play by the rules of publishing or perishing. Chase added that law professors tend to make more money than professors in many other fields in the academy, so law professors have another reason for having to pay the publishing dues ("The Legal Scholar" 66).

Jarvis extended the idea that Chase and others have advocated, specifically maintaining that scholarship should be "the single most important item on [law professors'] professional agendas" (72). In the context of the legal field, Jarvis asserted that "only law professors have the possibility of becoming and remaining authentic academics" (74). For instance, unlike practicing lawyers, academic lawyers have flexible professional time, resources for research, and research assistants (Jarvis 75–76). Jarvis made the point that research should be law professors' top priority not only "the year before they come up for tenure" but rather throughout their scholarly careers (76). If a lawyer in practice seeks to transition to the academy, that individual most likely will need to publish at least one article to make the case for suitability for working in the academy (Hernández 517, Jesson 450–51, Zietlow 511). In a similar vein, a lawyer already in the academy who seeks to move to another university should be "a prolific writer" (Secunda 128).

Research has proved so significant that measuring its impact has been a major concern. For example, citation counts for research published in legal journals have been viewed as important since the 1980s (Ruhl et al. 782–83). Additionally, J. B. Ruhl et al. of Vanderbilt University argued that citation counts for research published in non-legal journals also should be considered valuable as measuring research impact (783–85).

In part because many lawyers have designated research as a major dimension of the law professor persona, these lawyers have argued over the particulars of legal scholarship. For instance, Anthony T. Kronman of Yale University argued that scholarship should be the pursuit of truth (967–68). Cramton argued for a "modernistic view of tentative and evolving truth" in scholarship, as well as for backing away from advocacy writing (5, 7–8). Additionally, Cramton bemoaned the point that the prolific scholar would gain prestige and migrate up the ladder of law school hierarchy, regardless of the quality of the research the scholar had done (14). Here, Cramton was arguing against a quantity-over-quality approach to advancement in the legal academy.

An anonymous party, who wrote under the pseudonym Lawprofblawg, and Darren Bush of the University of Houston suggested that, despite noble statements about "the joy of writing or service to society," external validation was likely the primary reason for doing scholarship (333). Often, academic writers were focused on superficial metrics like numbers of citations, placement of work in high-status journals, and the writers' own reputations among peers (Lawprofblawg & Bush 333). Lawprofblawg and Bush felt that external validation might be the worst motivation for doing scholarship (331).

Richard Posner of the University of Chicago Law School addressed the various types of scholarship, including doctrinal scholarship and interdisciplinary scholarship (1113, 1119). As Posner observed, doctrinal scholarship is the traditional mode of legal scholarship, supposedly independent of other disciplines, by which law professors consider legal authorities and refine an understanding of what legal doctrine is now and should be in the future (1113–14). On the other hand, interdisciplinary scholarship considers law in light of other scholarly fields such as those in the humanities and social sciences (Posner 1119). Interdisciplinary scholarship was beginning to enter the legal academy in the 1970s and 1980s (Ulen 403). Posner concluded that, although doctrinal scholarship "should remain the core of legal scholarship," both types of scholarship could have a home within the research dimension of the law professor persona and that law schools should attempt to further that end (1113, 1129–30).

Shortly thereafter, Edward L. Rubin of U.C. Berkeley concurred with some, although not all, of Posner's earlier discussion of interdisciplinary legal scholarship. Indeed, Rubin noted the overlap of law and other areas of knowledge such as natural science, literary criticism, moral philosophy, and social science (524–41). Although he accepted the potential value of interdisciplinary scholarship in certain cases, Rubin still drew lines between legal scholarship and scholarship in other fields. For instance, Rubin argued that, while legal scholarship was prescriptive, natural and social science scholarship was descriptive, literary criticism was interpretive, and moral philosophy was categorically prescriptive (565). According to Rubin, in most cases, differing assumptions about methodology proved too much for legal scholarship to rely upon the approaches of other fields (565). Regardless of whether one accepts Rubin's distinctions among the approaches of the non-legal fields that he considered, Rubin's focus on scholarship, much like Posner's, did help advance the notion of the importance of the scholarly dimension of the law professor persona because, one way or another, the law professor would generate scholarship.

As web logs, or blogs, became more common during the 2000s, lawyers argued about whether blogging could be a form of scholarship and, if so, at what level of quality. Admitting that not every legal idea should "be expanded to seventy-five pages and... festooned with copious footnotes and citations," Douglas A. Berman of Ohio State University pointed out that blogs offered a medium for concise legal scholarship (1048–49, 1051–53). Nancy Levit of the University of Missouri-Kansas City (953), along with Lawrence B. Solum of the University of Illinois (1072–73), observed that law review articles had cited blogs on many occasions, so blogs had something to do with scholarship. The blog was a medium for the distribution "of short-form, open-access, disintermediated legal scholarship" (Solum 1087). This observation meant that the blogosphere was noticing an emerging trend toward shorter legal scholarship that was readily available on the Internet and had less screening by intermediaries like law review editorial boards (Solum 1082–86).

Noting that the blogging risks of "possible embarrassment, understated criticisms, and preemption" of ideas were too high, Kate Litvak of the University of Texas argued that blogs were not, in most cases, the best way for scholars to gain feedback on their writing (1069). Litvak also opined that the quality of most comments on blogs was often "very low—not even close to something you can hear at a conference or read in a referee report" (1069).

Beyond the considerations of Cramton, Posner, Rubin, and the lawyers who have discussed blogs, other lawyers have argued the specifics of how new law professors should engage in legal scholarship, thus again maintaining the belief that the law professor persona has a key research dimension. Robert Abrams of Wayne State Law School offered a few tips, including the need for writing regularly and avoiding "[b]usy work" like "[b]ar journal articles, survey pieces, glorified op-ed pieces appearing in non-law reviews, law alumni magazine articles, previews of U.S. Supreme Court cases, non-substantive book reviews, [and] segments of commission reports or studies" (1–2). Abrams urged the new law professor to focus on "[h]igher orders" like "[a]ffirmative thesis articles, law reform articles, book chapters…, frontal attacks on the citadel of major legal doctrine, reconciliation of theory with practice articles, [and] longer works such as monographs and books" (2). Sherri L. Burr of the University of New Mexico School of Law suggested the importance of a scholarly agenda of interests and choosing to write from that set of interests (155–58). Burr maintained that "what gives you the most satisfaction" should guide selection from the set of interests (159). Still, the legal academy may push back against those who would advance "radical ideas or non-normative jeremiads by forcing them to moderate their arguments or forgo truly radical ideas until after tenure or forever" (Maynard 250).

Abrams also advanced several points about self-motivation for writing and the tenure politics that can follow writing. Addressing self-motivation and paraphrasing a colleague, Abrams noted that "the first step in writing is to take off your shoes. Then you crawl under your desk with a hammer and nails and nail the shoes to the floor. Finally, you sit down at the desk, insert your feet into the shoes, and tie your shoes on again" (8). In terms of tenure politics, Abrams offered "a series of three propositions":

1. Productive writers receive tenure.
2. Non-writers are denied tenure.
3. In cases not governed by the two primary rules the most important determinant in tenure decisions is the quantity of credible writing produced by the candidate. (11)

The sum total of the analysis was the following: "Write early and often!" (Abrams 13). This view reflected the German idea of *sitzfleisch*, literally "'sitting meat' or 'sitting flesh,'" which is one's ability to sit for the duration to complete the work that needs to be done (Schultheis).

Once one had completed some scholarship, whatever its nature might be, one could use contemporary technology to promote one's work. For instance, writing during the 2000s, Levit observed that Internet repositories such as the Social Science Research Network and Bepress Legal Repository helped to make the academic writing of lawyers more accessible (971). Indeed, with global access, websites allowed one's scholarship to reach a much broader audience than was possible in earlier decades.

Other lawyers have reviewed critically some aspects of legal scholarship. For example, Robert Stevens of Haverford College questioned the audience of legal scholarship. Stevens queried whether the law professor would write academic work that professors in other fields might read or pragmatic work that lawyers in the world of practice might use in their work ("American Legal Scholarship" 446). Stevens cautioned that law professors could not be all things to all people ("American Legal Scholarship" 445). Additionally, Marc Rohr of Nova University suggested that some law schools might place too much emphasis on scholarship at the cost of law students' educational experiences because not all scholarship benefits students (102–04). Nonetheless, by placing great emphasis on the research dimension of the law professor persona, lawyers further have emphasized their construction of the law professor persona as that of a scholar.

As vital as research has continued to remain as a dimension of the law professor persona, advocates of the scholar model have argued that the public function dimension still should remain important, although its importance ought not to be as great as that of the research dimension (Bard 733). This public function dimension has several strands, one of which is the production of scholarship helpful to the world of legal practice (Edwards, "The Growing Disjunction" 38; Hricik & Salzmann 765). Such scholarship should "prescribe ways effectively to improve law's ability to serve society" (Edwards, "Another Look" 1499). While such scholarship may have "a good dose of theory," this scholarship should give "due weight to doctrine" to be of utility to legal practitioners (Edwards, "The Growing Disjunction" 45–46). Justice Roger J. Traynor, an associate justice on the California Supreme Court, noted that judges and members of the practicing bar sometimes call upon law review scholarship in judicial opinions and in briefs to the court (6). Naturally, academic lawyers are frequently the authors behind law review articles. The point is that academic lawyers should offer practicing lawyers views on "how the legal regime works" so that practicing lawyers can call upon such views in legal argumentation (Edwards, "The Growing Disjunction" 56).

Another strand of the public function dimension of the law professor persona is "devot[ing] a substantial component of [one's] work life to selfless public service" (Bard 749). Such public service can include improving social conditions for individuals who are unable to help themselves (Bard 749), as well as offering consultation to government entities (Stevens, "American Legal Scholarship" 446). For example, a law professor who teaches in the area of torts might offer services to a legislative committee that is drafting a major new statute related to products liability law. This type of service not only could assist consumers who may be unaware of the limitations of state products liability law, but the service also would help legislators who would learn from the professor's expertise and thus be able to produce a more effective statute. Besides providing such benefits, participating in this service would set positive examples for law students who are on the verge of entering the profession (Bard 749). In a post-Watergate world, where the ethos of the legal profession has been an ongoing matter of concern, this example-setting is important (Bard 749).

Furthermore, acting as a public intellectual, the law professor might offer commentary on legal matters in the news, a service that educates both the news media and the public and, as Erwin Chemerinsky, then of Duke University, noted, offers the professor an audience much larger than the typical law school class (Gajda 219). The professor also might distribute commentary for lay people directly to a large audience through a blog (Bashman 1259). Social media like Facebook and Twitter can be other outlets for commentary, although the professor should be careful to remain professional in using such media (McPeak 227–32).

Finally, if not commenting on a particular case through various media, the law professor might become more involved with influencing law in action. The professor could aim to persuade practicing attorneys and judges to change the law, particularly at the level of the U.S. Supreme Court (Fontana 327–28). Alternatively, the professor even could take on the occasional high-profile case at the trial or appellate level, especially if the case were to go to the U.S. Supreme Court (Kurland 357–60, Entin 522–23).

While, under the scholar model of the law professor, lawyers have constructed a generally uniform persona, some tension periodically may manifest itself among the various dimensions of this persona. During the 1960s, Thomas F. Bergin of the University of Virginia offered what has become a classic explanation of the tension between teaching future lawyers and engaging in scholarship. Although the law professor may teach a favorite jurisprudential seminar, the professor is also supposed to teach law students something useful for working in the world of legal practice, a process which Bergin described as "Hessian-training" (638). Unlike jurisprudential teaching, teaching useful for legal practice often conflicts with the type of research that the law professor does (Bergin 638). From this perspective, the tension may be impossible to cure (Costello 391). Clark Byse of Harvard, then visiting at Boston University, posited that, because a law professor's research can inform the professor's teaching and vice versa, teaching and research should not be in great tension (29–31). Thus, a law professor ought to be able to teach law students something useful for lawyering and also engage in research on the law. Whether Bergin or Byse made the better argument has remained an unresolved matter.

As this section of Chapter V has illustrated, much as in the periods from 1870 to 1920 and from 1920 to 1960, in the period from 1960 to the present, advocates of the law professor as scholar persona have argued that the law professor persona should continue to include the dimensions of a full-time dedication to the job, teaching duties, production of research, and a public function. Although slightly more tolerance of limited legal practice has continued from the period between 1920 and 1960, in the period since 1960, the scholar persona of the law professor clearly has not been primarily oriented in the direction of legal practice.

In presenting their ideal law professor persona as the scholar, lawyers who have embraced this position have done so primarily through Aristotelian rhetoric. This rhetoric has involved the advancing and supporting of claims. The texts studied here did not suggest sustained consideration on the part of the pro-scholar advocates of a competing position for the purpose of understanding underlying concerns. Indeed, the rhetoric largely ignored the pro-practitioner discourse that will receive attention in the next section of this chapter. As such, the lawyers generally were not calling upon invitational rhetoric.

One exception to the generally Aristotelian nature of the discourse examined above would be the offering of examples from one's personal experience, which several of the lawyers noted above did. This type of discursive strategy is more common to non-Aristotelian rhetoric of a feminist vein (Foss & Foss, "Personal Experience" 39). Another exception would be a degree of awareness that, under the public function dimension, at least some scholarship should be helpful to the world of legal practice, something that attorneys who have supported the practitioner persona would support. However, as the next section of this chapter will show, pro-practitioner attorneys have perceived scholarship useful to the world of legal practice to be in short supply.

The Law Professor as Practitioner

Although the above rhetoric indicates substantial support for the scholar persona of the law professor, not all lawyers have accepted this persona. Instead, some lawyers have argued vigorously for the merits of a practitioner persona.

In seeking to construct this alternative persona, lawyers have called upon Aristotelian rhetoric because these lawyers have been making and supporting claims to advance their position, which have included a vigorous refutation of the pro-scholar position. Through Aristotelian rhetoric, these lawyers have offered two major claims: (1) legal education, through the scholar model, has failed to educate future lawyers adequately and (2) the practitioner model would be a more effective approach to legal education. To support these major claims that have outlined the practitioner persona, the pro-practitioner lawyers have offered various types of evidence. The following discussion examines the arguments that have developed this practitioner persona.

To begin with, pro-practitioner lawyers have argued passionately that legal education, through the scholar model, has failed to train prospective lawyers adequately for the practice of law. This critique has come from as high up as the U.S. Supreme Court. In the mid-1970s, Chief Justice Warren E. Burger took U.S. legal education to task for not satisfactorily training law students to function as competent courtroom lawyers (227, 232). Calling upon "conversations extending over the past twelve to fifteen years at judicial meetings and seminars, with literally hundreds of judges and experienced lawyers," Burger estimated that perhaps "from one-third to one-half of the lawyers who appear in the serious [legal] cases are not really qualified to render fully adequate representation" to clients (234). Burger listed witness examination and handling of evidence as examples of skills that many lawyers had not mastered (234–35). Picking up on rhetoric from the period from 1870 to 1920 that drew comparisons between legal education and education in other fields, Burger pointed out that "[t]he medical profession does not try to teach surgery simply with books; more than 80% of all medical teaching is done by practicing physicians and surgeons" (232).

Scott Turow, a practicing lawyer in Chicago, also focused on the technical side of law school, arguing, "To put it plainly, law school is not lawyer school." Turow observed, "The best teachers of legal skills are those who use them, and it would have been pointless for my Harvard Law School professors to attempt to instruct me about the execution of tasks they themselves may barely know how to perform." Indeed, "law school does *not* teach students to think like lawyers"; it instead teaches students "to think like law professors" (Turow). According to Turow, something essential was missing from law school.

Pro-practitioner advocates have taken issue with the research performance of the law professor who has adopted the scholar persona and how that performance has done little to prepare students for practical legal writing. For instance, Judge Patricia M. Wald, a judge on the U.S. Court of Appeals for the District of Columbia Circuit, noted that "[a]ble advocacy writing has little in common with a long, discursive paper on some abstract facet of the law" (42). Wald pointed out that this latter type of writing commonly has a home in "law review 'think' pieces" (42), which, as observed above, have become an important component of one dimension of the scholar persona of the law professor. Wald went as far as to explain that "experience teaches... that too few law review articles prove helpful in appellate decision making. They tend to be too talky, too unselective in separating the relevant from the irrelevant, too exhaustive, too exhausting, too hedged, too cautious about reaching a definite conclusion" (42). Clearly, from Wald's perspective, the orientation toward law review writing by professors who have adopted the scholar persona has not been in the interest of preparing law students to write as practicing lawyers.

Critiques of the academy's great interest in scholarly writing, particularly the law review article, have also come from the highest level of the federal judiciary. For instance, Justice Stephen Breyer of the U.S. Supreme Court observed, "[T]here is evidence that law review articles have left terra firma to soar into outer space" (33). Breyer added, "I do worry about the academic world losing touch with the profession" (33).

In more colorful language, Chief Justice John Roberts, then holding the same position on the U.S. Supreme Court that Burger had held decades earlier, offered another critique. Responding to a question during an interview, Roberts maintained the following:

> Pick up a copy of any law review that you see—and the first article is likely to be, you know—the influence of Immanuel Kant on evidentiary approaches in eighteenth century—Bulgaria or something—which I'm sure was of great interest to the academic that wrote it, but isn't of much help to the—to the bar. Now, I—I hasten to add I don't think there's anything wrong with that. If the—the academy wants to deal with the legal issues at a particularly abstract and philosophical level—that's great, and that's their business—but they shouldn't expect that it would be of any particular help or even interest to members of the practicing bar—or judges. (30:47–31:32)

Roberts admitted, "You know, it's their business, but—people ask me, you know, what the last law review article I read was, and I have to think very hard before coming up with one" (32:03–32:14).

Away from the bench, Brent E. Newton, deputy staff director for the U.S. Sentencing Commission, continued the critique of the efficacy of legal education, again with attention to the focus on academic writing. Newton argued that the law professor, increasingly the holder of a Ph.D. as well as a law degree, was spending a voluminous amount of time writing esoteric scholarship that was irrelevant to law students, the practicing bar, and the judiciary

("Preaching" 130–32, 113–25). More-elite law schools were more likely to hire professors with Ph.D.s than less-elite law schools (McCrary et al. 545–46). Newton observed that the scholarship by such professors was for other law professors ("Ninety-Five Theses" 126). Moreover, in addition to "lack[ing] practical skills," the professor even had a sense of "indifference toward (or in some cases outright disdain for) both practicing attorneys and practical components of the law school faculty such as clinicians" (Newton, "Preaching" 113). Such a law professor, preoccupied with scholarly interests, hardly could prepare students for the practice of law.

In light of critiques such as the foregoing, lawyers have argued that the practitioner model would be a more effective approach to legal education than the scholar model. In order to address the unsatisfactory status quo, Burger maintained that, at least in the case of trial practice, "trial advocacy must be learned from trial advocates" (232). U.S. legal education could learn from the hands-on approach that England has employed in the training of its legal advocates (Burger 228–30), and the practitioner persona would work credibly with such an approach. Ideally, this type of approach would help address the level of incompetence that Burger and others have claimed to have observed.

From her perspective, Wald offered several benefits that law students would gain from the law professor who credibly had assumed the practitioner persona to teach. For instance, Wald stressed that law school graduates should understand how claims progress through the system so that graduates would know whether to litigate a particular claim; not all claims can be litigated at acceptable costs, financial or otherwise (36). Also, in noting the importance of trial experience, Wald quoted her former mentor, Judge Jerome Frank, for the point "that focusing on [teaching] appellate opinions, to the detriment of [teaching] what happened in the trial court, was 'like the difference between kissing a girl and reading a treatise on osculation'" (43). Further, practical experience can allow law graduates to understand the human dimensions of legal practice (P. Wald 38). As Wald noted, too much technical training at the expense of learning how to deal "with real clients, witnesses and even judges and court personnel" is detrimental to legal practice because lawyers need to know how to interact with other human actors in the legal world (38). Wald's argument suggests that the appropriate professor to help law students down this path would be the one who successfully could assume the practitioner persona.

Breyer and Roberts added their thoughts for improvement, too, suggesting the value of practical research. Breyer expressed his perspective that the legal profession worked best when professors produced research that commented on the law, practicing lawyers used that research to advance clients' goals through sharing the professors' views with the bench, and judges considered the professors' views as articulated by practicing lawyers (33–34). Of course, for practicing lawyers and judges to use the commentary on the law well, they would need to be able to understand it, so the commentary presumably would need to be practice-oriented. Roberts also urged research useful to lawyers outside of the academy, stating the following during the above-noted interview: "But I—I do think that—if the academy is interested in having an influence—on—on the practice of law, on the development of law—that they—they would be wise to sort of stop and think, 'Is—is this area of research going to be of—of help to anyone—other than other—academics?'" (31:39–32:02).

For his part, Newton issued a call for law faculties that included significant numbers of members who possessed extensive experience in the practice of law ("Preaching" 149–50). Specifically, Newton called for "at least two-thirds of the faculty" to have "a significant amount of meaningful practical experience" in law ("Preaching" 149–50). Such experience would be at least a decade and perhaps more (Newton, "Preaching" 150).

Other legal communicators have concurred with this sentiment of practicality. Judge Sherman G. Finesilver of the U.S. District Court for the District of Colorado argued for the benefits of learning law from professors who have adopted the practitioner persona. Finesilver declared that students become more involved in learning from experienced practitioners because such practitioners can offer realistic experiences that relate directly to "the role of a functioning attorney" (1062). Such practical experience should enhance the relevance of law school for many law students and better help prospective lawyers understand "both the immediate analytic aspects as well as the larger social context of each case" (Finesilver 1062, 1071).

Support for the practitioner persona and its accompanying level of expertise has come from the state bench as well as from the federal bench. Judge Judith Ann Lanzinger of the Ohio Court of Common Pleas considered the benefits of the law professor's adopting the persona of a judicial practitioner. Lanzinger's argument was that, via adding "depth and breadth to the law school curriculum," judges could "enrich the law school itself by balancing faculty who have limited practical experience" (107, 103). Specifically, such judges might teach Trial Advocacy and other litigation-related courses (Lanzinger 99). If law schools without judicial experience on the faculty were to consider employing judges part-time, the law professor persona would take a turn for the practical, which would benefit students (Lanzinger 105).

Although lawyers in the world of practice have been the dominant voices in the call for the practitioner model of the law professor and the purported benefits to law students and the legal field that would come with such an approach, lawyers in the academy have not always avoided such rhetoric. One example was Hugh W. Silverman of the University of Windsor, who offered some suggestions that made their way into the U.S. conflict over the construction of the law professor. Silverman contended that practical experience would allow a law professor effectively to teach the overlapping nature of branches of law like contracts and torts that frequently come together in practice, much more so than in law school classes usually divided up artificially by areas of law (430). Silverman explained that "[t]he practitioner who has whetted his teeth upon the various skills and arts of the law has a storehouse of knowledge and insight into the nature and practice of the law, and can readily assess the needs of the lawyer who is about to enter that arena" (430).

Silverman offered several possibilities in which the practitioner could bring realistic experience to class. For instance, rather than relying upon hypothetical situations to provide instruction, in teaching Contracts, the practitioner could instruct students in drafting contracts, in teaching Torts, the practitioner could offer examples from torts trials, and, in teaching Civil and Criminal Procedure, the practitioner likewise could present examples from experience (Silverman 430, 431). Additionally, because the practitioner with trial experience could offer law students a perspective apart from that via which students only would consider appellate law, the practitioner approach would broaden the education of law students (Silverman 431).

One special situation in which lawyers have argued that the practitioner persona of the law professor can be especially helpful in establishing professorial ethos and thus more effective legal education is clinical legal education, which goes back at least as far as the 1960s (Leleiko 515). Clinical legal education involves "integrating the law school with the judicial, legislative and administrative processes of a community" (Leleiko 512). Generally, the law school runs the equivalent of a public interest law firm in which students work on real-life legal problems under the supervision of experienced attorneys (Leleiko 513). Such an environment affords students the opportunities to connect with local communities and sometimes even to work with social movements (McDougall 327, 334). At numerous law schools, "a rigid divide" has existed between individuals who teach clinics and individuals who teach doctrinal courses (Chemerinsky 40), and clinical teachers often have had lower institutional status (Berger 129; Edwards, "The Role" 292).

According to supporters of clinical legal education, the benefits for students are many. For example, Steven H. Leleiko of New York University School of Law explained that clinical legal education provides direct legal experience for law students, offers a different perspective on the law from that found in traditional law school classes, opens up students' minds to social change, enhances students' capacities, allows students to assume responsibility in their chosen profession sooner, helps with "a broad range of public service activities and the administration of civil and criminal justice," and challenges law students simultaneously to employ multiple "intellectual capacities" (511–12). Of course, clinical legal education can be only as good as the quality of the supervision and the nature of the opportunities that law students receive in the process (Leleiko 517).

For such experiences to have a chance to take place, the professor must assume the persona of a practitioner because the scholar persona does not fit with the specific means of legal instruction in the clinic. This is an example of a case in which persona and ethos have a relationship (Cherry 402), as the assumed persona of the practitioner would help the professor develop ethos with the audience of law students. If the audience is pragmatically-oriented and the performance is skillful, the audience's perception of ethos most likely will be positive. In turn, windows to learning will be more likely to open. Thus, the material consequences of the professor's assumed persona include a strong professorial ethos and an audience more open to instruction.

As the arguments of these lawyers, including the lawyers on the bench, show, discontent with the scholar persona of the law professor remains. Giving a hearty nod to the practical qualities that they desire in legal education, lawyers have advanced a spirited case for the practitioner persona to have at least some space within the law school. The rhetoric of this persona has remained defiant.

In seeking to develop their ideal law professor persona as a practitioner, lawyers who have adopted this position have employed Aristotelian rhetoric. This rhetoric has consisted of advancing and supporting claims, including a spirited refutation of the scholar model. The texts studied here did not suggest any serious consideration of the pro-scholar position for the purpose of understanding underlying concerns.

The Law Professor as Scholar/Practitioner Hybrid

For the period from 1960 to present, despite the extensive amount of literature on the ideal law professor persona, this study did not locate much rhetoric that supported hybrid models. Nonetheless, several modest scholar/practitioner hybrid personas or fragments thereof made cameo appearances in the discourse and now receive attention. To their Aristotelian rhetoric, the proponents of the hybrid personas or fragments thereof added a notable touch of invitational rhetoric.

Randall T. Coyne of the University of Oklahoma articulated a hybrid persona mainly academic in nature, but with a serious practitioner ingredient. From an academic position, Coyne advocated representing, on a regular basis, and generally pro bono, indigent individuals such as those charged with capital crimes or waiting to be executed (97–98). Presumably, this pro bono representation could take place with regard to other legal matters, too.

Although Coyne promoted much-needed legal representation, he admitted that such representation was not a law professor's "primary academic mission" (109). This representation was connected to the public function dimension of the law professor persona (Coyne 97), one dimension of a multi-dimensional persona. Besides a public function, Coyne's model also consisted of a full-time dedication to the job, teaching duties, and the development of research (97). Coyne's persona closely tracked the scholar persona, but, in advocating for regular pro bono work, Coyne advocated for more than the occasional pro bono effort and thus went beyond the scholar persona.

Another hybrid persona that appeared was that of the visitor to the other side of the scholar/practitioner divide. Edward D. Re, formerly of the U.S. Court of International Trade and then of St. John's University Law School, argued that the law professor without hands-on legal experience should take a sabbatical to "learn about the daily practice of law" (97). Such a sabbatical in practice should last at least one semester, but preferably one full school year (Re 97). With this type of sabbatical, the inexperienced professor would acquire hands-on experience and be able to pass on that experience to law students and colleagues (Re 97–98). For his proposal, Re received the concurrence of Amy B. Cohen of Western New England College School of Law, who did not necessarily limit the sabbatical idea to professors who lacked any practical experience at all (643). Emily Zimmerman of Drexel University suggested that some time in practice could be one way for academics to fulfill a continuing practice experience (CPE) requirement (140–41, 176). With some time in practice, although not fully able to assume the practitioner persona, the individual who generally assumed the scholar persona nonetheless would be able to perform a more credible nod to the practical part of the legal field.

The other version of the visitor persona involved attorneys from practice who would take sabbaticals to teach law, an idea which former U.S. Solicitor General Seth P. Waxman promoted (1911). Presumably, such visitors from practice would learn more about the workings of academic law. With some time teaching at the university, although not fully able to assume the scholar persona, the individual who generally assumed the practitioner persona nonetheless would be able to perform a more credible nod to the academic part of the legal field.

Meanwhile, Waxman also briefly maintained that law schools should "hire gifted people who have been successful in practice, public and private" as "practitioner-scholars who are fully integrated into the academic faculty" (1912). This articulation alluded to Harlan F. Stone's argument during the period from 1870 to 1920 that a law professor should be both one who has practiced law and a scholar ("The Importance" 206). However, Waxman made his point only briefly, and thus this hybrid fragment lacked the benefit of development.

While relatively few in number given the high volume of rhetoric about the ideal role of the law professor since 1960, these scholar/practitioner hybrid personas or fragments thereof suggested a notable touch of invitational rhetoric in addition to the more common Aristotelian rhetoric of advancing and supporting of claims. From a mainly academic perspective, Coyne acknowledged the importance of ongoing hands-on legal experience (97–98). The proponents of the visitor persona in its different forms recognized the value of time spent on the other side of the scholar/practitioner divide (Re 97, Cohen 642, Zimmerman 144–49, Waxman 1911). Zimmerman suggested that adoption of this persona "could foster a closer relationship between the legal academy and the world of law practice" (149). Waxman, from a practitioner perspective, reached out to academically-oriented lawyers, suggesting that lawyers should "speak with each other without shouting" and aim to "enrich the understanding of colleagues in other disciplines within the endeavor of law" (1912). Thus, several glimmers of the invitational emerged among the usual points of advocacy.

Conclusion

As this chapter has explained, the conflict between lawyers who have supported the scholar model of the law professor and lawyers who have supported the practitioner model has continued in the period since 1960. Although advocates of the scholar model have become slightly more accepting of limited practical experience, this model is generally the same model that Langdell, Ames, and their allies articulated in the late nineteenth century and into the early twentieth century. As in previous historical periods, the practitioner model has had a focus on field-tested skills and abilities that the professor can bring to the classroom for the benefit of law students. Although the scholar model has become the established ideal within the legal academy, advocates of the practitioner model have continued to try to advance their model, even if they seem to realize that this model will remain the minority perspective for the foreseeable future. The fact that, for the large amount of rhetoric published on the ideal law professor persona, only limited hybrid models emerged from the texts located for this era indicates that the lines of conflict have remained rather sharp.

The Aristotelian rhetoric that lawyers generally have continued to employ in the period since 1960 has not helped the tension in the field. Largely without listening to the major competing view in the conflict over the ideal law professor persona, lawyers in academia have tended to advance their own position, which often has involved rehashing familiar arguments from previous historical periods and only fine-tuning some of the details of these arguments, such as what types of legal scholarship are appropriate. To some observers, this approach might appear appropriate because lawyers in academia are currently in the position of power in the legal field regarding decision-making that surrounds the law professor persona and may be able to afford communicating in this unilateral manner. On the other hand, lawyers in the world of practice have tended to critique the view of lawyers in the academy while advancing a rather different view of the law professor persona. In this ongoing exercise of either arguing to members of one's own group or arguing to members of one's own group while also critiquing another group's position, even when that other group is not listening, the parties are not seriously addressing each other's underlying concerns such as intellectualism and practicality.

Some slight refinement to this general observation about Aristotelian rhetoric in the conflict is important. In the sample of texts studied, not every line consisted completely of Aristotelian rhetoric. For example, in considering how to address various teaching issues in law school, Susan J. Becker offered some personal examples from her own classroom (440), a strategy more common to non-Aristotelian rhetoric of a feminist vein (Foss & Foss, "Personal Experience" 39). In also addressing teaching issues, Angela Gilmore offered her personal experience with being openly lesbian (94–97), Angelique

Townsend EagleWoman shared her personal experience with being Native American (269), and Brian S. Clarke discussed his personal experience of struggling with depression and anxiety (410–14). Also, a degree of awareness that, under the public function dimension of the scholar persona, at least some scholarship should be helpful to the world of legal practice appeared. Moreover, while only making brief appearances, several hybrid perspectives or fragments thereof emerged, suggesting the possibility of compromise. On a slightly optimistic note, then, the discourses just noted did leave the door cracked open for other types of communication to enter the conflict. Still, in the sample of texts studied, this rhetoric was not the norm, as persuasion dominated.

In 1987, Chief Justice William H. Rehnquist of the U.S. Supreme Court observed the following about the legal field:

> I like to think of the profession of law as a multi-legged stool—one leg is the practicing bar, another leg is the judiciary, another leg is the academic lawyers, another leg the government lawyers. No leg of the stool can support the profession by itself, and each leg is heavily interdependent on the others. (157)

Rehnquist's legs on this multi-legged stool fall into two main categories: scholar and practitioner. Generally, the leg in the scholar category represents the academics, while the legs in the practitioner category represent the members of the practicing bar, both in private practice and government work, and the judiciary.

Regrettably, since the conflict over the construction of the ideal law professor persona in the United States has been ongoing at least since the end of the nineteenth century, the legs of the stool have not been coexisting successfully with each other for a long time. As suggested earlier, many academic lawyers look down upon practicing lawyers, and many lawyers in legal practice criticize lawyers in the academy (Edwards, "The Growing Disjunction" 35). Indeed, while some academics have come to "scorn the practicing lawyer and his work" (Wellington 329), some members of the practicing bar have become "resentful of the attitudes" that those academics have toward the bar (Allen 132).

Effective communication is essential in many professional situations, and the field of law offers no exception to this general principle. In research on law professors in the United States during the 1960s, 1970s, and early 1980s, Douglas D. McFarland observed that legal academics and practitioners had come to "live in different rhetorical worlds" ("Students and Practicing Lawyers" 105). Specifically, these players in the legal field came to develop "little or no understanding" of each other and even became "hostile to one another" (McFarland, "Students and Practicing Lawyers" 105). Although each camp continued to disseminate its rhetoric, the other camp failed to process that rhetoric because the views of the camps were so different (McFarland, "Self-Images...: Rethinking the Schism" 260). Quite simply, the communication was not working well (McFarland, "Students and Practicing Lawyers" 106). Since this communication had not been moving the situation forward, observers reasonably could expect nothing more than minor change, if that at all (McFarland, "Students and Practicing Lawyers" 106–07).

Given the analyses in the last three chapters of this book, one can make essentially the same assessment about discourse on the ideal U.S. law professor persona both from the late nineteenth century to the period of McFarland's study and from the period of McFarland's study to the present time. Dating back to the nineteenth century, the communication problem has been even more historically extensive than McFarland's work maintained, and this problem has persisted since McFarland completed his research. In short, lawyers have clashed with each other and also talked past each other, making only a few concessions.

While McFarland declined to offer any potential suggestions for improving this less-than-constructive communication (*Self-Images...: Rethinking Legal Education* 207), Francis A. Allen acknowledged, "Dialogue concerning the methods and emphasis of law training... is indispensable to the continuing adaptation of legal education to the world in which it finds itself" (131). In also suggesting dialogue, Seth P. Waxman stressed the need for attorneys to "speak with each other without shouting" (1912). Indeed, these statements hint at part of the underlying problem with the communication in the present period of the conflict. Although the camps have been disseminating their rhetoric, they often have not attempted to listen deeply enough to understand each other, and, if they have listened at all, the purpose has been to offer rebuttal. Either way, understanding underlying concerns like intellectualism and practicality has been missing. The Aristotelian approach to the rhetorical process has not proved as helpful as one might like, but fortunately other approaches to rhetoric are available to participants involved in the conflict over the construction of the ideal law professor persona in the United States. Consequently, this book next will suggest, as part of another approach, the process of invitational rhetoric, which will add a dialogic dimension to the communication. Ultimately, invitational rhetoric, along with a healthier version of Aristotelian rhetoric, will pave the way for cooperative rhetoric, an approach which employs both the much-needed dialogue and the persuasion already employed in the legal field.

Works Cited in Chapter V

Abrams, Robert H. "Sing Muse: Legal Scholarship for New Law Teachers." *Journal of Legal Education*, vol. 37, 1987, pp. 1–13.

Ahmad, Nadia B. "'Blood, Sweat, Tears': A Muslim Woman Law Professor's View on Degenerative Racism, Misogyny, and (Internal) Islamophobia from Preeclampsia and Presumed Incompetent to Pandemic Tenure." *FIU Law Review*, vol. 16, 2021, pp. 13–74.

Allen, Francis A. "The Prospects of University Law Training." *Journal of Legal Education*, vol. 29, 1978, pp. 127–38.

Arriola, Elvia Rosales. "Amor y Esperanza: A Latina Lesbian Becomes a Law Professor." *Journal of Legal Education*, vol. 66, 2017, pp. 484–92.

Bard, Robert L. "Legal Scholarship and the Professional Responsibility of Law Professors." *Connecticut Law Review*, vol. 16, 1984, pp. 731–51.

Bashman, Howard J. "The Battle over the Soul of Law Professor Blogs." *Washington University Law Review*, vol. 84, 2006, pp. 1257–61.

Becker, Susan J. "Advice for the New Law Professor: A View from the Trenches." *Journal of Legal Education*, vol. 42, 1992, pp. 432–46.

Berger, Todd A. "Three Generations and Two Tiers: How Participation in Law School Clinics and the Demand for 'Practice-Ready' Graduates Will Impact the Faculty Status of Clinical Law Professors." *Journal of Law and Policy*, vol. 43, 2013, pp. 129–55.

Bergin, Thomas F. "The Law Teacher: A Man Divided against Himself." *Virginia Law Review*, vol. 54, 1968, pp. 637–57.

Berman, Douglas A. "Scholarship in Action: The Power, Possibilities, and Pitfalls for Law Professor Blogs." *Washington University Law Review*, vol. 84, 2006, pp. 1043–60.

Binford, Warren. "How to Be the World's Best Law Professor." *Journal of Legal Education*, vol. 64, 2015, pp. 542–61.

Boyle, Robin A. "Employing Active-Learning Techniques and Metacognition in Law School: Shifting Energy from Professor to Student." *University of Detroit Mercy Law Review*, vol. 81, 2003, pp. 1–30.

Breyer, Stephen G. "Response of Justice Stephen G. Breyer." *NYU Annual Survey of American Law*, vol. 64, 2008, pp. 33–35.

Brown, Heidi K. "The Emotionally Intelligent Law Professor: A Lesson from *The Breakfast Club*." *University of Arkansas at Little Rock Law Review*, vol. 36, 2013, pp. 273–317.

Burger, Warren E. "The Special Skills of Advocacy: Are Specialized Training and Certification of Advocates Essential to Our System of Justice?" *Fordham Law Review*, vol. 42, 1973, pp. 227–42.

Burr, Sherri L. "Reflections on a Scholarly Agenda for the Beginning Law Professor." *Saint Louis University Public Law Review*, vol. 10, 1991, pp. 155–59.

Byse, Clark. "Legal Scholarship, Legal Realism and the Law Teacher's Intellectual Schizophrenia." *Nova Law Review*, vol. 13, 1988, pp. 9–31.

Case, David W. "A Pedagogical Rationale for the Law Professor as Moot Court Coach." *Mississippi Law Journal*, vol. 89, 2020, pp. 367–406.

Chase, Anthony. "The Legal Scholar as Producer." *Nova Law Review*, vol. 13, 1988, pp. 57–67.

Chemerinsky, Erwin. "Why Not Clinical Education?" *Clinical Law Review*, vol. 16, 2009, pp. 35–41.

Cherry, Roger D. "Ethos versus Persona: Self-Representation in Written Discourse." *Written Communication*, vol. 15, 1998, pp. 384–410.

Christie, George C. "The Recruitment of Law Faculty." *Duke Law Journal*, vol. 1987, 1987, pp. 306–16.

Clarke, Brian S. "Coming Out in the Classroom: Law Professors, Law Students and Depression." *Journal of Legal Education*, vol. 64, 2015, pp. 403–15.

Cohen, Amy B. "The Dangers of the Ivory Tower: The Obligation of Law Professors to Engage in the Practice of Law." *Loyola Law Review*, vol. 50, 2004, pp. 623–73.

Coleman, Clare Keefe, and William Albertson. "Teaching International Law Students: A Collaboration between a Law Professor and an ESL Specialist." *Journal of Law & Education*, vol. 50, 2021, pp. 1–34.

Costello, John L. "Another Visit to the Man Divided: A Justification for the Law Teacher's Schizophrenia." *Journal of Legal Education*, vol. 27, 1975, pp. 390–417.

Coyne, Randall T. "A Law Professor's Reflections on Representing Guantánamo Detainees." *Northeastern University Law Journal*, vol. 1, 2009, pp. 97–110.

Crabb, John H. "On Integrating Law with the Academic World." *Journal of Legal Education*, vol. 14, 1962, pp. 329–42.

Cramton, Roger C. "Demystifying Legal Scholarship." *Georgetown Law Journal*, vol. 75, 1986, pp. 1–17.

D'Amato, Anthony. "The Decline and Fall of Law Teaching in the Age of Student Consumerism." *Journal of Legal Education*, vol. 37, 1987, pp. 461–94.

Darling-Hammond, Sean, and Kristen Holmquist. "Creating Wise Classrooms to Empower Diverse Law Students: Lessons in Pedagogy from Transformative Law Professors." *Berkeley La Raza Law Journal*, vol. 25, 2015, pp. 1–67.

"Doceō." *Oxford Latin Dictionary*, edited by P. G. W. Glare, Oxford UP, 1982, p. 568.

"Doctor." *Follett World-Wide Latin Dictionary*, edited by Edwin B. Levine et al., Follett, 1967, p. 125.

"Doctor." *A Latin-English Dictionary*, edited by Charlton T. Lewis and Charles Short, 1879, Oxford UP, 1975, p. 605.

"Doctrīna." *A Latin-English Dictionary*, edited by Charlton T. Lewis and Charles Short, 1879, Oxford UP, 1975, p. 605.

"Doctrix." *A Latin-English Dictionary*, edited by Charlton T. Lewis and Charles Short, 1879, Oxford UP, 1975, p. 605.

EagleWoman, Angelique Townsend (Wambdi A. WasteWin). "Balancing between Two Worlds: A Dakota Woman's Reflections on Being a Law Professor." *Berkeley Journal of Gender, Law & Justice*, vol. 29, 2014, pp. 250–74.

Edwards, Harry T. "Another Look at Professor Rodell's *Goodbye to Law Reviews*." *Virginia Law Review*, vol. 100, 2014, pp. 1483–1511.

---. "The Growing Disjunction between Legal Education and the Legal Profession." *Michigan Law Review*, vol. 91, 1992, pp. 34–78.

---. "The Role of Legal Education in Shaping the Profession." *Journal of Legal Education*, vol. 38, 1988, pp. 285–93.

Entin, Jonathan L. "The Law Professor as Advocate." *Case Western Reserve Law Review*, vol. 38, 1988, pp. 512–36.

Finesilver, Sherman G. "The Tension between Practical and Theoretical Legal Education: A Judge's View of the Gap." *Brigham Young University Law Review*, vol. 1977, 1977, pp. 1061–71.

Fontana, David. "What Do Constitutional Law Professors Do?" *Wisconsin Law Review*, vol. 2020, 2020, pp. 317–41.

Foss, Karen A., and Sonja K. Foss. "Personal Experience as Evidence in Feminist Scholarship." *Western Journal of Communication*, vol. 58, 1994, pp. 39–43.

Gajda, Amy. "The Law Professor as Legal Commentator." *The Journal of the Legal Writing Institute*, vol. 10, 2004, pp. 209–43.

Gilmore, Angela. "How Amendment 1 (North Carolina's Anti-Marriage Equality Constitutional Amendment) Helped Me Become a Better Law Professor." *Law & Sexuality*, vol. 22, 2013, pp. 91–101.

Greene, Susan. "Knitting 101: Why Law Professors Should Share Their Hobbies with Their Students." *Journal of Legal Education*, vol. 68, 2019, pp. 751–53.

Hantzis, Catharine W. "Kingsfield and Kennedy: Reappraising the Male Models of Law School Teaching." *Journal of Legal Education*, vol. 38, 1988, pp. 155–64.

Hernández, Tanya K. "Placing the Cart before the Horse: Publishing Scholarship before Entering the Legal Academy." *Michigan Journal of Race & Law*, vol. 7, 2002, pp. 517–22.

Hervey, John G. "The Juris Doctor Degree... An Inquiry into Some Reasons Advanced against Adoption." *The Student Lawyer Journal*, vol. 11, 1966, pp. 11–13, 28–31.

---. "Law School Graduates Should Receive 'Professional Doctorates'... Time for a Change from LL.B. to J.D. Degree." *The Student Lawyer Journal*, vol. 10, 1965, pp. 5–8, 27.

Hricik, David, and Victoria S. Salzmann. "Why There Should Be Fewer Articles like This One: Law Professors Should Write More for Legal Decision-Makers and Less for Themselves." *Suffolk University Law Review*, vol. 38, 2005, pp. 761–87.

Jarvis, Robert M. "Why Law Professors Should Not Be Hessian-Trainers." *Nova Law Review*, vol. 13, 1988, pp. 69–78.

Jesson, Lucinda. "So You Want to Be a Law Professor." *Journal of Legal Education*, vol. 59, 2010, pp. 450–53.

Johnson, Alex M. "Think like a Lawyer, Work like a Machine: The Dissonance between Law School and Law Practice." *Southern California Law Review*, vol. 64, 1991, pp. 1231–60.

"Juris Doctor Information." *The Student Lawyer Journal*, vol. 12, 1967, p. 24.

Kronman, Anthony T. "Foreword: Legal Scholarship and Moral Education." *Yale Law Journal*, vol. 90, 1981, pp. 955–69.

Kurland, Adam Harris. "Court's in Session: A Law Professor Returns to the Majestic Chaos of a Criminal Jury Trial." *Howard Law Journal*, vol. 52, 2009, pp. 357–73.

Lanzinger, Judith Ann. "Judges Teaching in Law School: Who, What, Where, and Why Not?" *Journal of Legal Education*, vol. 43, 1993, pp. 96–107.

Lawprofblawg and Darren Bush. "LAW REVIEWS, CITATION COUNTS, and TWITTER (Oh my!): Behind the Curtains of the Law Professor's Search for Meaning." *Loyola University Chicago Law Journal*, vol. 50, 2018, pp. 327–64.

Leflar, Robert A. "The Law Teacher's Place in the American Legal Profession." *Journal of the Society of Public Teachers of Law*, vol. 8, 1964, pp. 21–30.

Leleiko, Steven H. "Legal Education—Some Crucial Frontiers." *Journal of Legal Education*, vol. 23, 1971, pp. 502–27.

Levit, Nancy. "Scholarship Advice for New Law Professors in the Electronic Age." *Widener Law Journal*, vol. 16, 2007, pp. 947–82.

Litvak, Kate. "Blog as a Bugged Water Cooler." *Washington University Law Review*, vol. 84, 2006, pp. 1061–70.

Manley, Stewart. "Degree (Un)Equivalencies: The Confounding Case of the Juris Doctor." *Journal of Legal Education*, vol. 68, 2019, pp. 392–415.

Maynard, Goldburn P. "Killing the Motivation of the Minority Law Professor." *Minnesota Law Review*, vol. 107, 2022, pp. 245–96.

McCrary, Justin, et al. "The Ph.D. Rises in American Law Schools, 1960–2011: What Does It Mean for Legal Education?" *Journal of Legal Education*, vol. 65, 2016, pp. 543–79.

McDougall, Harold. "The Rebellious Law Professor: Combining Cause and Reflective Lawyering." *Journal of Legal Education*, vol. 65, 2015, pp. 326–51.

McFarland, Douglas D. "Self-Images of Law Professors: Rethinking the Schism in Legal Education." *Journal of Legal Education*, vol. 35, 1985, pp. 232–60.

---. "Students and Practicing Lawyers Identify the Ideal Law Professor." *Journal of Legal Education*, vol. 36, 1986, pp. 93–107.

McFarland, Douglas Dale. *Self-Images of Law Professors: Rethinking Legal Education*. 1983. University of Minnesota, Ph.D. dissertation.

McPeak, Agnieszka. "The Internet Made Me Do It: Reconciling Social Media and Professional Norms for Lawyers, Judges, and Law Professors." *Idaho Law Review*, vol. 55, 2019, pp. 205–32.

Meyerson, Michael I. "Law School Culture and the Lost Art of Collaboration: Why Don't Law Professors Play Well with Others?" *Nebraska Law Review*, vol. 93, 2015, pp. 547–91.

"Minnesota Adopts J.D. Degree." *The Student Lawyer Journal*, vol. 12, 1967, p. 24.

Moliterno, James E. "Exporting American Legal Education." *Journal of Legal Education*, vol. 58, 2008, pp. 274–89.

Newton, Brent E. "The Ninety-Five Theses: Systemic Reforms of American Legal Education and Licensure." *South Carolina Law Review*, vol. 64, 2012, pp. 55–141.

---. "Preaching What They Don't Practice: Why Law Faculties' Preoccupation with Impractical Scholarship and Devaluation of Practical Competencies Obstruct Reform in the Legal Academy." *South Carolina Law Review*, vol. 62, 2010, pp. 105–56.

Posner, Richard A. "The Present Situation in Legal Scholarship." *Yale Law Journal*, vol. 90, 1981, pp. 1113–30.

Power, Garrett. "In Defense of the J.D." *Journal of Legal Education*, vol. 20, 1967, pp. 67–70.

Re, Edward D. "Law Office Sabbaticals for Law Professors." *Journal of Legal Education*, vol. 45, 1995, pp. 95–98.

Rehnquist, William H. "The Legal Profession Today." *Indiana Law Journal*, vol. 62, 1987, pp. 151–57.

Rieke, Richard D., et al. *Argumentation and Critical Decision Making*. 6th ed., Pearson, 2005.

Roberts, John. "A Conversation with Chief Justice Roberts." Interview by J. Harvie Wilkinson. *C-SPAN*, 25 June 2011, www.c-span.org/video/?300203-1/conversation-chief-justice-roberts. Accessed 28 June 2023.

Rohr, Marc. "A Law School for the Consumer." *Nova Law Review*, vol. 13, 1988, pp. 101–05.

Rubin, Edward L. "Law and and the Methodology of Law." *Wisconsin Law Review*, vol. 1997, 1997, pp. 521–65.

Ruhl, J. B., et al. "Total Scholarly Impact: Law Professor Citations in Non-Law Journals." *Journal of Legal Education*, vol. 69, 2020, pp. 782–815.

Rutledge, Njeri Mathis. "Walking the Tightrope: Reflections of a Black Female Law Professor." *Campbell Law Review*, vol. 43, 2021, pp. 233–41.

Schultheis, Emily. "*Sitzfleisch*: The German Concept to Get More Work Done." *BBC*, 4 Sept. 2018, www.bbc.com/worklife/article/20180903-to-have-sitzfleisch---its-a-professional-compliment. Accessed 28 June 2023.

Schuwerk, Robert P. "The Law Professor as Fiduciary: What Duties Do We Owe to Our Students." *South Texas Law Review*, vol. 45, 2004, pp. 753–813.

Secunda, Paul M. "Tales of a Law Professor Lateral Nothing." *University of Memphis Law Review*, vol. 39, 2008, pp. 125–51.

Silverman, Hugh W. "The Practitioner as a Law Teacher." *Journal of Legal Education*, vol. 23, 1971, pp. 424–39.

Smith, George P. "Much Ado about Nothing—The J.D. Movement." *The Student Lawyer Journal*, vol. 11, 1966, pp. 8–10, 26–27.

Snow, C. P. *The Two Cultures and the Scientific Revolution*. Cambridge UP, 1959.

Solum, Lawrence B. "Blogging and the Transformation of Legal Scholarship." *Washington University Law Review*, vol. 84, 2006, pp. 1071–88.

Stein, Jay W. "The Juris Doctor." *Journal of Legal Education*, vol. 15, 1963, pp. 315–20.

Stevens, Robert. "American Legal Scholarship: Structural Constraints and Intellectual Conceptualism." *Journal of Legal Education*, vol. 33, 1983, pp. 442–48.

---. *Law School: Legal Education in America from the 1850s to the 1980s*. U of North Carolina P, 1983.

---. "Legal Education: The Challenge of the Past." *New York Law School Law Review*, vol. 30, 1985, pp. 475–90.

Stone, Harlan F. "The Importance of Actual Experience at the Bar as a Preparation for Teaching Law." *American Law School Review*, vol. 3, 1912, pp. 205–11.

Tamer, Christine, and Melissa Shultz. "The Adaptable Law Professor: Ten Tips for Keeping the Magic of an Oral Argument Competition Alive on Zoom." *Syllabus*, vol. 52, 2021, qa.americanbar.org/groups/legal_education/publications/syllabus_home/volume-52-2020-2021/syllabus-winter-2021-52-2/adaptable-law-professor. Accessed 28 June 2023.

Traynor, Roger J. "To the Right Honorable Law Reviews." *UCLA Law Review*, vol. 10, 1962, pp. 3–10.

Turow, Scott. "Law School v. Reality." *The New York Times Magazine*, 18 Sept. 1988, www.nytimes.com/1988/09/18/magazine/law-school-v-reality.html. Accessed 28 June 2023.

Ulen, Thomas S. "The Unexpected Guest: Law and Economics, Law and Other Cognate Disciplines, and the Future of Legal Scholarship." *Chicago-Kent Law Review*, vol. 79, 2004, pp. 403–29.

Wald, Eli. "A Thought Experiment about the Academic 'Billable' Hour or Law Professors' Work Habits." *Marquette Law Review*, vol. 101, 2018, pp. 991–1018.

Wald, Patricia M. "Teaching the Trade: An Appellate Judge's View of Practice-Oriented Legal Education." *Journal of Legal Education*, vol. 36, 1986, pp. 35–44.

Waxman, Seth P. "Rebuilding Bridges: The Bar, the Bench, and the Academy." *University of Pennsylvania Law Review*, vol. 150, 2002, pp. 1905–13.

Weaver, Richard M. *The Ethics of Rhetoric*. Henry Regnery, 1953.

Wellington, Harry H. "Challenges to Legal Education: The 'Two Cultures' Phenomenon." *Journal of Legal Education*, vol. 37, 1987, pp. 327–30.

Zietlow, Rebecca E. "Writing Scholarship While You Practice Law." *Michigan Journal of Race & Law*, vol. 7, 2002, pp. 511–16.

Zimmerman, Emily. "Should Law Professors Have a Continuing Practice Experience (CPE) Requirement?" *Northeastern University Law Journal*, vol. 6, 2013, pp. 131–87.

CHAPTER VI

In Support of Invitational Rhetoric as a Propitious Discursive Form

The past three chapters have sketched out a picture in which, at least since the late nineteenth century, advocates of the differing personas of the law professor have advanced their positions through Aristotelian rhetoric, yet this conflict has continued to the present time without much improvement in the communication. As communication and legal scholar Douglas D. McFarland explained, although the lawyers in the contemporary portion of the conflict have advanced their own positions, in general, these lawyers have not listened to each other carefully to understand the relevant positions in the discourse ("Students and Practicing Lawyers" 106). When the lawyers have listened at all, they mainly have done so to point out why different perspectives are "wrong." Indeed, McFarland predicted that the future of such discourse would involve only "marginal change" at best ("Students and Practicing Lawyers" 106–07). Because, to a large extent, this is a communication problem, the situation calls for a communication approach.

The work of communication scholars Sonja K. Foss and Cindy L. Griffin, in which the authors laid out a theory of an alternative to the millennia-old traditional Western concept of rhetoric as persuasion, is one such approach that can be of value to the lawyers embroiled in the ongoing conflict. This alternative approach to rhetoric offers the audience of the rhetoric a chance "to enter the rhetor's world and to see it as the rhetor does" without the necessity of a win-lose decision (Foss & Griffin, "Beyond Persuasion" 5). A *rhetor* is a communicator such as a speaker. In the type of communication that Foss and Griffin proposed, the speaker refrains from judging the perspectives of other participants in the communication, and the other participants refrain from judging the perspective of the speaker ("Beyond Persuasion" 5). Rather than seeking to change other participants' perspectives, the speaker seeks to help the other participants understand the speaker's perspective (Foss & Griffin, "Beyond Persuasion" 5). Then the other participants become empowered because they have an opportunity to express themselves while the original speaker listens. Foss and Griffin termed this alternative type of rhetoric *invitational rhetoric* ("Beyond Persuasion" 5).

Since its publication, Foss and Griffin's work on invitational rhetoric has received scholarly attention in the field of communication and become significant for a variety of reasons. For example, M. Lane Bruner argued that Foss and Griffin's study of invitational rhetoric has "played an important role in revealing how women have been excluded from much of traditional rhetorical scholarship" (188). Also, Bruner added that the study "contributed substantially to an understanding of the constraining and enabling features of identification practices" (188), and Irwin Mallin and Karrin Vasby Anderson observed that the study revived discussion about how modes of rhetoric can be "most productive" to the parties involved (121). As Mallin and Anderson noted, invitational rhetoric is consequential "because it offers a new frame of reference for what argument can and should accomplish [and] assigns rhetors new responsibilities" outside those responsibilities of Aristotelian rhetoric (124). Jeffrey W. Jarman and Kelly M. McDonald observed the utility of the values, including equality, immanent value, and self-determination, on which Foss and Griffin explicitly based their work (207).

Beyond the field of communication, invitational rhetoric has been influential. For instance, invitational rhetoric has made contributions to multiple other fields such as "English literature and composition, education, public relations, environmental studies, and business and management" (Daughton & Buzzanell xiv). Invitational rhetoric also has made an initial contribution to law (Pedrioli, "A New Image" 185–87). Furthermore, around the world, invitational rhetoric has been employed "in a variety of situations marked by strong disagreement or conflict," including those in which participants have sought to integrate refugees after civil war, to facilitate discourse between people who support and people who oppose abortion, and to address hyper-partisanship in politics (Foss & Griffin, "Metatheoretical Foundations" 59). Because of the attention that invitational rhetoric has received, additional consideration of invitational rhetoric is appropriate to further understand how it might be of service to human communicators (Bile 63), including lawyers who have had a difficult time communicating successfully with each other.

Accordingly, this chapter maintains that, despite some limitations, invitational rhetoric can be a propitious form of discourse for helping lawyers improve their communication regarding the ideal law professor persona. To develop this position, the chapter will consider the traditional Aristotelian notion of rhetoric and some limitations of that notion, invitational rhetoric as a potential alternative to Aristotelian rhetoric, and finally both critiques of invitational rhetoric and some responses to those critiques. The next chapter then will illustrate how invitational rhetoric can be helpful for lawyers presently involved in the conflict over the construction of the ideal law professor persona. In presenting an argument for the propitious nature of invitational rhetoric as a tool for improving the status of the conflict between two major groups of lawyers, this chapter will exemplify the tension between taking a position on invitational rhetoric and communicating in an invitational manner. Such can be the paradoxical, and thus intriguing, nature of rhetoric.

While Chapters VI and VII will address invitational rhetoric, invitational rhetoric is one key step in the ultimate suggested approach of this book, not the ultimate approach itself. In a legal field that assumes Aristotelian rhetoric, invitational rhetoric alone would be inadequate. Invitational rhetoric focuses on the dialogue that has been missing from the communication regarding the construction of the ideal law professor persona, but, because the legal field works principally with Aristotelian rhetoric, Aristotelian rhetoric also calls for some consideration. Accordingly, Chapters VI and VII will pave the way for a discussion and application of cooperative rhetoric in Chapter VIII. As Chapter VIII will observe, cooperative rhetoric embraces both the dialogue of invitational rhetoric and the persuasion of Aristotelian rhetoric. Invitational rhetoric will help develop the theoretically underdeveloped dialogic dimension of cooperative rhetoric, the dimension of cooperative rhetoric more needed in the ongoing conflict over the ideal law professor persona, and cooperative rhetoric, in considering persuasion as well as dialogue, ultimately will be a better fit for the legal field than invitational rhetoric. Indeed, invitational rhetoric and cooperative rhetoric can benefit from each other. Hence, the attention paid to invitational rhetoric in this chapter and the following chapter will be important because this attention will develop a stronger understanding of cooperative rhetoric.

The Aristotelian Notion of Rhetoric and Its Limitations

Traditionally, *rhetoric* has involved attempting to persuade an audience to accept an advocate's position. In his fourth-century B.C. treatise *On Rhetoric*, Aristotle defined the term *rhetoric* as "an ability, in each [particular] case, to see the available means of persuasion" (36). Hence, in a given situation, a skilled advocate endeavors to find multiple modes of persuasion rather than just one (Golden et al. 28). Much more recently, but still in the Aristotelian vein, communication scholar Michael Leff described the term *rhetoric* as an endeavor whose goal is persuasion (6). The study of Aristotelian rhetoric dates back to the ancient world, specifically to fifth-century B.C. Athens, and, ever since male Greek citizens of that era called upon rhetoric in the process of bringing and defending legal suits, debating matters of public policy, and speaking on special occasions, rhetoric has been essential (Golden et al. 6, 8).

Such Aristotelian rhetoric involves justifying why a particular position is appropriate. Today, for instance, rhetoric manifests itself in political debates and legal trials and appeals (Golden et al. vii), as well as in advertising (Larson 5, 8). Indeed, some forms of rhetoric are more fully supported with evidence than others. In many situations, advocates seek to change the views of audiences to serve the advocates' own ends. One can think of politicians who want to gain or retain office, lawyers who want to win large contingency fees, and advertisers who seek to sell a seemingly endless stream of consumer products. Not only do such examples of Aristotelian rhetoric often involve justifying why a particular position is "right" (Makau & Marty 84), but frequently, by necessity, such examples involve explaining why another position is "wrong."

One situation that illustrates Aristotelian rhetoric well is intercollegiate debate. In this forum, advocates compete against each other to win the vote of the judge of the debate round (Hobbs et al. 81). At stake in the end are trophies and bragging rights among teammates and competitors. For many students, victory is the bottom line in this activity.

Some communication scholars, including those who have acted on a developing feminist consciousness in this area of study (Carlson 17–18), have critiqued the persuasion-based understanding of Aristotelian rhetoric. For instance, these scholars have maintained that, when a speaker seeks to change the minds of audience members, the speaker implicitly, if not explicitly, can seek to dominate audience members (Foss & Griffin, "Beyond Persuasion" 3). In such circumstances, the concern is not for the members of the audience, but for achieving the speaker's goal of influence. Often, these attempts at domination rely upon patriarchal lines of rhetoric and even become embodied in social institutions like the law (Crenshaw, "The Normality of Man" 182–83).

Along the same lines, scholars have observed that Aristotelian rhetoric frequently is steeped in confrontation (Palczewski, "Special Issue" 164). Indeed, Aristotelian rhetoric can be "an adversarial activity governed by war metaphors and infused with a win-lose ideology" (Mallin & Anderson 121). Terms like *attack*, *defend*, and *counterattack* play key roles in the discussion and practice of Aristotelian rhetoric (Palczewski, "Special Issue" 164). Thus, David Zarefsky described rhetoric as the practice of engaging in "verbal conflict" (288–89). To the alarm of some scholars, the rhetoric-as-war understanding of discourse has proven prominent (Palczewski, "Argument in an Off Key" 1), especially since the "winner" of such war-like rhetoric often feels accomplished at the expense of the "loser" (Makau & Marty 84). On a relatedly brutal note, Wayne Brockriede even drew an analogy between heated Aristotelian rhetoric and rape (2–3).

As one would expect, such problems with Aristotelian rhetoric often play out in law and politics. In court, many lawyers adopt a win-lose mentality and the metaphor of war. Going toward an extreme, some lawyers attempt to mislead jurors about the nature of evidence at trial (Makau & Marty 85). This combative approach to discourse occurred in the impeachment trial of President Bill Clinton in 1999, and, following that proceeding, many individuals questioned "how deeply committed the participants on both sides...were to creating an environment conducive to reaching the most reasoned, fair, and informed decision possible" (Makau & Marty 85–86). Again, the focus was on winning the rhetorical event.

Some scholars have critiqued Aristotelian rhetoric further by noting that it often has not been as welcoming of personal testimony or experience as Aristotelian rhetoric has been of other forms of evidence like "facts, examples, expert testimony and statistics" (Pickering 1). Within the domain of Aristotelian rhetoric, "facts, examples, expert testimony and statistics" frequently are considered "objective" and thus have assumed a higher status than personal testimony (Pickering 1, 19). Although not all scholars have agreed about the value of personal testimony in rhetoric (MacKinnon 535, Elshtain 612), or even how carefully to consider personal experience (Pickering 1), some scholars have maintained that personal experience can be "the consciousness that emerges from personal participation in events" or even one's own "'experience as [one's] truth'" (Foss & Foss, "Personal Experience" 39). Consideration of personal experience is helpful because it can lead to deeper understanding of discursive participants and can open the door to multiple truths (Foss & Foss,

"Personal Experience" 41). While individuals can call upon personal experience in private discourse, some scholars have noted that personal experience also can play a role in public discourse (Pickering 3).

Finally, scholars have commented that Aristotelian rhetoric many times does not adhere to principles such as equality, immanent value, and self-determination, principles to which many feminists and other individuals adhere (Foss & Griffin, "Beyond Persuasion" 4). Foss and Griffin described these principles in the following way: *equality* as the absence of "domination and elitism," *immanent value* as the uniqueness "of all living beings," and *self-determination* as the right of "individuals to make their own decisions about how they wish to live their lives" ("Beyond Persuasion" 4). Without consideration of principles like these, Aristotelian rhetoric can lack a sufficient degree of humanity.

Invitational Rhetoric as a Potential Alternative to Aristotelian Rhetoric

Given the potential for domination, confrontation, frequent lack of recognition of personal experience, and exclusion of certain important principles that can come with Aristotelian rhetoric, Foss and Griffin introduced *invitational rhetoric* ("Beyond Persuasion" 5). Foss and Griffin defined this term as "an invitation to understanding as a means to create a relationship rooted in equality, immanent value, and self-determination" ("Beyond Persuasion" 5). Invitational rhetoric offers the audience a chance "to enter the rhetor's world and to see it as the rhetor does" (Foss & Griffin, "Beyond Persuasion" 5). As noted above, a *rhetor* is a communicator such as a speaker. When communicating invitationally, the speaker refrains from judging the perspectives of other participants in the communication process, and the other participants attempt to refrain from judging the perspective of the speaker (Foss & Griffin, "Beyond Persuasion" 5). Instead of seeking to change other participants' perspectives, the speaker tries to help the other participants understand the speaker's perspective (Foss & Griffin, "Beyond Persuasion" 5). Then the other participants become empowered because they have a chance to express themselves while the original speaker listens. Invitational rhetoric allows communicators "to clarify positions, explore issues and ideas, or articulate beliefs and values" (Griffin 336). Such a process can change participants' understandings, even if it does not change their views (Foss & Griffin, "Metatheoretical Foundations" 69).

The process of invitational rhetoric, which can be similar to bilateral dialogue (Bile 62), is about offering perspectives and not about telling others to take a given action or understand why their ideas are flawed (Foss & Griffin, "Beyond Persuasion" 7–10; Mallin & Anderson 130). Because, as Irene P. Faass noted, this is a process of rhetoric as inquiry (220), any change in perspective that takes place occurs when members of the audience choose to make such change, and they do so without the influence of a speaker who presses for that change (Foss & Foss, *Inviting Transformation* 13–14). Unlike politics and law, no "winner" prevails, and no "loser" feels the sting of defeat. Of note, invitational rhetoric is about a constructive communication process, not a specific content or substantive result. Since a prescribed content would violate the invitational spirit of invitational rhetoric, the exact content of the rhetoric is up to the communicators.

Although invitational rhetoric will not succeed in all cases in which communicators employ it, when invitational rhetoric is to succeed, it tends to consist of at least three external conditions: safety, value, and freedom (Foss & Griffin, "Beyond Persuasion" 10). Foss and Griffin defined these conditions in the following manner: *safety* as "the creation of a feeling of security and [absence of] danger for the audience," *value* as "the acknowledgment that audience members have intrinsic or immanent worth," and *freedom* as "the power to choose or decide" ("Beyond Persuasion" 10–13). To the work of Foss and Griffin, Foss and fellow scholar Karen A. Foss added openness as a fourth condition that helps foster invitational rhetoric; Foss and Foss defined *openness* as "seek[ing] out and consider[ing] as many perspectives as possible" (*Inviting Transformation* 39).

To help foster the conditions of safety, value, freedom, and openness that can lead to invitational rhetoric, Foss and Foss suggested the process of *re-sourcement*, which refers to finding a new source of "energy and inspiration" (*Inviting Transformation* 44). Re-sourcement involves disengaging oneself from an interaction frame of conquest or conversion of one's audience and then encountering the audience via a non-conquest and non-conversion interaction frame (Foss & Foss, *Inviting Transformation* 44–48).

In attempting to show how invitational rhetoric can work, Foss and Griffin offered several examples of successful invitational rhetoric in differing communication situations such as interpersonal communication and public address situations. One such example involved two individuals with drastically opposing perspectives on abortion. Encountering each other at an airport in New York, a woman, who supported abortion, and a man, who opposed abortion, began to scream at each other until they almost needed to be separated (Foss & Griffin, "Beyond Persuasion" 14). One hour later, as the woman boarded a bus, she discovered that the only available seat was next to the man with whom she had just had the verbal altercation (Foss & Griffin, "Beyond Persuasion" 14). Instead of resuming the same type of discourse, the woman began to ask the man about his life, and the man responded in kind (Foss & Griffin, "Beyond Persuasion" 14). While neither changed her or his perspective, over the course of the dialogue, each developed a deeper understanding of and appreciation for the other (Foss & Griffin, "Beyond Persuasion" 15). In a case where Aristotelian rhetoric had proven destructive, invitational rhetoric succeeded in fostering the external conditions of safety, value, and freedom (Foss & Griffin, "Beyond Persuasion" 15), as well as openness. Each speaker promoted safety by acknowledging a differing perspective on a highly charged issue, value by respecting the holding of a different point of view, and freedom by recognizing that the other speaker could continue to believe as she or he chose regarding this subject (Foss & Griffin, "Beyond Persuasion" 15). Also, each speaker promoted openness by looking at a different perspective.

Another example of successful invitational rhetoric that Foss and Griffin offered involved the manner in which Adrienne Rich, Alice Walker, and Audre Lorde handled acceptance of the 1974 National Book Award in Poetry. Although all three women had received nominations for the award, only Rich received the actual award (Foss & Griffin, "Beyond Persuasion" 13). However, when Rich accepted the award, she did so on behalf of herself, Walker, and Lorde, noting, "'We, Audre Lorde, Adrienne Rich, and Alice Walker, together accept this award in the name of all the women whose voices have gone and still go unheard in a patriarchal world'" (Foss & Griffin, "Beyond Persuasion" 13). In expressing their own perspective in this manner, the poets fostered the external conditions of safety, value, freedom, and openness. The poets promoted safety by recognizing the one-winner approach of the judges of the National Book Awards, the value of the members of the extended audience by noting the personal sacrifices of many audience members, and freedom by acknowledging that the audience could choose its own course of action in response to the speech (Foss & Griffin, "Beyond Persuasion" 13–14). Also, the poets promoted openness by placing their perspective in a communication context of differing perspectives on the matter at hand.

While the contemporary communication environment, in which multiple interactions may happen at once, presents challenges to communicators

(Turner & Foss 22–23, Foss & Turner 157–58), invitational rhetoric can be beneficial to communicators who attempt to employ it. For instance, invitational rhetoric is particularly well-suited for fostering "cooperative, nonadversarial, and ethical communication" because invitational rhetoric accepts multiple perspectives as valid (Foss & Griffin, "Beyond Persuasion" 15–16). Although not necessarily limited to this type of situation, invitational rhetoric is especially helpful when one is engaged in discourse with another person with whom one has an ongoing relationship (Mallin & Anderson 130–31), such as a significant other (Longtin & Binion 378), a family member (Pariera & Turner 186), a colleague at work (Alexander & Hammers 6), an adult patient (Longtin & Binion 378), or a parent of a minor patient (Make & Lauver 2). In contrast, if one goes to court in a large city and hopes never to see one's opponent after the trial, then Aristotelian rhetoric may be more appropriate (Mallin & Anderson 130). Nonetheless, the bus example above indicates that invitational rhetoric can be helpful with strangers, too.

As well as being available for in-person settings, including those with more than two communicators (J. Johnson et al. 385–86, 394–95), invitational rhetoric can be available for mediated settings, such as those found on social media, which can involve numerous communicators (Orbe & Orbe 29–31). Invitational rhetoric also can serve a purpose in other communication contexts, including those that feature artistic performances (Bates & Schrader 51).

Additionally, invitational rhetoric validates the personal experiences and testimonies of individuals. Invitational speakers do not have to be physicians, scientists, or attorneys to have valuable experiences to share with other invitational communicators. Common experience, whether from the lives of women or men, or from the lives of more-privileged or less-privileged individuals, can have merit in invitational rhetoric. Invitational communicators can call upon such experiences to present their own personal truths about life.

Moreover, invitational rhetoric gives women and other outsiders, as well as individuals empathetic to the situations of such outsiders, a resource to employ in attempting "to transform systems of domination and oppression" (Foss & Griffin, "Beyond Persuasion" 16). Foss and Foss suggested that invitational rhetoric can help a communicator to understand the positions of individuals, such as neo-Nazis, whose perspectives are hateful to many people (*Inviting Transformation* 18). With a better understanding of such perspectives, the communicator then may go about attempting to change the conditions that foster hateful perspectives (Foss & Foss, *Inviting Transformation* 18–19). Accordingly, invitational rhetoric offers several important benefits to communicators.

Critiques of Invitational Rhetoric and Some Responses to Such Critiques

Despite its various positive attributes, invitational rhetoric has been the subject of critiques from communication scholars who have questioned the viability of this alternative form of discourse. To begin with, M. Lane Bruner expressed concern that invitational rhetoric sets up a false dichotomy between "'patriarchal'" rhetoric and "'feminist'" rhetoric (187, 190). As Bruner described the terms, the former term refers to rhetoric that is "'dominating,' 'controlling,' 'competitive,' and views the audience as an 'enemy,'" while the latter term refers to rhetoric that is "'nurturing,' 'affirmative,' promoting self-determination, mutual respect, camaraderie, and views the audience as a 'friend'" (187). With this reading of invitational rhetoric, feminist rhetoric becomes limited to "'perspective offering'" and is helpful in a very narrow range of situations (Bruner 187). This critique suggests that feminists and others who employ invitational rhetoric may be able to do no more than present their views of the world, while speakers who employ Aristotelian rhetoric will be able, at a minimum, to have a chance of getting the results they want.

Bruner's key point was that Foss and Griffin's work reified traditional gender stereotypes instead of critiquing them (188). Essentially, according to Bruner, invitational rhetoric takes for granted the false gender dichotomies that devalue women (189). As Bruner viewed invitational rhetoric, women then are unable to become "aggressive..., confrontational, directly persuasive, or intent on changing the opinions of collectives" (189). Instead, women must be "motherly, nurturing, [and] relatively non-adversarial" (Bruner 189). Accordingly, "women cannot aggressively seek change while at the same time nurturing their communities" because the dichotomy of either seeking change or being nurturing would prevent seeking change and being nurturing from happening simultaneously (Bruner 194).

Given his understanding of invitational rhetoric, Bruner called for *limit work* (196). This idea refers to scholarship that constantly questions gender stereotypes (Bruner 196). Refusing to see "feminist" rhetoric as enabling and "patriarchal" rhetoric as constraining, such limit work sees all rhetoric as potentially enabling and constraining (Bruner 196). The end goal is to emancipate "all subjects from unnecessarily constraining gender stereotypes" (Bruner 187).

Beyond Bruner's false dichotomy critique, composition scholar Richard Fulkerson, joining the discussion among communication scholars, maintained that invitational rhetoric is self-contradictory (204). Indeed, perspective-offering suggests that speakers hope their audiences will adopt the perspectives offered (Fulkerson 204–05). According to Fulkerson, the speakers want the audience to accept their evidence and refutation of opposing points of view (205). This process implicates the invitational speakers in Aristotelian rhetoric (Fulkerson 204). Here Fulkerson essentially claimed that Foss and Griffin sought to have their cake and eat it as well. Fulkerson maintained that, if feminists really adopted invitational rhetoric, they could not expect social change to occur via such rhetoric.

Additionally, Fulkerson noted that invitational rhetoric leaves open the door to the notion that altering the views of others is always unethical (205). While he admitted that Foss and Griffin acknowledged the potential value of non-invitational rhetoric, Fulkerson also observed that Foss and Griffin called upon an authority who believed that having the intention of changing other individuals was an act of violence (204–05). The authority was feminist scholar Sally Miller Gearhart, who, in her writing, had described persuasion as "the *conquest* model of human interaction" (196). Fulkerson faulted Gearhart's position for ignoring situations that do not employ conquest. For example, Fulkerson pointed out that teachers try to change students for the better, just as expert speakers try to change novice speakers for the better (205). Fulkerson added that, in writing the "Letter from Birmingham Jail," Martin Luther King, Jr., was not "engaged in a patriarchal act of violence" and that Susan B. Anthony's speeches were not "immoral imposition" (205).

Moreover, Fulkerson critiqued invitational rhetoric for maintaining that all perspectives have value. For instance, Fulkerson doubted that Foss and Griffin would regard an abusive spouse's beliefs as "'right for him at the time'" (205). Fulkerson added that he suspected that Foss and Griffin would not abandon their "beliefs that rape and racism are moral evils" (205). In short, Fulkerson faulted invitational rhetoric for what he saw as opening wide the door to "complete moral relativism," something to which he believed the proponents of invitational rhetoric would not subscribe (205–06).

In addition, Fulkerson complained about the conservative nature of invitational rhetoric (206). As Fulkerson saw it, invitational rhetoric allows for the "shar[ing], exchang[ing], under[standing], and respect[ing]" of viewpoints (206). However, the speakers do not take any action (Fulkerson 206). Unfortunately, when no change takes place, sexist and patriarchal policies and procedures remain in effect (Fulkerson 206). Such a consequence disproportionally impacts members of marginalized communities (Chick 323). From Fulkerson's perspective, an example of this understanding might be women who desire to see political change but who, constrained by invitational rhetoric, are unable to advocate for that change.

In light of his critique of invitational rhetoric, Fulkerson called for a different conceptualization of rhetoric. Indeed, Fulkerson acknowledged a need for a reduction in the level of adversariness and an increase in the number of voices who want to speak without being threatened (213). Unlike invitational rhetoric, which Fulkerson read as only calling for the offering of perspectives (213), a kinder and gentler rhetoric instead would allow for change. In looking for an alternative to both Aristotelian rhetoric and invitational rhetoric, Fulkerson turned to Aristotelian rhetoric, but he desired a more humane version of that type of rhetoric.

To illustrate what he meant by a kinder and gentler rhetoric, Fulkerson gave the example of a student whose swimming club activities he had dismissed as "essentially frivolous" (215). Fulkerson indicated that his student wrote a rejoinder in her journal, claiming that he was wrong in dismissing her activities (215). To make her case, the student pointed out the difficulty of performing such feats as floating on one's back, extending a leg straight up in the air, twisting around without moving the leg, diving down, and having both feet come together as they enter the water (Fulkerson 215). Among other points, the student added that the swimming team gave her valuable physical activity, allowed her to vent frustration, and helped her self-confidence (Fulkerson 215). Noting how the student changed his opinion of her activity, Fulkerson argued that rhetoric can be contentious and still be productive (215). Fulkerson maintained that invitational rhetoric would have done little to change his mind in this situation because his student only would have "'offered' her opinion" about the swimming team (215).

On a note related to Fulkerson's critique of invitational rhetoric as too conservative, Jeffrey W. Jarman and Kelly M. McDonald took the position that invitational rhetoric is unsuitable for deliberative rhetoric such as undergraduate debate. To develop this position, the authors called upon Thomas G. Goodnight's notion of spheres of argument, which consist of "different standards of argumentation and proof" (Jarman & McDonald 206). These spheres include the personal, the public, and the technical spheres (Goodnight 215).

While the personal sphere is more concerned with individual affairs, "[t]he public sphere is where the community comes together to resolve important and pressing problems" (Jarman & McDonald 207). The technical sphere includes specialized rhetoric like undergraduate debate, but rhetoric in this sphere can help students prepare for the public sphere because rhetoric that allows for resolution of issues takes place in both spheres (Jarman & McDonald 207).

Jarman and McDonald maintained that the values of invitational rhetoric, including equality, immanent value, and self-determination, are better suited for the private sphere than the public sphere because these values do not help in decision-making (207). Hence, due to its lack of a focus on decision-making, invitational rhetoric is ill-suited for implementation in the public sphere, which the authors understood as a forum for problem-solving.

In addition to the various critiques of invitational rhetoric outlined above, invitational rhetoric can be the subject of at least two other critiques. One such critique is that, because invitational rhetoric relies upon the willingness of the parties involved, when the parties are unwilling to engage in invitational rhetoric, it cannot be helpful. The example of two law faculty members who have sharply different views about the future of the legal academy is illustrative. The law and economics scholar, who studies the law from an economics perspective, might continue to look down his nose at the fluid, experience-based work of his feminist colleague, and the feminist scholar may look down her nose at the mathematical models of the law and economics scholar. If both parties are unwilling to attempt to understand each other, then invitational rhetoric will not be possible.

A lack of willingness to participate in invitational rhetoric may be especially present if one party has greater power than the other party (Lozano-Reich & Cloud 221–22). The party with the greater power, benefiting from having that power, simply may lack the motivation to communicate invitationally with the party that has less power (Lozano-Reich & Cloud 221–22). For example, a mayor of a large city might refuse to speak with community leaders from a small, lower-income section of the city, in part because the mayor has the support of powerful members of the local business community and believes that he does not need the support of residents of the small, less-privileged portion of the city in the next election.

Another such critique is that invitational rhetoric brings with it the risk that parties may hurt each other in some way. This would be the case if the law and economics scholar and the feminist scholar were to attempt to engage in invitational rhetoric and then allow their passionate feelings about their own work and the work of other scholars to derail the invitational process. The two scholars might end up shouting at each other instead of listening to each other. Hence, risk is an inherent part of invitational rhetoric.

While some of the above-noted critiques do make insightful points, an analysis of these critiques suggests that invitational rhetoric is indeed a propitious, but not an entirely risk-free, form of discourse. Several items help to explain this. To begin with, despite Bruner's concern of a false dichotomy between "'patriarchal'" and "'feminist'" rhetoric (187, 190), invitational rhetoric does not establish two rigid extremes. Although Foss and Griffin faced the need of distinguishing invitational rhetoric from Aristotelian rhetoric to explain invitational rhetoric, the authors did not state that, in terms of communication, men are patriarchal and women are invitational. If this were the case, then the authors indeed would be reifying gender stereotypes and in turn patriarchal norms. However, the authors did not preclude individuals who might identify as other than feminist from holding the values of equality, immanent value, and self-determination. While patriarchy may not adopt such principles, the authors did not contend that all men were opposed to such principles, nor did the authors maintain that all women accepted these principles.

Foss and Griffin responded to Bruner's concern specifically. They noted the following:

> Although invitational rhetoric is constructed largely from feminist theory, the literature in which its principles and various dimensions have been theorized most thoroughly, we are not suggesting that only feminists have dealt with and developed its various components or that only feminists adhere to the principles on which it is based.... We also do not want to suggest that the rhetoric we propose describes how all women communicate or that it is or can be used only by women.... The rhetoric we describe is a rhetoric used at various times by some women and some men, some feminists and some non-feminists. ("Beyond Persuasion" 5)

The initial explanation of a genre of rhetoric, here invitational rhetoric, required that the authors make distinctions between two genres, but nowhere were Foss and Griffin so rigid as Bruner suggested.

Foss and Griffin were not the only scholars who made this point. Mallin and Anderson read Foss and Griffin's research as recognizing that both women and men can employ invitational rhetoric (122). According to Mallin and Anderson, the terms "'feminist'" and "'patriarchal'" apply not to gender stereotypes, but to "critical and political agendas," whether women, men, or both enact such agendas (123). This understanding further suggests that Foss and Griffin's perspective did not assume that "the minds of men and women are fundamentally different" (Condit & Williams 1). Indeed, Foss and Griffin left open the possibility that different types of men and women could employ invitational rhetoric. Accordingly, invitational rhetoric grants anyone who is willing to speak invitationally equal access to the identity of an invitational speaker (Crenshaw, "The Arguer's Identity" 22).

If, as Foss, Griffin, and others maintained, invitational rhetoric is a less rigid and polarizing concept than Bruner claimed, then Bruner's concern that this type of rhetoric harms women is not well-founded. Indeed, women can call upon invitational rhetoric, as well as Aristotelian rhetoric, when needed. Foss and Griffin noted that "persuasion is often necessary" ("Beyond Persuasion" 5). Given these points, women are not reduced merely to offering their perspectives. Rather, they can invite, and they also can persuade. When speakers employ invitational rhetoric, they can call upon this genre of rhetoric to question "assumptions about rhetoric, confounding and challenging stereotypes" (Mallin & Anderson 123).

By way of an aside, qualifying the implementation of Aristotelian rhetoric in this context is important. In light of the critiques of Aristotelian rhetoric that Foss, Griffin, and other scholars have provided, one might endeavor to employ, in situations that require persuasion, a more humane version of Aristotelian rhetoric to avoid being controlling, dominating, and confrontational. For example, intent to change is problematic when it involves control and domination and when such intent devalues individuals and their perspectives (Foss & Griffin, "Beyond Persuasion" 2–3; Mallin & Anderson 123). This reading leaves open the door to employing Aristotelian rhetoric in a more ethical manner than the manner in which speakers often have employed it, and ideally any implementation of Aristotelian rhetoric would be less war-like and more respectful to other parties to the communication. Hence, as noted above, invitational rhetoric does not close the door to Aristotelian rhetoric.

This qualification aside for now, Bruner's call for limit work, noted above and which refused to see "feminist" rhetoric as enabling and "patriarchal" rhetoric as constraining (196), was in accord with invitational rhetoric. Indeed, as indicated above, invitational rhetoric recognizes that a given rhetoric can be both enabling and constraining. The constant questioning of gender stereotypes can be a part of invitational rhetoric, provided that the invitational speakers agree to engage in discourse with each other over such a topic. Hence, invitational rhetoric addresses Bruner's concern on this issue.

Beyond Bruner's false dichotomy critique, Fulkerson's claim that an argument for invitational rhetoric does involve a degree of inherent tension has some merit. Given the genre of academic writing in the humanities, which usually entails making an argument, Foss and Griffin had little choice about how to present their work on invitational rhetoric. If they wanted scholars in the field of communication to read their work, a communication journal was an appropriate venue for that work. To satisfy the generic constraints of such a journal, the authors essentially had to make an argument. However, as their calling upon the word *proposal* in the title of their paper would suggest, Foss and Griffin did not write a domination-based article in the spirit of Aristotelian rhetoric at its worst ("Beyond Persuasion" 2). While the authors implicated themselves in Aristotelian rhetoric, they also took the opportunity to offer their perspective on a subject significant to them. Thus, although the authors had to conform to generic requirements to present their perspective, such a constraint on their rhetoric did not deny the value of invitational rhetoric.

On a related note, although Foss and Griffin might have wanted their audience to accept their perspective, the authors did not attempt to force it on their audience. Rather, Foss and Griffin presented their perspective of invitational rhetoric and left choice and action up to the audience. No win-lose scenario emerged. An invitational speaker can hold a perspective that the speaker wishes a fellow participant in invitational rhetoric would adopt, but, at the same time, the speaker can respect both the process of invitational rhetoric and the autonomy of the fellow participant. While an adherent of a particular perspective might desire that an audience adopt the adherent's perspective, the adherent still can focus on encouraging the audience to understand the adherent's perspective and on trying to understand the audience's perspective. Such an approach can enrich the audience's understanding of a given topic of discussion.

Additionally, Foss and Griffin's work did not claim that altering the views of others is always unethical. Fulkerson maintained that, since Foss and Griffin called upon feminist scholar Sally Miller Gearhart for authority, Foss and Griffin, like Gearhart, assumed that any implementation of intentional persuasion was unethical. While Gearhart did write that intentionally changing others is a form of domination and thus assumed to be unethical (196), Fulkerson's reading of Foss and Griffin is a guilt-by-association argument. Scholars can call upon each other's work for inspiration without adopting every aspect of that work as their own. Indeed, Foss and Griffin specifically stated, "[W]e believe that persuasion is often necessary" ("Beyond Persuasion" 5). Accordingly, rather than assuming that all attempts to alter the views of others are unethical, Foss and Griffin did leave open the door to persuasion, even though their work focused on invitational rhetoric. In light of this understanding of invitational rhetoric, Fulkerson's support of persuasion in situations like the classroom and civil rights cases is in line with Foss and Griffin's understanding of a range of types of rhetoric.

Moreover, Fulkerson's faulting invitational rhetoric for opening wide the door to "complete moral relativism," as he described it (205–06), was not accurate because Foss and Foss offered a compromise that can employ invitational rhetoric and Aristotelian rhetoric at different points. As noted above, Foss and Foss suggested that invitational rhetoric can help a participant understand the positions of individuals, such as neo-Nazis, whose perspectives are hateful to many people (*Inviting Transformation* 18). For example, such individuals may have had difficult life experiences and blamed those experiences on given groups of people. With a better understanding of such positions, the participant in invitational rhetoric then can go about attempting to change the conditions that foster such hateful perspectives (Foss & Foss, *Inviting Transformation* 18–19). This approach is not the same as Fulkerson's description of "complete moral relativism" (205–06).

In addition, invitational rhetoric does not have to be as conservative as Fulkerson suggested it must be. Participants in invitational rhetoric can do more than sharing, understanding, and respecting different viewpoints. If the participants decide to act after having been part of invitational rhetoric, they are free to do so. If the participants do not decide to act, they are free to refrain from doing so. Under these circumstances, the only change may be the deeper understanding participants have of differing viewpoints. However, if the participants do decide to act, greater transformation is a possibility. Invitational rhetoric does not preclude such change from happening.

Furthermore, some consideration is appropriate for the two final critiques of invitational rhetoric summarized above. In terms of the first of these two final critiques, which observed that invitational rhetoric cannot be helpful when the parties are unwilling to participate in the invitational process, willingness to employ invitational rhetoric is indeed a prerequisite for the success of invitational rhetoric. When the parties will not interact with each other in an invitational manner, invitational rhetoric is simply not possible.

If a more powerful party will not communicate invitationally with a less powerful party, another rhetorical strategy besides invitational rhetoric, as communication scholars have theorized it, may be more appropriate. For instance, Jill Swiencicki explained that, if an invitation is turned down, particularly by a more powerful party such as a government leader, the party who extended the invitation may share the experience in a manner that informs members of the public of the experience and leaves open the possibility that they will try to improve the situation (160–61). As such, if the big city mayor continues to decline the offer to participate in invitational rhetoric that community leaders from a small, less-privileged part of the city have extended, the community leaders may share their experience of refusal with civic groups across the city that may be predisposed to encourage the mayor to communicate productively with the leadership of the less-privileged part of the city. The need to employ a discursive strategy besides invitational rhetoric, as communication scholars have understood it, suggests the limitations of invitational rhetoric.

In terms of the second of the final two critiques summarized above, which observed that invitational rhetoric brings with it the risk that parties may hurt each other in some way, parties who attempt to participate in invitational rhetoric can end up hurting each other. However, this is an accurate point about any type of human communication, not just invitational rhetoric. Overall, these two final critiques point to some of the limitations of invitational rhetoric.

Nonetheless, when the parties are willing to interact with each other and can avoid heated discourse, invitational rhetoric can help the parties push the limits of imagination and open doors to new possibilities. As the above analysis shows, while invitational rhetoric does have some limitations, it also has various merits. Particularly for, but not exclusively for, individuals who are frustrated with trying more conventional means of discourse like Aristotelian rhetoric, invitational rhetoric can open doors to understanding and perhaps even meaningful change.

Conclusion

As this chapter has maintained, invitational rhetoric is a propitious form of discourse. The critiques of invitational rhetoric do not deny its viability as a potential alternative to Aristotelian rhetoric in various situations. While invitational rhetoric comes with limitations, such as the prerequisite of willingness and the potential for harm if participants are not careful to respect each other, invitational rhetoric has a number of merits, including being a resource for both men and women, functioning as a helpful means of understanding the circumstances that shape other individuals' beliefs, not precluding in situations of Aristotelian rhetoric the attempt at changing minds, and allowing for change free of persuasive pressure when the invitational communicators so desire such change. Although a humane version of Aristotelian rhetoric remains an ethical option in many situations, invitational rhetoric, since it accepts multiple perspectives as valid, presents an opportunity for fostering "cooperative, non-adversarial, and ethical communication" (Foss & Griffin, "Beyond Persuasion" 15–16). Invitational rhetoric also gives women and other outsiders another way of attempting to alter oppressive social systems.

As such, invitational rhetoric can work successfully as a means of human communication. While employing invitational rhetoric may not necessarily be easy, neither is employing Aristotelian rhetoric (Foss & Griffin, "Metatheoretical Foundations" 69). Given the value of invitational rhetoric, this discursive genre has merit as both a rhetorical theory and a rhetorical practice, and Foss and Griffin's proposal for an invitational rhetoric deserves the attention it has received.

In the next chapter, this book will explain how the merits of invitational rhetoric make this rhetorical genre a viable means of approaching the communication impasse that has developed between advocates of the scholar and practitioner personas of the law professor. Indeed, the lawyers in that conflict could benefit from the advantages of strong, ongoing relationships with each other, and invitational rhetoric would offer lawyers the chance to develop new relationships (Bone et al. 446). Much discursive effort may be required to facilitate understanding (Foss & Griffin, "Metatheoretical Foundations" 69–70), but the role of the law professor should be worthy of that effort for lawyers.

Works Cited in Chapter VI

Alexander, Bryant Keith, and Michele Hammers. "An Invitation to Rhetoric: A Generative Dialogue on Performance, Possibility, and Feminist Potentialities in Invitational Rhetoric." *Cultural Studies ←→ Critical Methodologies*, vol. 19, 2019, pp. 5–14.

Aristotle. *On Rhetoric: A Theory of Civic Discourse*. Translated by George A. Kennedy, Oxford UP, 1991.

Bates, Sophia N., and Valerie Lynn Schrader. "Sharing 'The Music of My Soul': Invitational Rhetoric in the Musical *Memphis*." *Kentucky Journal of Communication*, vol. 40, 2021, pp. 45–62.

Bile, Jeffrey Thomas. "Communication, Advocacy, Argumentation, and Feminisms: Toward a Dialectical Partnership." *Speaker and Gavel*, vol. 32, 1995, pp. 55–70.

Bone, Jennifer Emerling, et al. "Beyond Traditional Conceptualizations of Rhetoric: Invitational Rhetoric and a Move toward Civility." *Western Journal of Communication*, vol. 72, 2008, pp. 434–62.

Brockriede, Wayne. "Arguers as Lovers." *Philosophy and Rhetoric*, vol. 5, 1972, pp. 1–11.

Bruner, M. Lane. "Producing Identities: Gender Problematization and Feminist Argumentation." *Argumentation and Advocacy*, vol. 32, 1996, pp. 185–98.

Carlson, A. Cheree. "Creative Casuistry and Feminist Consciousness: The Rhetoric of Moral Reform." *Quarterly Journal of Speech*, vol. 78, 1992, pp. 16–32.

Chick, Daniel M. "Memorializing Senator McCain's 'Uncivil Tongue': Invitational Rhetoric and the Problem of Confrontation and Violence." *Southern Communication Journal*, vol. 86, 2021, pp. 320–34.

Condit, Celeste M., and Melanie Williams. "Gender Differences and Argumentation: A Positional Account of the Reception of Genetics Arguments." *Speaker and Gavel*, vol. 32, 1995, pp. 1–12.

Crenshaw, Carrie. "The Arguer's Identity: A Feminist Perspective on the Practice of Argumentation Theory." *Speaker and Gavel*, vol. 32, 1995, pp. 13–25.

---. "The Normality of Man and Female Otherness: (Re)Producing Patriarchal Lines of Argument in the Law and the News." *Argumentation and Advocacy*, vol. 32, 1996, pp. 170–84.

Daughton, Suzanne, and Patrice M. Buzzanell. Foreword. *Inviting Understanding: A Portrait of Invitational Rhetoric*, edited by Sonja K. Foss and Cindy L. Griffin, Roman & Littlefield, 2020, pp. xiii–xvi.

Elshtain, Jean Bethke. "Feminism Discourse and Its Discontents: Language, Power, and Meaning." *Signs: Journal of Women in Culture and Society*, vol. 7, 1982, pp. 603–21.

Faass, Irene P. "Shades of Gray: Alternative Metaphors for Argumentation." *Arguing Communication and Culture: Selected Papers from the Twelfth NCA/AFA Conference on Argumentation*, edited by Thomas Goodnight, National Communication Association, 2002, pp. 219–21.

Foss, Karen A., and Sonja K. Foss. "Personal Experience as Evidence in Feminist Scholarship." *Western Journal of Communication*, vol. 58, 1994, pp. 39–43.

Foss, Sonja K., and Karen A. Foss. *Inviting Transformation: Presentational Speaking for a Changing World.* 2nd ed., Waveland, 2003.

Foss, Sonja K., and Cindy L. Griffin. "Beyond Persuasion: A Proposal for an Invitational Rhetoric." *Communication Monographs*, vol. 62, 1995, pp. 2–18.

Foss, Sonja K., and Cindy L. Griffin. "The Metatheoretical Foundations of Invitational Rhetoric: Axiological, Epistemological, and Ontological Explorations." *Inviting Understanding: A Portrait of Invitational Rhetoric*, edited by Sonja K. Foss and Cindy L. Griffin, Roman & Littlefield, 2020, pp. 59–73.

Foss, Sonja K., and Jeanine Warisse Turner. "Challenges to the Enactment of Invitational Rhetoric in the Age of Mobile Communication Technologies." *Inviting Understanding: A Portrait of Invitational Rhetoric*, edited by Sonja K. Foss and Cindy L. Griffin, Roman & Littlefield, 2020, pp. 157–79.

Fulkerson, Richard. "Transcending Our Conception of Argument in Light of Feminist Critiques." *Argumentation and Advocacy*, vol. 32, 1996, pp. 199–217.

Gearhart, Sally Miller. "The Womanization of Rhetoric." *Women's Studies International Quarterly*, vol. 2, 1979, pp. 195–201.

Golden, James L., et al. *The Rhetoric of Western Thought.* 6th ed., Kendall, 1997.

Goodnight, G. Thomas. "The Personal, Technical, and Public Spheres of Argument: A Speculative Inquiry into the Art of Public Deliberation." *Journal of the American Forensic Association*, vol. 18, 1982, pp. 214–27.

Griffin, Cindy L. *Invitation to Public Speaking.* 2nd ed., Thomson Wadsworth, 2006.

Hobbs, Jeffrey Dale, et al. "Intercollegiate Debate as Invitational Rhetoric: An Offering." *Contemporary Argumentation and Debate*, vol. 21, 2000, pp. 76–94.

Jarman, Jeffrey W., and Kelly M. McDonald. "Invitation Declined: A Response to Intercollegiate Debate as Invitational Rhetoric." *Arguing Communication and Culture: Selected Papers from the Twelfth NCA/AFA Conference on Argumentation*, edited by Thomas Goodnight, National Communication Association, 2002, pp. 205–11.

Johnson, Jenell, et al. "'Keep Talking, I Keep Changing My Mind': The Value of Invitational Rhetoric for Focus Group Research." *Western Journal of Communication*, vol. 85, 2021, pp. 381–99.

Larson, Charles U. *Persuasion: Reception and Responsibility*. 7th ed., Wadsworth, 1995.

Leff, Michael. "The Habitation of Rhetoric." *Argument and Critical Practices: Proceedings of the Fifth SCA/AFA Conference on Argumentation*, edited by Joseph W. Wenzel, Speech Communication Association, 1987, pp. 1–8.

Longtin, Krista, and Kelsey Binion. "Creating Choice and Building Consensus: Invitational Rhetoric as a Strategy to Promote Vasectomies in the United States." *Rhetoric of Health & Medicine*, vol. 4, 2021, pp. 367–87.

Lozano-Reich, Nina M., and Dana L. Cloud. "The Uncivil Tongue: Invitational Rhetoric and the Problem of Inequality." *Western Journal of Communication*, vol. 73, 2009, pp. 220–26.

MacKinnon, Catherine A. "Feminism, Marxism, Method and the State: An Agenda for Theory." *Signs: Journal of Women in Culture and Society*, vol. 7, 1982, pp. 515–44.

Makau, Josina M., and Debian L. Marty. *Cooperative Argumentation: A Model for Deliberative Community*. Waveland, 2001.

Make, Jeremy, and Adam Lauver. "Increasing Trust and Vaccine Uptake: Offering Invitational Rhetoric as an Alternative to Persuasion in Pediatric Visits with Vaccine-Hesitant Parents (VHPs)." *Vaccine: X*, vol. 10, 2022, pp. 1–9.

Mallin, Irwin, and Karrin Vasby Anderson. "Inviting Constructive Argument." *Argumentation and Advocacy*, vol. 36, 2000, pp. 120–33.

McFarland, Douglas D. "Students and Practicing Lawyers Identify the Ideal Law Professor." *Journal of Legal Education*, vol. 36, 1986, pp. 93–107.

Orbe, Mark P., and Gabrielle L. Orbe. "Progressive Political Leadership through an Orientation of Invitational Rhetoric: An Analysis of the Twittersphere of 'The Squad.'" *Journal of Contemporary Rhetoric*, vol. 12, 2022, pp. 17–33.

Palczewski, Catherine Helen. "Argument in an Off Key: Playing with the Productive Limits of Argument." *Arguing Communication and Culture: Selected Papers from the Twelfth NCA/AFA Conference on Argumentation*, edited by Thomas Goodnight, National Communication Association, 2002, pp. 1–23.

---. "Special Issue: Argumentation and Feminisms." *Argumentation and Advocacy*, vol. 32, 1996, pp. 161–69.

Pariera, Katrina L., and Jeanine W. Turner. "Invitational Rhetoric between Parents and Adolescents: Strategies for Successful Communication." *Journal of Family Communication*, vol. 20, 2020, pp. 175–88.

Pedrioli, Carlo A. "A New Image in the Looking Glass: Faculty Mentoring, Invitational Rhetoric, and the Second-Class Status of Women in U.S. Academia." *Hastings Women's Law Journal*, vol. 15, 2004, pp. 185–215.

Pickering, Barbara A. "Women's Voices as Evidence: Personal Testimony in Pro-Choice Films." *Argumentation and Advocacy*, vol. 40, 2003, pp. 1–22.

Swiencicki, Jill. "Rhetorics of Invitation and Refusal in Terry Tempest Williams's *The Open Space of Democracy*." *Women's Studies in Communication*, vol. 38, 2015, pp. 151–66.

Turner, Jeanine Warisse, and Sonja K. Foss. "Options for the Construction of Attentional Social Presence in a Digitally Enhanced Multicommunicative Environment." *Communication Theory*, vol. 28, 2018, pp. 22–45.

Zarefsky, David. "Future Directions in Argumentation Theory and Practice." *Perspectives on Argumentation: Essays in Honor of Wayne Brockriede*, edited by Robert Trapp and Janice Schuetz, Waveland, 1990, pp. 287–97.

CHAPTER VII

Invitational Rhetoric and the Conflict over the Construction of the Ideal Law Professor Persona

As Chapter V observed, the various legs of the stool of the legal profession, in Chief Justice William H. Rehnquist's terms (156), have not coexisted successfully with each other. Of major contention have been lawyers' expectations for the ideal law professor persona. In light of this conflict, many academic lawyers have looked down upon practicing lawyers, and, in turn, many legal practitioners have criticized legal academics (Edwards, "The Growing Disjunction" 35).

In mid-1980s research that focused on discourse from the 1960s, 1970s, and early 1980s, communication and legal scholar Douglas D. McFarland argued that legal academics and practitioners were "liv[ing] in different rhetorical worlds" ("Students and Practicing Lawyers" 105). These lawyers came to develop "little or no understanding" of each other and even became "hostile to one another" (McFarland, "Students and Practicing Lawyers" 105). Although each camp continued to produce Aristotelian rhetoric regarding the law professor role, the other camp failed to process that rhetoric because the views of the camps were sharply divergent (McFarland, "Self-Images . . . : Rethinking the Schism" 260). In addition to reinforcing the conclusions of McFarland's research, Chapters III, IV, and V of this book have explained how one can make the same point about legal discourse regarding the law professor persona both from the late nineteenth century to the period of McFarland's study and from the period of McFarland's study to the present time. Overall, as a two-way phenomenon, the communication has been strikingly ineffective (McFarland, "Students and Practicing Lawyers" 106).

Although the traditional approach to rhetoric has not proved as helpful as it might have, other approaches to rhetoric are available to participants involved in the conflict over the construction of the law professor persona in the United States. Specifically, invitational rhetoric offers participants in this ongoing controversy a chance to step back from their own perspectives and focus on learning about other perspectives in the discourse. In developing such a prospect, this chapter will look at how invitational rhetoric might play out in legal communication among advocates of differing perspectives on the ideal law professor persona, consider the benefits of such communication among lawyers involved in this conflict, and address some potential concerns regarding implementation of invitational rhetoric in this situation.

As previously noted, invitational rhetoric is one key step in the ultimate suggested approach of this book, not the ultimate approach itself. Chapter VIII will address how cooperative rhetoric can call upon both invitational rhetoric and Aristotelian rhetoric to improve the communication process in the conflict over the law professor persona. As such, the application of invitational rhetoric will inform the ensuing discussion of cooperative rhetoric in the next chapter. Additionally, the application of invitational rhetoric in this chapter will be about suggesting a more constructive communication process, not a specific content, to the present participants in the ongoing conflict. Since a prescribed content would violate the spirit of invitational rhetoric, the exact content of the rhetoric will be up to the invitational communicators.

How Invitational Rhetoric Might Unfold in the Conflict over the Ideal Law Professor Persona

While invitational rhetoric might play out successfully in different conflicts common in the legal field, at this point, the conflict studied in this book is of particular interest. To sketch out how invitational rhetoric could unfold among lawyers involved in the conflict over the construction of the law professor persona, this section of the chapter will consider four aspects of participating in invitational rhetoric: incentives for it, contexts that can enable it, a process for it, and possible change in discursive content that could emerge from it.

First, for lawyers from the academy and lawyers from the world of practice to participate in invitational rhetoric and foster a better understanding of differing views on the role of the law professor, the lawyers would need some incentive. This incentive exists in the major goals of legal education. Legal scholars R. Randall Kelso and Charles D. Kelso offered four major goals of legal education that can explain how academic lawyers and practicing lawyers can find the incentive to communicate more effectively about legal education in general and the law professor persona more specifically. According to Kelso and Kelso, four major goals of legal education are the following: advancing scholarship on the law, graduating students who are able to perform the roles that practicing lawyers perform, developing in law students the skills of legal problem-solving, and motivating law students to enter the ongoing discussion among members of the legal community about what the law is now and should become in the future (12–15).

These goals generally have appeal for both academics and practitioners. Although academic lawyers may be more interested in scholarship and practicing lawyers may be more interested in the roles that practicing lawyers perform, these particular goals are significant to both groups. For instance, some academic lawyers have admitted that scholarship should inform the practice of law (Hricik & Salzmann 765), a prospect that has immediate significance for practicing lawyers who could benefit from pre-existing thinking on relevant legal topics. Indeed, practitioners cannot be experts in all areas of the law (Ames 143). From this perspective, scholarship needs to do something outside the academy. If scholarship does not, the credibility of academics comes into question among members of the practicing bar. An important relationship exists, then, between scholarship and the roles that lawyers perform in practice.

Furthermore, the skills of legal problem-solving apply to both law school discussions and the everyday world of legal practice. At one level or another, both academics and practitioners deal with legal problems, and both groups would want future lawyers to know how to approach these legal problems. Again, this point touches on the relevance of legal education, but it also touches on a basic set of professional skills upon which practitioners rely. Thus, legal problem-solving skills are of interest to lawyers of an academic nature and lawyers of a more practical nature.

Additionally, discussion about what the law is and what it should become is another area of overlap. Thoughtful and learned discussions on the role of the law are well-suited to the writing of law review articles, an activity that would appeal to academic lawyers, but these discussions can have a meaningful impact on the lives of practicing lawyers because those lawyers must interact with the processes of the law on a daily basis. Hence, a working understanding of the present and future states of the law should have appeal to both lawyers inside and outside the academy.

Given the general appeal of the noted goals of legal education to both academic lawyers and practicing lawyers, some room for common ground exists. This common ground provides the incentive for lawyers from the two groups to employ invitational rhetoric about legal education. As focused more particularly on the subject matter of this book, this common ground would facilitate consideration of the appropriate role of the law professor in furthering the major goals of legal education. Regarding the overlapping goals considered above, the law professor has, by way of professional status, a significant influence on legal scholarship, the skills of legal problem-solving, and discussing the role of the law in society. As noted previously, legal scholarship can inform the roles that practicing lawyers perform. Accordingly, academic lawyers and practicing lawyers do have an incentive to try to communicate more productively about the role of the law professor in legal education.

Second, lawyers in favor of the scholar persona of the law professor and lawyers in favor of the practitioner persona of the law professor who find an incentive to communicate invitationally would need to be able to communicate with each other in a context conducive to invitational rhetoric. Such a context would have physical and discursive dimensions. In terms of the physical dimension, lawyers often meet during law school campus lectures, bar association functions, and the day-to-day work of public service functions of the bar (Leflar 22, 24). While law journals could continue to provide forums for addressing the conflict that historically has played out in law journals, encouraging lawyers to communicate in person probably would be more effective since casually dismissing the views of someone who is physically present in the same context is often difficult.

In terms of the discursive dimension of the context, lawyers would need to foster the external conditions of safety, value, freedom, and openness that communication scholars Sonja K. Foss and Cindy L. Griffin ("Beyond Persuasion" 10) and Sonja K. Foss and Karen A. Foss (*Inviting Transformation* 39) articulated. To foster safety, or "the creation of a feeling of security and [absence of] danger for the audience" (Foss & Griffin, "Beyond Persuasion" 10–13), lawyers would need to feel free from the courtroom clash that often comes with traditional legal advocacy. When one is in court to try or appeal a case, one functions in a situation in which one's views on a given matter constantly come under critique. As such, attempting to communicate invitationally right after the close of a heated trial or appeal would not be the best approach for fostering safety. Rather, bar association meetings, award functions, and civic functions would be more appropriate environments.

To foster value, or "the acknowledgment that audience members have intrinsic or immanent worth" (Foss & Griffin, "Beyond Persuasion" 10–13), lawyers again would need to avoid the clash of the courtroom or other often hostile environments like a negotiation situation between two divorcing spouses. In environments somewhat free of this type of clash, such as those mentioned in the prior paragraph, lawyers likely would be more open to respecting each other as people. In this type of situation, value of other lawyers would be possible.

Additionally, lawyers would want to foster freedom, or "the power to choose or decide" (Foss & Griffin, "Beyond Persuasion" 10–13). For lawyers, achieving this external condition should not be too difficult, at least in one sense. Especially for lawyers who practice advocacy, making up one's own mind on issues is not a difficult matter. However, lawyers also would need to learn to respect the right of others to make up their own minds. Some trial lawyers, much like some undergraduate debaters, might tend to expect audiences to accept the viewpoints presented. Of course, audiences have their own minds. Just as a jury can decide as it wishes, so can other lawyers. Recognizing this point might be a challenge for some lawyers, but enough quality communications with other parties as fellow humans, not as opponents, would help in this matter.

In addition to fostering safety, value, and freedom through their discourse, lawyers would want to foster the external condition of openness, or "seek[ing] out and consider[ing] as many perspectives as possible" (Foss & Foss, *Inviting Transformation* 39). Given that the legal field is one of advocacy, this external condition may be a challenge for lawyers to achieve. Again, a trial or appellate lawyer is accustomed to advocating a position vigorously on behalf of a client. Nonetheless, lawyers committed to treating each other respectfully should be willing to listen to each other to understand one another effectively. Acquiring multiple understandings of the ideal law professor persona would be a function of having communicated with various other lawyers in an invitational manner. Thus, while facing a challenge, lawyers willing to listen carefully could achieve openness. In a situation in which lawyers could accomplish the external conditions of safety, value, freedom, and openness, the lawyers would stand a good chance of communicating in an invitational manner.

Third, the process of invitational rhetoric would be an attempt to understand the views of individuals with different perspectives on the ideal law professor persona. Change of views would be a possibility that may come from the process, but, in the absence of change, participating lawyers still would have the opportunity to develop positive ongoing professional relationships that they often have not enjoyed to date. At a minimum, willing lawyers would be able to understand more effectively the parties whom they have come to ignore or dismiss with uninformed argument, rhetorical behavior that Chapters III, IV, and V illustrated in depth.

While the process of invitational rhetoric is not precise, the following is a suggestion of how the process might unfold between two individuals with different views of the role of the law professor. A communication consultant would lay out this general process for the participating lawyers. As the consultant would explain, the process most likely would begin in an informal manner at a gathering where academic lawyers and practicing lawyers would be present, such as a gathering mentioned above. After the usual pleasantries, the two lawyers, located in a comfortable setting, would take turns explaining their views on the topic, and each lawyer would have the opportunity to enter the other lawyer's world and see it as the other lawyer would see it (Foss & Griffin, "Beyond Persuasion" 5). When speaking, one lawyer would refrain from judging the perspective of another lawyer in the discussion, and the other lawyer would attempt to refrain from judging the perspective of the lawyer who was speaking (Foss & Griffin, "Beyond Persuasion" 5). Instead of change, the focus of the communication would be understanding (Foss & Griffin, "Beyond Persuasion" 5).

The communication consultant would explain that the first lawyer, taking the initiative, could outline the particulars of how she saw the role of the law professor. Meanwhile, the second lawyer would make the effort to place his own views of the role of the law professor aside and also make an effort to understand the views of the first lawyer, which might include the need for the law professor to be a scholar. The second lawyer would have to listen carefully and might even want to take some brief notes. If done politely, the second lawyer, almost becoming an active student of the views of the first lawyer, could ask the first lawyer to pause in her discussion and address a few points of clarification. Communication scholars Irwin Mallin and Karrin Vasby Anderson termed this type of active listening *reflective listening* (129). The idea is that, throughout the process, the second lawyer would gain a developing understanding of the first lawyer's explanations. While some points of clarification could be helpful, the second lawyer, upon receiving clarifications, then would need to make sure the first lawyer would be able to complete her explanation.

Most likely, this step in the process would take more than just a few minutes, especially since the second lawyer would want to allow the first lawyer to explain why she viewed the role of the law professor as she did. At the end of this process, the second lawyer should be able to explain accurately and in some detail the first lawyer's views to the first lawyer.

The communication consultant would note that, after the first lawyer had a chance to explain her view of the law professor role and the second lawyer had inquired about any points of clarification, the second lawyer then would have an opportunity to outline the particulars of how he saw the law professor role. Meanwhile, the first lawyer would try to place her personal views of the role of the law professor aside and focus on understanding the views of the second lawyer, which might include a need for the law professor to be a practitioner. The first lawyer would have to listen carefully and might desire to take some notes. As before, except with roles reversed, the first lawyer, essentially becoming an active student of the views of the second lawyer, could ask the second lawyer to pause in his explanation and address a few matters of clarification. Throughout the process, the first lawyer would gain a developing understanding of the second lawyer's explanations. Although a few points of clarification could be helpful, the first lawyer, upon receiving clarifications, would need to make sure the second lawyer would be able to complete his explanation. This step in the process probably would take time, especially since the first lawyer would want to allow the second lawyer to explain why he viewed the role of the law professor as he did. At the end of this process, the first lawyer should be able to explain accurately and in some detail the second lawyer's views to the second lawyer.

During both stages of the process of invitational rhetoric, gaining more than a superficial understanding would be important, as the communication consultant would explain to the participating lawyers, because a deeper understanding can get at interests, rather than just at general viewpoints. Interests are concerns that motivate people, and understanding another party's interests can help one connect more effectively with that party (Fisher et al. 41–43). As suggested above, asking why a party sees something in a particular manner can be one productive way of understanding that party's interests (Fisher et al. 44).

Looking for underlying common interests would be helpful for the two hypothetical lawyers. For example, the second lawyer might ask the first lawyer why she feels that the law professor should be a scholar, and the first lawyer might point out that the academy requires that law schools produce scholarship. Also, the first lawyer might ask the second lawyer why he feels that the law professor should be a practitioner, and the second lawyer could indicate that future lawyers need to learn from lawyers who have performed the tasks that the future lawyers will perform. In this case, two underlying interests are a requirement of functioning within the present academic system and a need for future lawyers to learn to practice law. Although a deeper understanding might not result in the changing of minds, the knowledge of each other's underlying interests and the explanations that accompany them could allow parties to come to respect each other as professionals. Each party would know that the other party's views were not random and devoid of an explanation. This result could be an improvement in the communication between academic lawyers and practicing lawyers.

This hypothetical example of invitational rhetoric is just one possibility via which the process might unfold. For instance, the consultant would note that a similar process also could take place in small groups, in which one lawyer would explain that lawyer's views and also address points of clarification. In this scenario, another lawyer then would assume that role. The process would repeat itself until all lawyers in the group had had time to express their views. In this manner, each participant would have a chance to speak and carefully listen for understanding. This would not always be an easy task, but if lawyers, knowing that they all would have a chance to talk at some point, were willing to listen to each other, the door to understanding could begin to open.

Fourth, possible change in discursive content is another part of invitational rhetoric that should receive some attention. Invitational rhetoric does not always result in change of content, but, if conducted in a willing and respectful manner, the process can help professional relationships to develop. While the development of such relationships is itself often beneficial, in certain cases, invitational rhetoric also can lead to some change in content (Foss & Foss, *Inviting Transformation* 13–14).

Such potential change may take place if lawyers, upon gaining a deeper understanding of other lawyers' interests, come to see value in some of those interests in relation to their own interests. For example, an academic lawyer might decide that more interaction with the world of practice could make her scholarship more accurate and relevant. Also, a practicing lawyer might decide that some legal scholarship could inform the world of legal practice, and the lawyer might even take an interest in writing a scholarly article on some aspect of his legal specialty that has been troubling him for decades. If enough lawyers in one group begin to see value in the interests of lawyers in the other group and vice versa, openness to some change would become a possibility.

A prescription for the content of the invitational rhetoric among lawyers would be inconsistent with the assumptions of invitational rhetoric, which is not a top-down communication approach in which a consultant tells participants what the content should be. Foss and Griffin described invitational rhetoric, in part, as "an invitation to understanding" ("Beyond Persuasion" 5), not a requirement for adopting a message. However, several examples, while not exhaustive, can illustrate the possibilities of invitational rhetoric as a means of fostering constructive communication among lawyers regarding the ideal role of the law professor.

For instance, lawyers might decide to devise a law professor persona based on a hybrid persona from the period 1870 to 1920 or 1960 to the present. One such approach might be akin to that of Albert M. Kales, who argued for a restricted amount of practical experience for the law professor ("Should the Law Teacher" 255). Assuming a distinction between taking care of clients and taking care of cases, such a persona would view client care as more business than law and something that would take a large amount of a lawyer's time (Kales, "Should the Law Teacher" 254). This possible model could suggest that a law professor should handle cases, not clients, and to such cases the law professor would bring expertise in a given area (Kales, "Should the Law Teacher" 255). By being able to test legal hypotheses, as some might call them, through litigation, the law professor would have a better understanding of the legal world, and such an understanding would allow the law professor to become a better teacher (Kales, "Should the Law Teacher" 259–60). Accordingly, this persona would balance scholarly and practical interests.

Another possible hybrid model might be akin to that of Harlan F. Stone from the same period as the Kales model. Such an approach could embrace both the scholar and the practitioner (Stone, "The Importance" 206). This model would note that, because logical and practical considerations are part of practicing law, the law professor should be familiar with both types of considerations (Stone, "The Importance" 207). This persona could embrace Stone's belief that "[t]he law teacher has indeed missed his calling who has nothing to offer his students but the solution of the purely intellectual problems of the law" ("The Importance" 208). In short, this law professor persona could be that of "a well-rounded lawyer" (Stone, "The Importance" 210), or one who has practiced law and now desires to teach law within a university setting.

Besides the hybrid possibilities in which the law professor resides in an academic setting and either continues a limited practice of law or has practiced law extensively in the past, another possibility may emerge from invitational rhetoric regarding the ideal law professor persona. For instance, law schools could accept multiple personas simultaneously. The scholar model discussed in Chapters III, IV, and V might become one track to tenure in the law school, while the practitioner model discussed in the same chapters might become another track to tenure. The former model would meet the law school's requirement of producing scholarship for the university, and the latter model would meet the law school's requirement of developing practice-ready graduates for the world of legal practice. For this dynamic to work on an equitable basis, the lawyers who would develop such an approach may note that, in contrast to the situations in many present-day law schools (Alfieri 1074, Joy & Kuehn 230), both professor models would have equal status. Neither scholarship nor skills training would assume higher status, as each would serve a vital purpose.

The Benefits of Invitational Rhetoric as a Means of Addressing the Conflict over the Ideal Law Professor Persona

Invitational rhetoric offers multiple benefits to lawyers who have communicated about the ideal law professor persona. These benefits relate to this long-standing conflict but also go beyond the conflict. As suggested above, successful invitational rhetoric would allow lawyers to come to understand each other more thoroughly on legal education topics that include, but are not limited to, the ideal law professor persona. With deeper understanding, which has been a key ingredient missing from the communication studied in this book, lawyers could make more-informed decisions about how they want their field, including its educational component, to function. Along with greater understanding come greater possibilities for new approaches to old challenges.

Not only would invitational rhetoric allow lawyers to come to greater understandings of their colleagues' views on legal education, especially regarding the ideal law professor persona, but invitational rhetoric also would offer lawyers the chance to develop new relationships (Bone et al. 446). As Foss and Griffin emphasized, invitational rhetoric can be "a means to create a relationship" ("Beyond Persuasion" 5). Thus, if certain lawyers enter the world of other lawyers at a deep enough level, the lawyers involved may find something of value in those communicative interactions and seek to continue the communication. Although ongoing relationships would not develop in every instance, in some instances, lawyers might choose to further their communication through ongoing relationships. When lawyers live and work in the same community, whether they work on university campuses or in law firms, ongoing relationships can be of great value, particularly when lawyers need to address larger challenges like law reform issues. Also, lawyers of differing stripes have the future of legal education at stake because academic lawyers work in that environment, and the environment is supposed to prepare future lawyers for the world of legal practice. Ideally, lawyers in a particular relationship would not only gain an understanding of other perspectives on the persona at the front of the law school classroom, but the lawyers would deepen their interactions on other legal, or even non-legal, subjects of importance. The implications of invitational rhetoric could be widespread.

Furthermore, because invitational rhetoric accepts multiple perspectives as valid, it is particularly well-suited for fostering "cooperative, nonadversarial, and ethical communication" (Foss & Griffin, "Beyond Persuasion" 15–16). In the legal field, which often, although not always, gives pride of place to the more combative manifestations of Aristotelian rhetoric, lawyers could improve their skills by interacting with each other in a different manner on some occasions. Indeed, lawyers have to work with court and office personnel, each other, and sometimes other professionals like expert witnesses. While successful lawyers have to function within an adversarial system, learning to communicate in other ways when possible would add an important human dimension to legal practice, particularly when listening to the perspectives of others can be helpful to one's work. This point is especially salient when one is communicating with another person with whom one has an ongoing relationship (Mallin & Anderson 130–31), such as a court clerk or opposing counsel.

On a related note, because invitational rhetoric is a process of rhetoric as inquiry (Faass 220), any change in perspective that takes place occurs when members of the audience choose to make such change, and they do so without the influence of a speaker who presses for that change (Foss & Foss, *Inviting Transformation* 13–14). For many lawyers, this type of communication will not be intuitive. However, not all types of communication require that communicators try to change each other. Indeed, a break from the world of persuasion, a world that often still calls for "right" and "wrong" answers to sometimes complex problems, would be enjoyable for many overworked attorneys. Avoiding the pressure of persuasion would be a healthy change. Instead, when communicating under an invitational paradigm, lawyers would have the chance to make up their minds on matters like the ideal law professor persona free of pressure.

Accordingly, invitational rhetoric offers lawyers multiple benefits. This genre of rhetoric presents an opportunity for greater understanding of perspectives on legal education, including perspectives regarding the ideal law professor role. Moreover, invitational rhetoric also offers the chance for relationship-building and more humane, relaxed discourse.

Potential Concerns with Applying Invitational Rhetoric to the Conflict over the Ideal Law Professor Persona

Although invitational rhetoric offers multiple benefits to lawyers that would include and go beyond gaining a greater understanding of the various perspectives on the ideal law professor persona, one might raise a few concerns regarding the implementation of invitational rhetoric in the manner suggested above. Some consideration of such concerns is now appropriate, and this section of the chapter will show how the concerns are not obstacles to improving the ongoing conflict in the legal field about the ideal law professor persona.

For instance, one could point out that, because invitational rhetoric relies upon the willingness of the lawyers involved, when the lawyers are unwilling to engage in invitational rhetoric, invitational rhetoric cannot be helpful. If both parties are unable to make attempts to understand each other, then invitational rhetoric will not be possible.

This is a fair point. When two parties do not desire to communicate productively with each other, invitational rhetoric, by definition, is impossible. Some lawyers, perhaps those deeply entrenched within an adversarial system, will not want to participate in invitational rhetoric. However, different lawyers see the world differently, and other lawyers may choose to participate in invitational rhetoric, seeing this genre of rhetoric as a welcome change from the normal discourse of the legal field.

Additionally, although many lawyers are skillful at speaking, one might ask whether lawyers really can listen well. After all, good listening is a key part of invitational rhetoric. Despite much of the confrontational communication in the legal field, effective listening is crucial for lawyers (Ala-Kortesmaa & Isotalus 175). For instance, lawyers have to listen to clients who enter law offices in need of assistance with legal matters. A client with extensive assets who seeks estate planning requires a lawyer who can carefully listen to that client's needs. Likewise, a client who requires assistance with defense against criminal charges needs a lawyer who can listen carefully to the client's perspective of what, if anything, happened, as well as perhaps to the perspectives of witnesses. During trial, each attorney needs to listen carefully to the other attorney's witness examinations to make evidentiary objections. To be effective, each of the above lawyers needs information from another individual or other individuals. Also, judges spend time listening to lawyers who argue cases and to witnesses. Indeed, effective legal actors must call upon listening skills in a variety of contexts.

Some such listening skills are used in an adversarial context like court. However, lawyers could endeavor to transfer such skills to a non-adversarial context like one open to invitational rhetoric and then develop the skills in that context. While there would be no need to find fault with the communication to which lawyers would listen, the need to understand would remain. Lawyers could place additional emphasis on further understanding. As such, lawyers could build upon some of their pre-existing skills, even those for which they are often less well-known, to communicate in an invitational manner.

Finally, since parties to invitational rhetoric are not advocating the merits of their views, invitational rhetoric is not the most effective type of rhetoric for decision-making. This is an accurate point. In some cases, invitational rhetoric can lead to change because one party may be willing to adopt a view of another party. However, because invitational rhetoric does not focus on advocacy, the following chapter will offer a discussion of cooperative rhetoric, which embraces both understanding and advocacy. Nonetheless, since invitational rhetoric can foster the understanding necessary for improved communication and, in turn, successful cooperative rhetoric, the general lack of appropriateness of invitational rhetoric for explicit decision-making does not deny the value of invitational rhetoric.

Conclusion

As this chapter has explained, invitational rhetoric can be one effective means of helping lawyers meet the challenge of communicating in a more successful manner regarding the ideal law professor persona. With attention to four aspects of participating in invitational rhetoric, including incentives for it, contexts that can enable it, a process for it, and possible change in discursive content that could emerge from it, the chapter has looked at how invitational rhetoric could play out in communication among supporters of differing perspectives on the law professor persona. The chapter also considered the benefits of invitational rhetoric among lawyers involved in this conflict and addressed some potential concerns with implementation of invitational rhetoric in the conflict.

Although invitational rhetoric may not be the magic solution to a long and ongoing conflict among members of the legal profession in the United States, this genre of rhetoric offers a theoretically sound means by which lawyers can begin to open doors to new possibilities. When the norm consists of "little or no understanding" of other parties to the communication, as McFarland described the phenomenon ("Students and Practicing Lawyers" 105), and an often hostile clash of viewpoints, understanding can be of great value to legal communicators. The need for such understanding is a need that invitational rhetoric is well-suited to address. Still, while in some cases invitational rhetoric alone can lead to change, invitational rhetoric is most likely not the final step in addressing the ongoing conflict among lawyers regarding the construction of the ideal law professor persona. Because invitational rhetoric is not the most effective type of rhetoric for decision-making, cooperative rhetoric now calls for attention.

Works Cited in Chapter VII

Ala-Kortesmaa, Sanna, and Pekka Isotalus. "Relational Tensions and Optimal Listening in the Communication Relationships of American and Finnish Legal Professionals." *Journal of Intercultural Communication Research*, vol. 43, 2014, pp. 173–93.

Alfieri, Anthony V. "Against Practice." *Michigan Law Review*, vol. 107, 2009, pp. 1073–92.

Ames, James Barr. "The Vocation of the Law Professor." *American Law Register*, vol. 48, 1900, pp. 129–46.

Bone, Jennifer Emerling, et al. "Beyond Traditional Conceptualizations of Rhetoric: Invitational Rhetoric and a Move toward Civility." *Western Journal of Communication*, vol. 72, 2008, pp. 434–62.

Edwards, Harry T. "The Growing Disjunction Between Legal Education and the Legal Profession." *Michigan Law Review*, vol. 91, 1992, pp. 34–78.

Faass, Irene P. "Shades of Gray: Alternative Metaphors for Argumentation." *Arguing Communication and Culture: Selected Papers from the Twelfth NCA/AFA Conference on Argumentation*, edited by Thomas Goodnight, National Communication Association, 2002, pp. 219–21.

Fisher, Roger, et al. *Getting to Yes: Negotiating Agreement without Giving In*. 2nd ed., Penguin, 1991.

Foss, Sonja K., and Karen A. Foss. *Inviting Transformation: Presentational Speaking for a Changing World.* 2nd ed., Waveland, 2003.

Foss, Sonja K., and Cindy L. Griffin. "Beyond Persuasion: A Proposal for an Invitational Rhetoric." *Communication Monographs*, vol. 62, 1995, pp. 2–18.

Hricik, David, and Victoria S. Salzmann. "Why There Should Be Fewer Articles like This One: Law Professors Should Write More for Legal Decision-Makers and Less for Themselves." *Suffolk University Law Review*, vol. 38, 2005, pp. 761–87.

Joy, Peter A., and Robert R. Kuehn. "The Evolution of ABA Standards for Clinical Faculty." *Tennessee Law Review*, vol. 75, 2008, pp. 183–232.

Kales, Albert M. "Should the Law Teacher Practice Law?" *Harvard Law Review*, vol. 25, 1912, pp. 253–69.

Kelso, R. Randall, and Charles D. Kelso. *Studying Law: An Introduction*. West, 1984.

Leflar, Robert A. "The Law Teacher's Place in the American Legal Profession." *Journal of the Society of Public Teachers of Law*, vol. 8, 1964, pp. 21–30.

Mallin, Irwin, and Karrin Vasby Anderson. "Inviting Constructive Argument." *Argumentation and Advocacy*, vol. 36, 2000, pp. 120–33.

McFarland, Douglas D. "Self-Images of Law Professors: Rethinking the Schism in Legal Education." *Journal of Legal Education*, vol. 35, 1985, pp. 232–60.

---. "Students and Practicing Lawyers Identify the Ideal Law Professor." *Journal of Legal Education*, vol. 36, 1986, pp. 93–107.

Rehnquist, William H. "The Legal Profession Today." *Indiana Law Journal*, vol. 62, 1987, pp. 151–57.

Stone, Harlan F. "The Importance of Actual Experience at the Bar as a Preparation for Teaching Law." *American Law School Review*, vol. 3, 1912, pp. 205–11.

CHAPTER VIII

Cooperative Rhetoric: A Possible Future for the Conflict over the Construction of the Ideal Law Professor Persona

As several of the foregoing chapters have detailed, at least since the late nineteenth century, Aristotelian rhetoric has played a dominant role in the construction of the U.S. law professor persona. In the Aristotelian tradition, lawyers have advocated different positions on the ideal law professor persona. However, Chapters III, IV, and V noted that Aristotelian rhetoric has led to communication often devoid of understanding of other perspectives. Chapters VI and VII looked to invitational rhetoric as a potential approach to improving this conflict. One of the main benefits of invitational rhetoric is that it can help willing participants develop greater understanding of the perspectives that other communication participants hold, and a related benefit is that such rhetoric can help lawyers develop positive ongoing relationships.

Although invitational rhetoric can help address some of the limitations of Aristotelian rhetoric, invitational rhetoric alone admittedly is not well-suited for decision-making, as the previous chapter observed. If no decision comes from the process of invitational rhetoric, the legal field still would benefit from deciding what kind of law professor persona the profession should retain or adopt. Some members of the contemporary legal academy, particularly those whose rhetoric received attention in Chapter V, may say that, given the prominence of the scholar persona in legal education today, the field already has made its choice. However, the foregoing chapters developed communication and legal scholar Douglas D. McFarland's point that parties to this type of decision have developed "little or no understanding" of each other ("Students and Practicing Lawyers" 105). Although the camps have continued to disseminate rhetoric, for the most part, they have failed to process each other's rhetoric at any real depth (McFarland, "Self-Images...: Rethinking the Schism" 260). This type of communication suggests that the decision has not been as informed as it could have been. While the legal field may opt to retain the scholar persona, the field may decide, with further reflection, upon the practitioner persona, both personas, another option, or a combination of multiple options. Of note, deeper understanding of other perspectives can prepare decision-makers in law to make more-informed choices on this matter.

Because of the limits of Aristotelian rhetoric in fostering understanding and invitational rhetoric in fostering more structured decision-making, another genre of rhetoric would be of great value to legal decision-makers. Specifically, *cooperative rhetoric* combines the best of both Aristotelian rhetoric and invitational rhetoric, which can "complement and inform one another" (Woodyard, "Competition and Control" 22–23). In short, this approach allows participants to come to understand other participants' perspectives and also allows the participants the chance to argue the merits of such perspectives to arrive at a decision. Cooperative rhetoric answers what communication scholar Jeanine Czubaroff characterized as the "persistent call [of decades of prior communication research] for an enlarged conception of rhetoric" ("Dialogue" 60).

In light of the opportunity that cooperative rhetoric presents, this chapter explains how cooperative rhetoric can be of value to lawyers who have participated in the ongoing conflict over the construction of the ideal law professor persona. To do so, the chapter will examine cooperative rhetoric as invitational rhetoric informs it; outline *collaborative law*, a type of alternative dispute resolution often used in family law cases, as a precedent for the implementation of cooperative rhetoric in the legal field; and then explain how cooperative rhetoric could work in the conflict over the ideal law professor persona.

Cooperative Rhetoric as Invitational Rhetoric Informs It

Communication scholars have used a variety of terms to speak of the concept of cooperative rhetoric. For instance, Josina M. Makau and Debian L. Marty employed *cooperative argumentation* (88), Irwin Mallin and Karrin Vasby Anderson used *constructive argument* (127), Steven E. Daniels and Gregg B. Walker called upon *collaborative learning* (55), Walker and Daniels also called upon *collaborative argument* (141–42), and Jeanine Czubaroff employed *dialogical argumentation* ("Justice and Argument" 19). Despite contemporary interest in the rhetorical genre, composition scholar Richard Fulkerson, joining the discussion among communication scholars, showed that the genre is not entirely new; in the *Topics*, Aristotle referenced the idea of common purpose in rhetoric (Fulkerson 212). For the sake of consistency, this book will employ the term *cooperative rhetoric*. This section of the chapter provides an overview of cooperative rhetoric and shows how invitational rhetoric contributes to cooperative rhetoric.

Under the theory of cooperative rhetoric that communication scholars have developed, communicators focus on addressing the problem at hand as opposed to "winning" the argument (Mallin & Anderson 124). Cooperative rhetoric is "a process of reasoned interaction intended to help participants and audiences make the best assessments or the best decisions in any given situation" (Makau & Marty 87). In terms of an analogy, one might envision "a group of mountain climbers concerned for their mutual safety" and thus interested in testing "two ropes in every conceivable way and then select[ing] for their common use the stronger one" (Ehninger & Brockriede 15). Of course, more than two ropes may be available. Because parties to the rhetoric are collaborators, not opponents, in addressing problems (Mallin & Anderson 127), or perhaps seeking to "achiev[e] an end product" (Mitchell et al. 9), the parties see themselves as mutual resources (Makau & Marty 88). Through the process of cooperative rhetoric, a communicator "offers her ideas rather than imposing them, and builds upon her interlocutor's ideas rather than tearing them down" (Mallin & Anderson 130). Naturally, listening is a key part of this process, too (Makau, "Revisioning" 79; Mallin & Anderson 128–29). Accordingly, cooperative rhetoric seeks to offer "constructive and productive modes of communication" (Mallin & Anderson 127).

Furthermore, cooperative rhetoric emphasizes the interdependence of people and ideas (Makau & Marty 88). The cooperative potential of any given group of communicators is a function of "the significant value that parties place on their relationships with one another, their willingness to trust and share power, their desire for open and constructive communication, and their respect for creative approaches to" addressing problems (Daniels & Walker 63). This type of rhetoric can take place in various communication contexts, including group situations and interpersonal situations (Makau & Marty 93–95, 97–100), as well as in mediated situations (Tolman 19, Minei et al. 336–37). Consequently, cooperative rhetoric can "develop community building and cross-cultural communication competencies" (Makau, "A Conversation" 81).

As this description has illustrated, cooperative rhetoric is a combination of the best manifestations of invitational rhetoric and Aristotelian rhetoric. Because it allows both or all parties to explain themselves, cooperative rhetoric places emphasis on the dialogic focus of invitational rhetoric (Walker & Daniels 140–41). Additionally, since cooperative rhetoric then allows parties respectfully to advocate their positions to determine the most appropriate option or options for that situation, cooperative rhetoric places emphasis on the deliberative focus of Aristotelian rhetoric (Walker & Daniels 141). However, contrary to many situations in which Aristotelian rhetoric is employed, situations in which cooperative rhetoric succeeds involve a respectful tone and a willingness of the participants to yield to positions more conducive to addressing the problems at hand. Convictions matter, but so do relationships (Makau & Marty 91). Wayne Brockriede, in comparing communicators with lovers before scholars had focused on developing the idea of cooperative rhetoric, might have added that participants in cooperative rhetoric value their fellow participants enough to sacrifice some personal gain for the good of "a bilateral relationship" (5).

This understanding of cooperative rhetoric envisions a dialectic between dialogue and deliberation. In some cases, dialogue will encourage the communication more toward learning, and, in other cases, deliberation will encourage the communication more toward decision-making (Walker & Daniels 141). As with most any dialectic, some contradiction or tension exists between the two foci, yet, for cooperative rhetoric to work as a whole rhetorical unit, each focus needs to have a high level of interdependence with the other (Downey 143–46).

Nonetheless, on a critical note, one might query what would happen when some parties in a communication situation fail to cooperate (Czubaroff, "Justice and Argument" 23), or even to cooperate to a sufficient degree (Wei 11). One option is for a motivated party to set the example for other parties. By way of an analogy, even if oncoming night drivers refuse to dim their headlights, a frustrated driver might dim the lights on his own vehicle to try to prevent a major crash (Makau & Marty 90). One can sacrifice one's personal need for vindication and achieve a greater good (Makau & Marty 90). Such is the spirit of cooperative rhetoric. In addressing how cooperative decision-making could function in a competitive culture, Lani Guinier, a legal academic, stated, "'I think the best explanation is to model it'" (Makau & Marty 105).

Even if parties are willing to participate in cooperative rhetoric, at some point they still may reach an impasse. When the parties arrive at such an impasse, they may want to ask what sort of evidence might change someone's view; this inquiry could involve researching new evidence (Walker & Daniels 143). Sometimes thinking aloud can be another option for dealing with blocks in the communicative process (Walker & Daniels 143). Because cooperative rhetoric can be an ongoing process that evolves over time (Daniels & Walker 63), the impasse-bound parties may wish to return to work on their problem with fresh minds at a later date. Such is an understanding of cooperative rhetoric.

Despite the importance of dialogue to the cooperative process, the communication research cited above has not embraced invitational rhetoric vigorously. Of the major pieces of research on cooperative rhetoric addressed in this section, only the Mallin and Anderson piece explicitly made a sustained attempt to develop cooperative rhetoric in part based on invitational rhetoric. While Mallin and Anderson maintained that invitational rhetoric has value for understanding cooperative rhetoric (121), they included in their study various theories that inform cooperative rhetoric and did not focus specifically on invitational rhetoric. In light of the theoretical discussion of invitational rhetoric in Chapter VI and the potential insights for cooperative rhetoric that such a discussion can provide, invitational rhetoric deserves some additional consideration as a theory that can foster a more developed understanding of the dialogic dimension of cooperative rhetoric.

For instance, the external conditions that invitational rhetoric considers can help illustrate the environment in which cooperative communicators are supposed to be able to explain themselves and listen to others, eventually to make informed decisions. Mallin and Anderson noted this point in passing (124), but this insight calls for more than brief attention. In their theory of invitational rhetoric, Sonja K. Foss and Cindy L. Griffin maintained that safety, value, and freedom are three important external conditions ("Beyond Persuasion" 10). Foss and Griffin defined these conditions in this way: *safety* as "the creation of a feeling of security and [absence of] danger for the audience," *value* as "the acknowledgment that audience members have intrinsic or immanent worth," and *freedom* as "the power to choose or decide" ("Beyond Persuasion" 10–13). To the work of Foss and Griffin, Foss and colleague Karen A. Foss added openness as a fourth condition that helps foster the type of climate desired for invitational rhetoric or cooperative rhetoric; Foss and Foss defined *openness* as "seek[ing] out and consider[ing] as many perspectives as possible" (*Inviting Transformation* 39).

The external condition of openness, which Mallin and Anderson did not address in light of invitational rhetoric (124), is especially important to cooperative rhetoric. While a party to cooperative rhetoric needs to feel safe in the communication situation, of some value to the process, and free to choose for himself, the party also must remain open to new ideas. If a party refuses to be open to new ideas, the party may employ Aristotelian rhetoric, trying to persuade the other party of the "correctness" of the former's viewpoint. In this scenario, only the latter party remains open to change; the former does not. As Chapters III, IV, and V explained, this process by itself can be quite uninformed and thus counterproductive. No openness means no cooperative rhetoric. However, with openness, the parties develop the spirit of cooperative rhetoric, which is oriented toward informed decision-making, not just decision-making in general. Openness, then, is an important external condition needed in creating a climate for cooperative rhetoric.

Overall, an understanding of the conditions of safety, value, freedom, and openness, as Foss and Griffin explained with the interpersonal and public address examples summarized in Chapter VI, can produce the type of communication climate that encourages dialogue. When individuals feel unsafe, devalued, and constrained regarding decision-making and are closed-minded, they are unlikely to enter the process of dialogue. Without that dialogue, cooperative rhetoric fails. Thus, an understanding of these conditions, especially the condition of openness, can help establish a climate in which the understanding needed in cooperative rhetoric is likely to take place.

To foster these conditions of safety, value, freedom, and openness that can lead to invitational rhetoric, Foss and Foss suggested the process of *re-sourcement*, which refers to finding a new source of "energy and inspiration" for one's communication (*Inviting Transformation* 44). Re-sourcement involves disengaging oneself from an interaction frame of conquest or conversion of one's audience and then encountering the audience via a non-conquest and non-conversion interaction frame (Foss & Foss, *Inviting Transformation* 44–48). In other words, participants in the communication move away from trying to prove each other "wrong" and focus on opening themselves up to comprehending their respective views. In cooperative rhetoric, when one is temporarily focused on another party's understanding of a matter, one is necessarily less focused on advancing one's own viewpoint and can learn from one's fellow cooperative communicator. This type of understanding can suggest new insight that leads one to change and, ideally, improve one's own understanding of the problem at hand. With more information, decision-making can improve. As such, the notion of re-sourcement from invitational rhetoric enriches an understanding of cooperative rhetoric.

In addition to offering both the specific external conditions that can establish a climate for cooperative rhetoric and the concept of re-sourcement that helps bring about the needed external conditions, invitational rhetoric also validates the personal experiences and testimonies of many different individuals, not just of traditional experts such as physicians, scientists, and attorneys. This approach can lead to new insights from unexpected sources. Foss and Foss pointed out that one's personal experience often functions as one's personal truth ("Personal Experience" 39), and such experience comes from individuals of all types. When foregrounded in a discussion, personal experience gives voice to a variety of individuals and, in a cooperative rhetoric situation, this dynamic can enrich decision-making. The more relevant information the decision-makers have, the more-informed the decisions can be.

While not necessarily of great value to the conflict over the ideal law professor persona, in which the parties are lawyers and thus traditional experts, giving voice to non-traditional experts in other legal conflicts can provide for a more-informed decision-making process. For instance, in a legal conflict over logging in a particular forest, hearing from experts well-versed in the law and environmental science is not enough because non-traditional experts may live near the area in question. These non-traditional experts would have much to say about environmental policies that directly would impact the lives of those who live in the area. Not only is this process one of validating communication for the non-traditional experts in the situation, but the communication can provide more information regarding parties' experiences upon which decision-makers can make informed decisions. This is another aspect of invitational rhetoric that can help develop a theory of cooperative rhetoric.

The last portion of this section of the chapter has identified some aspects of invitational rhetoric that can provide for a richer understanding of the dialogic dimension of cooperative rhetoric. A better understanding of the external factors that give rise to invitational rhetoric provides a deeper understanding of the how those factors can foster dialogue within a cooperative rhetoric context. Re-sourcement adds to an understanding of refocusing on other parties to the communication, necessary for cooperative rhetoric to flourish. Also, the importance of voices of many backgrounds, valued in invitational rhetoric, points out that, as relevant, many voices should speak in a cooperative rhetoric situation so that the decision-makers can make more-informed decisions. Viewed through an invitational lens, the dialogic dimension of cooperative rhetoric becomes clearer.

Collaborative Law as Legal Precedent for the Implementation of Cooperative Rhetoric

Because the legal field in the United States, as well as in other common law jurisdictions, places great value upon precedent, having a precedent for the implementation of cooperative rhetoric in a law-related conflict like the conflict over the construction of the law professor persona is helpful. The idea of *collaborative law*, upon which this section of the chapter elaborates, provides such a precedent to suggest that cooperative rhetoric can function well within some law-related conflicts.

Collaborative law, a type of alternative dispute resolution (Tindall & Smith 690), is an approach to law that has developed since the early 1990s (Schwab 354–55). This approach focuses on "offering 'kinder and gentler' ways of helping parties resolve their differences" (Webb 315). Although sometimes used in other types of cases, such as those that involve employment and family business (O'Connell 539, Goodman 16–17), collaborative law is most often used in divorce cases (Schwab 354).

Founded upon "mutual self-interest" (Moses & Russ 23), collaborative law encourages parties to opt for non-litigation alternatives to resolve their disputes (Macfarlane 180). In agreeing not to litigate, parties sit down with each other and their lawyers, as well as perhaps another professional such as a mental health practitioner, to work out the best solution given the circumstances (Lande 1320–21, N. Smith 25), and the parties aim to do so without court intervention (Boyarin 500). The idea is to work together toward a settlement of the relevant issues and give the parties more control over, and thus more satisfaction regarding, the outcome of the process (Curtis, Daicoff 131). Parties who have contributed more to the process are more likely to comply with the final product (Daicoff 132).

Attorneys must ensure that the parties thoroughly understand the process of collaborative law (Hoffman & Schepard 96). The process is confidential and involves "full and timely disclosure of all relevant information" (Boyarin 505, Reynolds & Tennant 12). In collaborative law, the lawyers often act more as counselors than as advocates (Boyarin 506).

If litigation results, the lawyers, according to a pre-existing agreement with the clients typically called a collaborative law participation agreement, have to withdraw from the situation, so the litigation incentive for lawyers is absent (Boyarin 495, Schwab 358). Likewise, each attorney promises to withdraw from the case if the attorney learns that the attorney's client has undermined the collaborative process (Reynolds & Tennant 12).

In a hypothetical example, two collaborative lawyers and their clients would sit down for a four-way meeting that would address possible approaches to managing a divorce (Voegele et al. 984). In advance, the wife and the husband would have expressed their desires to their respective lawyers. Also in advance, the lawyers would have reviewed the available documents, such as deeds, mortgages, car payments, and records of credit card debt, to determine if their clients' desires had factual support. If possible, the attorneys would have tried to establish a collaborative relationship before the first four-way meeting (Voegele et al. 990).

To the first four-way meeting, which would help lay a foundation for the overall process (Voegele et al. 991), the parties would bring the supporting documents. At the meetings, the parties would aim to follow previously agreed upon agendas (Voegele et al. 993). While each lawyer would know that lawyer's client's interests in advance, at the first meeting, the lawyers and the parties would need to clarify each party's interests. This process would call for the type of active listening, namely reflective listening, described in the earlier discussion of applying invitational rhetoric (Mallin & Anderson 129). The parties would need to be open with each other about their interests (Voegele et al. 994). Specifically, the wife might want to keep a particularly efficient car; the husband might want to make sure he has custody of the children. Different options for addressing these issues would receive attention.

In addition to dialogue, some well-mannered advocacy of options would be necessary to the process. One lawyer could argue that, given her long daily commute, the wife would need the particularly efficient automobile, while the other lawyer might argue that, based on prior parenting experiences, the husband should have custody of the children. If some type of resolution were possible for certain issues, those issues would be taken off the table. If not, those issues might require additional consideration after the parties and lawyers had had a chance to take a break and think more carefully about each party's interests. In this case, subsequent meetings would be helpful. Either way, the parties and the lawyers would have to be willing to adjust their contentions throughout the process. For example, adjustments could include accepting a different family car that would meet the needs of a long commute and having primary custody of the children.

Again, in the process of working toward a resolution of some sort, the dialectic of understanding and advocacy would play out. Since the process is oriented toward problem-solving, rather than being purely adversarial in nature, the parties, having opted for collaborative law instead of the more expensive and combative traditional option of litigation, would focus on how they could find a reasonable conclusion to their marriage. This process would not be for individuals who seek the most lucrative or vengeful end to a marriage.

The practice of collaborative law has received formal recognition, including in law school curricula. Various law schools cover collaborative law in seminars on dispute resolution systems, professional ethics classes, and advanced classes on domestic relations law (Tesler, "Collaborative Family Law" 333). In the 2000s, some law schools began to offer stand-alone classes on collaborative law (Strickland 994). For instance, in 2003, Santa Clara University announced that its law school would be the first in the United States to offer a class specifically on collaborative law ("SCU School of Law Offers"). At about the same time, Loyola University of New Orleans was developing a year-long interdisciplinary course on collaborative practice that aimed to bring together graduate students in fields like law, psychology, social work, and business (Tesler, "Collaborative Family Law" 333). Courses like the one at Loyola University have both theoretical and practical dimensions because students study why collaborative practice can be effective and then apply that understanding to working on collaborative cases from the perspectives of the students' various disciplines (Tesler, "Collaborative Family Law" 333). With such experiences for students, continued expansion of the use of collaborative law in the law school curriculum was recommended (Engle 67).

Beyond the law school context, many legal communities and states have recognized collaborative law in one manner or another. Attorneys practice collaborative law across the United States, as well as in Canada, Europe, and Australia (Hoffman, Voegele et al. 975). In the United States, training for collaborative practice often takes place locally and thus is readily available (Daicoff 129). On a very formal level, several states adopted collaborative law statutes during the 2000s. Texas was the first state to do so (Tesler, "Collaborative Family Law" 334). North Carolina and California soon followed the Texas example with their own collaborative law statutes (Comes 572, 573). In 2010, Utah became the first state to adopt the Uniform Collaborative Law Act (UCLA), a model statute designed to bring uniformity to the area of collaborative law ("Collaborative Law Act"). In the ensuing years, many states across the Union, along with the District of Columbia, also adopted the UCLA ("Collaborative Law Act").

As an interdisciplinary process, collaborative law involves various fields like psychology, social work, and business (Tesler, "Collaborative Family Law" 330–33), but collaborative law also involves the field of communication. The description of collaborative law in the preceding pages suggests that collaborative law as an alternative legal process relates closely to cooperative rhetoric. Indeed, collaborative law is an example of how cooperative rhetoric can play out in a given field, here the field of law. In general, cooperative rhetoric explains how both understanding and advocacy are key ingredients in collaborative law. In the manner noted above, participants in collaborative law work to develop understanding of the interests of fellow participants and also employ advocacy to test ideas and move toward resolutions.

More specifically, in terms of the dialogic dimension of collaborative law, cooperative rhetoric, as invitational rhetoric informs it, has much to offer. Indeed, cooperative rhetoric addresses the external conditions of safety, value, freedom, and openness necessary for collaborative law to occur successfully. For instance, parties to collaborative law need to feel safe enough that they are willing to disclose documents and other information that normally would remain closely held before, and sometimes even during, the process of civil discovery, by which lawyers attempt to collect information to use as evidence during litigation. Conflicts notwithstanding, the parties also must be able to see some human value in each other because, without recognizing that each party has importance, the parties can allow their frustrations to dominate. Under these conditions, collaborative law would deteriorate into a more hostile process that would not be collaborative in nature.

Another external condition, freedom, also explains the climate necessary for collaborative law. When parties to collaborative law try to force resolutions on each other, the process becomes more akin to some manifestations of traditional civil litigation, in which parties, through their attorneys, try to force each other into a corner. For example, in civil litigation, an attorney might claim that her opponent's case would be without value at trial and insist that the opponent should counsel his client to take a minor settlement at once or risk getting nothing. Instead of cornering each other, parties in a collaborative process should recognize that both parties have the freedom to make personal choices, given the constraints of the situation. A collaborative process involves at least two parties empowered to make decisions.

The final external condition relevant to a productive climate for collaborative law is openness. When parties are open to new suggestions, the process can move forward. If a party rigidly insists that, due to transportation needs, the party must get a specific vehicle after a divorce, the process may not move forward. However, if that party is open to receiving a cash payment from the other party that will address the transportation needs, the process may move forward in a productive manner.

Just as the external conditions needed for cooperative rhetoric help explain the conditions needed for collaborative law, so does the concept of re-sourcement. Parties who wish to avoid the hostile confrontation common in traditional divorce proceedings need to be able to move their goals away from conquest and focus initially on understanding. Conquest does not address the potentially unknown interests of other parties, nor does it give one a chance to explain one's own interests. When parties find a new source of focus for the communication process, they can move away from traditional litigation models and toward less-destructive models.

Additionally, the importance of giving voice to non-traditional experts that is a part of the dialogic dimension of cooperative rhetoric is instructive in explaining collaborative law. In a traditional divorce case, the voices of the children easily might receive inadequate attention because the lawyers are zealously representing the parents while the parents are full of hate for each other. However, in a collaborative law situation, in which the parties have agreed to try to find a non-litigation resolution to the situation, the parties will arrive at a more-informed decision if they give voice to all individuals with a stake in the outcome. Such individuals would include children (Kelly 150–51, Emery 170). Just as the parents need a say, so do the other individuals whose futures are at stake in the decision-making process of collaborative law.

Despite these insights that cooperative rhetoric offers the communication aspect, particularly the dialogic dimension of the communication aspect, of collaborative law, lawyers have much to learn about how communication theory can inform collaborative law. A Westlaw database search of law reviews, bar journals, and similar publications for articles with titles that contained the term *collaborative law* produced one hundred eighteen articles. While ninety-eight of the articles at least contained the term *communication*, only one article contained the term *communication theory*, which appeared in a footnote that appropriately pointed to the lack of communication theory in legal education (Tesler, "Collaborative Law" 971). No articles contained the term *rhetorical theory* or *cooperative rhetoric*. Because fields other than psychology, business, and social work can contribute to a richer understanding of the process of collaborative law, lawyers would benefit from considering what communication theories like cooperative rhetoric have to say about collaborative law.

How Cooperative Rhetoric Can Be of Value to Lawyers Involved in the Conflict over the Ideal Law Professor Persona

In light of collaborative law as a precedent for the implementation of cooperative rhetoric in certain legal conflicts, lawyers involved in the ongoing conflict over the construction of the ideal law professor persona ultimately would stand to gain from employing cooperative rhetoric. To date, lawyers have filled volumes deliberating over the ideal law professor persona, but, because of the ongoing understanding problem addressed in Chapters III, IV, and V, lawyers initially would benefit from gaining a more complete understanding of the law professor persona by focusing on dialogue for a period of time. In short, at this point, Aristotelian rhetoric has had its time, and invitational rhetoric still awaits its time. Given its focus on understanding, invitational rhetoric is a medicinal genre of rhetoric appropriate for the immediate future. However, at some point in the future when willing lawyers have listened for understanding through invitational rhetoric, and if invitational rhetoric alone has not provided for sufficient decision-making, a need for some deliberation and decision-making still would remain. At that future moment, cooperative rhetoric, precedented by collaborative law, would come into play.

As Chapter VII suggested, a key incentive for parties to participate in this cooperative process is common ground regarding the goals for legal education. The previous chapter explained how some of the major goals of legal education, including producing legal scholarship, addressing the roles of practicing lawyers, developing the skills of legal problem-solving, and discussing what law is and should be (Kelso & Kelso 12–15), speak to the needs of both academic lawyers and practicing lawyers. By way of professional status, the law professor has an important influence on the furtherance of these goals. Accordingly, academic lawyers and practicing lawyers have an incentive to try to communicate more productively about the persona of the law professor in legal education.

Given this incentive for lawyers to participate in a cooperative process, a communication consultant would provide an overview of that process to the participating lawyers. As the consultant would note, lawyers often meet during law school campus lectures, bar association functions, and the day-to-day work of public service functions of the bar (Leflar 22, 24). The previous chapter illustrated how, with the general presence of safety, value, freedom, and openness, these situations offer the chance for invitational rhetoric to take place. Because of the constructive nature of these situations, the situations also offer the chance for cooperative rhetoric to transpire. In such a cooperative situation, lawyers would be able to focus on dialogue, and they also would be able to focus on respectful advocacy. This type of advocacy, informed through dialogue, could spill over from these situations into written forums like law journals and legal magazines, which then would spread the persuasion to a nationwide legal audience. A special symposium, later published in a law journal, would be another option.

The communication consultant would note that, through this procedure, willing lawyers would focus on effective approaches to the law professor persona most appropriate for contemporary legal education, rather than on personal egos and reputations. Given the long-standing Aristotelian assumptions of the legal system in the United States, spirited persuasion most likely would result at some point, but lawyers would do well to view their colleagues as resources rather than as opponents. Instead of promoting hostile advocacy, the goal would be to promote an effective approach to legal education, specifically regarding the law professor role. Lawyers and their ideas would interact, but in a constructive manner.

More specifically, the process between the two hypothetical lawyers from Chapter VII could look something like this. The communication consultant would explain that, one at a time, the lawyers would outline the particulars of how they saw the law professor persona in legal education. While one lawyer spoke, the other lawyer would try to put aside personal views and instead focus on understanding the other lawyer, which might include asking some questions. Then the roles would reverse. The active listening needed for this process is the reflective listening that Mallin and Anderson described in their study (129). This part of the process would be akin to the part of a collaborative law process in which parties to a divorce matter offer their understandings, interests, and suggested approaches to addressing the situation, except in the former situation the lawyers would not have their own counsel as the parties in the divorce matter would. Much like the parties to a collaborative law process, the parties to cooperative rhetoric would assume an approach that would seek to avoid the type of destructive rhetoric often found in litigation. Re-sourcement, via which parties focus on understanding each other's points, as opposed to verbal conquest, would be helpful here, too. At the end of this dialogic part of the process, the lawyers ideally should be able to explain accurately and in some detail the views they have come to understand via this portion of the process.

Subsequently, either on the same occasion or on another one, the lawyers would proceed to argue over the merits of their perspectives. As the consultant would note, this process would involve attempts to further the merits of the models on the table, but, in contrast to the process of persuasion studied in Chapters III, IV, and V, this process would involve two parties who have agreed to remain open to change to make an effective decision. For instance, the first lawyer might realize that the second lawyer made a good point about the need for law schools to graduate practice-ready individuals, and the first lawyer may want to modify, but not abandon, her own model. Likewise, the second lawyer might realize that, given that the contemporary law school exists within the university system, the first lawyer made a strong point that scholarship is important to the law professor persona and accordingly modify, but not abandon, his model. This part of the process would be akin to the part of a collaborative law process in which the lawyers and parties evaluate for merit the differing possible approaches to the situation. Just as in collaborative law, the parties in the conflict over the law professor persona would need to keep in mind the commitment to work on the problem and avoid threatening to take a more verbally hostile approach to the situation. In the case studied here, the cooperative lawyers could go back and forth, working out which points had some merit.

As the parties make strong points about the relative merits of their preferred models, the parties, now more-informed about the models on the table, might be willing to accept some changes based on the persuasion process. Much the same as in a collaborative law situation but with different content, such a process of persuasion that involves some give and take could help foster a workable model of the law professor that speaks to the various needs, including scholarly and practical, of the two major groups in this conflict. Eventually, at some point in the future, and as a function of having participated in cooperative rhetoric, lawyers would retain, alter, or even abandon the current law professor persona, that of the scholar.

Quite predictably, not all lawyers would be willing to participate in cooperative rhetoric, but some probably would be. Some of the lawyers who practice collaborative law would be excellent ambassadors for cooperative rhetoric as a means of improving communication regarding the ongoing conflict over the law professor persona, as well as communication regarding other significant issues in the legal world. Such lawyers could set the example and encourage more skeptical lawyers to try cooperative rhetoric on this issue or others of importance.

One inspiration for this type of cooperative approach might come from the consideration of differing concerns that several lawyers exhibited in their rhetoric in favor of hybrid personas of the law professor during the periods from 1870 to 1920 and 1960 to the present. For instance, Chapter III described a model in which the law professor would continue to practice law while teaching and thus be able to test legal hypotheses, as well as a model in which a lawyer with great practical experience would become a full-time professor (Kales, "Should the Law Teacher" 259; Stone, "The Importance" 210). This type of discourse hints at cooperative rhetoric because the discourse not only advocates a position but also acknowledges the concerns of differing parties in the conflict.

Various decisions regarding the law professor persona could result from this cooperative approach to rhetoric. Because a cooperative approach does not prescribe substantive results but rather suggests a process for communication and leaves content up to the parties to the communication, these potential results are merely illustrations of what might develop, not necessarily what has to develop. The purpose of the illustrations is to make the cooperative process more concrete at this point. In addition to inspiring the procedure, the Kales and Stone models of the law professor also would be possible substantive results of cooperative rhetoric. As Chapter VII noted in an invitational rhetoric context, these models would combine the need to produce scholarship with the need for some hands-on experience. Alternatively, the two different major law professor personas, the scholar and the practitioner, together might satisfy the requirements that the law school exist within the academy and prepare future practitioners for the legal profession. Since one persona would be appropriate for producing scholarship and the other persona would be appropriate for developing hands-on skills in law students, the personas together would be available to meet the different needs of law schools. Again, these are only some conceivable results that could come from cooperative rhetoric, but they illustrate how this type of process might generate results.

Supported by collaborative lawyers and other open-minded lawyers, cooperative rhetoric would come with several benefits. For instance, some lawyers would develop a greater appreciation for listening and understanding, which can be helpful in dealing with people in many contexts, including legal contexts. At the same time, lawyers would be able to call upon their existing skills of persuasion, ideally in a way that focuses more on the messages than on the messengers. Additionally, as a function of the communication, a well-thought-out decision regarding the ideal role of the law professor would be a real possibility, and lawyers would not simply be talking past each other as they have been for ages. This prospect is the key benefit that this book offers in addressing the main communication problem studied. Finally, as the practice of collaborative law suggests, this cooperative approach to rhetoric would be one that lawyers could rely upon in other situations in their professional lives, including negotiation situations.

Conclusion

This chapter has explained how cooperative rhetoric can be of value to lawyers involved in the ongoing conflict over the construction of the ideal law professor persona. The chapter has examined cooperative rhetoric as invitational rhetoric informs it, outlined collaborative law as an appropriate precedent for the implementation of cooperative rhetoric in the legal field, and shown how cooperative rhetoric could work in the conflict over the ideal role for the law professor. Consequently, this chapter has responded hopefully to Douglas D. McFarland's sobering observation that legal academics and practitioners had come to "live in different rhetorical worlds" ("Students and Practicing Lawyers" 105).

Works Cited in Chapter VIII

Boyarin, Yishai. "Generating 'Win-Win' Results: Negotiating Contracts in the Drafting Process of the Uniform Collaborative Law Act." *Hofstra Law Review*, vol. 38, 2009, pp. 495–536.

Brockriede, Wayne. "Arguers as Lovers." *Philosophy and Rhetoric*, vol. 5, 1972, pp. 1–11.

"Collaborative Law Act." *Uniform Law Commission*, www.uniformlaws.org/committees/community-home?communitykey=fdd1de2f-baea-42d3-bc16-a33d74438eaf&tab=groupdetails. Accessed 28 June 2023.

Comes, Diana M. "Meet Me in the Middle: The Time Is Ripe for Tennessee to Adopt the Uniform Collaborative Law Act." *University of Memphis Law Review*, vol. 41, 2011, pp. 551–96.

Curtis, Diane. "Collaborative Law—Solving Disputes the Friendly Way." *California Bar Journal*, Jan. 2005, archive.calbar.ca.gov/archive/Archive

.aspx?articleId=60136&categoryId=60037&month=1&year=2005. Accessed 28 June 2023.

Czubaroff, Jeanine. "Dialogue and the Prospect of Rhetoric." *The Review of Communication*, vol. 12, 2012, pp. 44–65.

---. "Justice and Argument: Toward Development of a Dialogical Argumentation Theory." *Argumentation and Advocacy*, vol. 44, 2007, pp. 18–35.

Daicoff, Susan. "Collaborative Law: A New Tool for the Lawyer's Toolkit." *University of Florida Journal of Law & Public Policy*, vol. 20, 2009, pp. 113–45.

Daniels, Steven E., and Gregg B. Walker. *Working through Environmental Conflict: The Collaborative Learning Approach*. Praeger, 2001.

Downey, Sharon D. "Rhetoric as Balance: A Dialectical Feminist Perspective." *Women's Studies in Communication*, vol. 20, 1997, pp. 137–50.

Ehninger, Douglas, and Wayne Brockriede. *Decision by Debate*. 2nd ed., Harper, 1978.

Emery, Robert E. "Easing the Pain of Divorce for Children: Children's Voices, Causes of Conflict, and Mediation—Comments on Kelly's 'Resolving Child Custody Disputes.'" *Virginia Journal of Social Policy and the Law*, vol. 10, 2002, pp. 164–78.

Engle, Jill C. "Collaborative Law in Legal Education: No Time like the Present." *Yearbook on Arbitration and Mediation*, vol. 2, 2010, pp. 65–88.

Foss, Karen A., and Sonja K. Foss. "Personal Experience as Evidence in Feminist Scholarship." *Western Journal of Communication*, vol. 58, 1994, pp. 39–43.

Foss, Sonja K., and Karen A. Foss. *Inviting Transformation: Presentational Speaking for a Changing World*. 2nd ed., Waveland, 2003.

Foss, Sonja K., and Cindy L. Griffin. "Beyond Persuasion: A Proposal for an Invitational Rhetoric." *Communication Monographs*, vol. 62, 1995, pp. 2–18.

Fulkerson, Richard. "Transcending Our Conception of Argument in Light of Feminist Critiques." *Argumentation and Advocacy*, vol. 32, 1996, pp. 199–217.

Goodman, Hayley R. "Divorcing Partners and Fighting Siblings: Using the Collaborative Law Model to Resolve Disputes in Family Businesses." *University of Miami Business Law Review*, vol. 30, 2021, pp. 1–28.

Hoffman, David A. "A Healing Approach to the Law: Collaborative Law Doesn't Have to Be an Oxymoron." *The Christian Science Monitor*, 9 Oct. 2007, www.csmonitor.com/2007/1009/p09s01-coop.html. Accessed 28 June 2023.

Hoffman, David A., and Andrew Schepard. "To Disclose or Not to Disclose? That Is the Question in Collaborative Law." *Family Court Review*, vol. 58, 2020, pp. 83–104.

Kales, Albert M. "Should the Law Teacher Practice Law?" *Harvard Law Review*, vol. 25, 1912, pp. 253–69.

Kelly, Joan B. "Psychological and Legal Interventions for Parents and Children in Custody and Access Disputes: Current Research and Practice." *Virginia Journal of Social Policy and the Law*, vol. 10, 2002, pp. 129–63.

Kelso, R. Randall, and Charles D. Kelso. *Studying Law: An Introduction*. West, 1984.

Lande, John. "Possibilities for Collaborative Law: Ethics and Practice of Lawyer Disqualification and Process Control in a New Model of Lawyering." *Ohio State Law Journal*, vol. 64, 2003, pp. 1315–84.

Leflar, Robert A. "The Law Teacher's Place in the American Legal Profession." *Journal of the Society of Public Teachers of Law*, vol. 8, 1964, pp. 21–30.

Macfarlane, Julie. "Experiences of Collaborative Law: Preliminary Results from the Collaborative Lawyering Research Project." *Journal of Dispute Resolution*, vol. 2004, 2004, pp. 179–227.

Makau, Josina M. "A Conversation about Communication Ethics with Josina M. Makau." *Exploring Communication Ethics: Interviews with Influential Scholars in the Field*, edited by Pat Arneson, Peter Lang, 2007, pp. 69–87.

---. "Revisioning the Argumentation Course." *Women's Studies in Communication*, vol. 15, 1992, pp. 79–91.

Makau, Josina M., and Debian L. Marty. *Cooperative Argumentation: A Model for Deliberative Community*. Waveland, 2001.

Mallin, Irwin, and Karrin Vasby Anderson. "Inviting Constructive Argument." *Argumentation and Advocacy*, vol. 36, 2000, pp. 120–33.

McFarland, Douglas D. "Self-Images of Law Professors: Rethinking the Schism in Legal Education." *Journal of Legal Education*, vol. 35, 1985, pp. 232–60.

---. "Students and Practicing Lawyers Identify the Ideal Law Professor." *Journal of Legal Education*, vol. 36, 1986, pp. 93–107.

Minei, Elizabeth M., et al. "Modern Day Digital Pen Pals: A Semester-Long Collaborative Online International Learning (COIL) Project." *Communication Teacher*, vol. 35, 2021, pp. 336–44.

Mitchell, Gordon R., et al. "The Debate Authors Working Group Model for Collaborative Knowledge Production in Forensics Scholarship." *Argumentation and Advocacy*, vol. 47, 2010, pp. 1–24.

Moses, Marlene Eskind, and Manuel Benjamin Russ. "A Paradigm Shift to Collaborative Law." *Tennessee Bar Journal*, vol. 55, 2019, pp. 23–25.

O'Connell, Johannah. "Don't Settle for 'the Devil You Know': The Benefits of Using Collaborative Law rather than Litigation to Resolve Employment Disputes." *Indiana Law Review*, vol. 49, 2016, pp. 533–53.

Reynolds, Douglas C., and Doris F. Tennant. "Collaborative Law—An Emerging Practice." *Boston Bar Journal*, vol. 45, Nov.–Dec. 2001, pp. 12–13, 27–29.

Schwab, William H. "Collaborative Lawyering: A Closer Look at an Emerging Practice." *Pepperdine Dispute Resolution Law Journal*, vol. 4, 2004, pp. 351–99.

"SCU School of Law Offers Exciting New Course." *Santa Clara University School of Law*, 25 Feb. 2003, law.scu.edu/news/scu-school-of-law-offers-exciting-new-course/. Accessed 28 June 2023.

Smith, Nanci A. "Divorce with Dignity: Using the Collaborative Law Approach to Achieve Procedural, Substantive and Psychological Satisfaction." *Vermont Bar Journal*, vol. 42, spr. 2016, pp. 24–26.

Stone, Harlan F. "The Importance of Actual Experience at the Bar as a Preparation for Teaching Law." *American Law School Review*, vol. 3, 1912, pp. 205–11.

Strickland, Elizabeth K. "Putting 'Counselor' Back in the Lawyer's Job Description: Why More States Should Adopt Collaborative Law Statutes." *North Carolina Law Review*, vol. 84, 2006, pp. 979–1012.

Tesler, Pauline H. "Collaborative Family Law." *Pepperdine Dispute Resolution Law Journal*, vol. 4, 2004, pp. 317–36.

---. "Collaborative Law: A New Paradigm for Divorce Lawyers." *Psychology, Public Policy and Law*, vol. 5, 1999, pp. 967–1000.

Tindall, Harry L., and Jennie R. Smith. "The Uniform Collaborative Law Act as a Teaching Tool." *Hofstra Law Review*, vol. 38, 2009, pp. 685–98.

Tolman, Elizabeth G. "Observing Cell Phone Use and Enhancing Collaborative Learning Using a Wiki." *Communication Teacher*, vol. 27, 2013, pp. 16–20.

Voegele, Gary L., et al. "Collaborative Law: A Useful Tool for the Family Law Practitioner to Promote Better Outcomes." *William Mitchell Law Review*, vol. 33, 2007, pp. 971–1027.

Walker, Gregg B., and Steven E. Daniels. "Dialogue and Deliberation in Environmental Conflict: Enacting Civic Science." *Environmental Communication Yearbook*, edited by Susan L. Senecah, Lawrence Erlbaum, 2004, pp. 135–52.

Webb, Stu. "Collaborative Law Introduction." *Pepperdine Dispute Resolution Law Journal*, vol. 4, 2004, p. 315.

Wei, Fang-Yi Flora. "Creating a Collaborative 'Hot Clock': Using Smart Phones to Motivate Students' Learning in News Interviewing and Reporting." *Communication Teacher*, vol. 30, 2016, pp. 11–16.

Woodyard, Kerith M. "Competition and Control: The Open Hand of Dialogue in a Closed-Fist Tradition." *The Forensic of Pi Kappa Delta*, vol. 87, 2002, pp. 13–24.

CONCLUSION

New Doors to Imperfect, but Positive, Communication

At least since the late nineteenth century, lawyers have contested the role of the U.S. law professor heavily. A persona analysis of legal texts written between 1870 and the present reveals that lawyers have constructed two major personas of the law professor: the scholar persona and the practitioner persona. While some lawyers have constructed several hybrid personas, these personas have had limited impact on the communication. In essence, the scholar and practitioner models have changed very little from their original forms in the period from 1870 to 1920, although the scholar model has become the dominant model in the legal academy. This information regarding personas answers the first research question of this study, which inquired about the expectations that U.S. lawyers have had for the ideal role that the law professor should perform as an educator.

In light of the consistent clash from the Aristotelian rhetoric upon which lawyers have relied, the research suggests that lawyers have not been listening effectively to each other, particularly since the rhetorical postures in the conflict often have been non-responsive to each other. This information answers the second research question of this study, which inquired how, if at all, lawyers have reconciled any competing visions about the law professor persona through communication. Clearly, lawyers have not done so.

Because lawyers have not reconciled their competing visions of the two major law professor personas via Aristotelian rhetoric, consideration of other types of rhetoric becomes helpful, and this study recommends cooperative rhetoric. Within cooperative rhetoric, invitational rhetoric offers lawyers a good chance of coming to understand each other more thoroughly. The details of the two major law professor personas analyzed in this study would be useful for participants in such an invitational process because these details provide relevant information about the views of participants in the conflict. Hence, invitational rhetoric should be a key aspect of improving the communication.

However, as helpful as invitational rhetoric alone can be in fostering understanding, the legal field values decision-making, and this pertains to the legal education branch of the field as well. While understanding is important, so is decision-making, which often calls upon Aristotelian rhetoric. With the lack of understanding between the two major groups in the conflict that Chapters III, IV, and V illustrated, a choice regarding the law professor persona that lawyers find productive is a decision that would benefit from some reconsideration. Thus, for improving this conflict, the book suggests the dialectical fusion of Aristotelian rhetoric and invitational rhetoric that produces cooperative rhetoric.

Given this ongoing communication, at stake will be the role that the law professor then will perform in the context of legal education. As noted earlier in this study, the central figure in the education of prospective lawyers, "the principal actor in the [law school] classroom" (Borthwick & Schau 195), is the law professor. The law professor can represent students' initial encounters with the legal field and can make "a positive impact" on law students (Ostrom 540). Of course, the law professor can make a negative impact on students, too. Either way, the law professor helps shape the way law students see the legal field since, when interacting with students, "the law professor... convey[s] a sense of what it means to be a lawyer" (Ostrom 540). The law professor is "both the gatekeeper[] and molder[] of the profession" (Borthwick & Schau 193). In this situation, the construction of the persona of the law professor will have an important impact on the performance of the persona.

The present research offers several contributions, both practical and academic in nature. First, as suggested above, the research expands upon knowledge of an ongoing communication problem among many lawyers regarding legal education and expectations for the role of the law professor in the United States. Lawyers have had, and continue to have, dueling visions of the ideal law professor persona, but, for the most part, these lawyers have not addressed, nor are they addressing, each other's concerns. For instance, advocates of the practitioner model have not spoken to the law professor's position in the university, and advocates of the scholar model have not spoken to the fact that most law graduates have hands-on occupations rather than academic occupations. Under the suggested approach of alternative types of rhetoric, willing lawyers could improve this conflict significantly. Because the phenomenon of study, "[t]he American law professor[,] is American legal education" (McFarland, "Self-Images . . . : Rethinking the Schism" 232), the significance for individuals who will entrust to the law professor their entry into the legal profession becomes readily apparent.

Second, this study begins the process of filling a major gap in communication research about legal education. Before this study, communication research on the law professor was limited to McFarland's 1980s work. The current study builds on that research by endeavoring to consider, in addition to legal rhetoric from the 1960s, 1970s, and early 1980s—decades and part of a decade whose rhetoric McFarland studied—legal rhetoric from the 1870s to the 1950s and from the mid-1980s to the present day. Indeed, McFarland suggested a future study of the law professor over time (*Self-Images . . . : Rethinking Legal Education* 237), and this current study offers such an angle on the law professor. The result is much stronger evidence of a major communication problem among lawyers of different stripes. Additionally, this book addresses another limitation in the research of McFarland, who admitted that "[t]he discussion in this dissertation should be read as descriptive rather than normative" (*Self-Images . . . : Rethinking Legal Education* 207). Because McFarland's study offered no suggestions for addressing the problem he identified in his sample of texts, more research was appropriate. The suggestions of invitational rhetoric to balance Aristotelian rhetoric and cooperative rhetoric as a dialectical relationship between invitational rhetoric and Aristotelian rhetoric speak to the normative gap in the research.

Third, this book demonstrates the benefits of addressing the first persona from a slightly different angle. While much of the existing communication research has focused on the performance of a first persona like that of a prophet, the current study illustrates in detail how communicators can fill volumes in the act of constructing a first persona rather than merely adopting a pre-existing first persona. The distinction is one between the first persona performed (FPP) and the first persona constructed (FPC). This distinction allows scholars to focus more on either the performance or the construction of personas. Of course, performance and construction are not mutually exclusive. For instance, once lawyers have constructed a law professor persona, conforming law faculty members would perform some version of that persona in the classroom. Of note, this first persona constructed approach to persona analysis would be useful in studying rhetoric in other areas besides legal education.

Fourth, this study broadens an understanding of invitational rhetoric. The book adds to the expanding body of research that engages invitational rhetoric at a practical level, and the book does so at great length. The present study explores a specific situation, the ongoing conflict over the ideal law professor persona, in which invitational rhetoric can be a productive rhetorical option. In working with a specific situation in the legal field, the study offers a more detailed approach to the actual process of invitational rhetoric, upon which Chapter VII elaborated. Thus, the present research, while grounded in theory, explores invitational rhetoric from a practical angle.

Fifth, this book enriches an understanding of cooperative rhetoric. The book calls upon invitational rhetoric to develop the dialogic dimension of cooperative rhetoric, which, when compared with the advocacy dimension of cooperative rhetoric in the conflict over the law professor persona, has been the dimension in need of greater attention. Additionally, by linking cooperative rhetoric to collaborative law, the study shows that cooperative rhetoric has a relevant precedent in the legal field and thus is appropriate for implementation in some situations in the field. Also, the study notes the added benefit that cooperative rhetoric can provide a theoretical understanding of part of the communication aspect of collaborative law.

In addition to offering the contributions noted above, the present research has uncovered several patches of fertile ground for potentially valuable future communication research. First, although the study takes a normative approach to a major communication problem among lawyers, the study does not involve empirical research to determine how lawyers would employ the suggestion of alternative types of rhetoric. Future work would do well to determine how lawyers actually respond to invitational rhetoric and cooperative rhetoric. One might begin such empirical research in a specific legal community and later conduct the research in other legal communities.

Second, while recognizing that members of outsider groups were largely absent from the early days of the conflict over the construction of the law professor persona, this study did not focus on determining how members of such groups have worked to overcome their construction as third personas, the omitted or marginalized parties, and gain rhetorical space in the legal field, particularly in the legal academy. For example, women had very little voice in the legal community during the period from 1870 to 1920, but many of the sampled texts from the period since 1960 have reflected women's voices. Clearly, women were entering the legal field and more specifically the legal academy. Thus, future research might focus on examining the rhetorical strategies of women during the 1960s and 1970s, for instance, to understand how women began to address the marginalization and gain rhetorical space in a field traditionally slow to change. Additional future research could do something similar with attention to race, class, and related topics.

Third, this research focuses on the tension between the academic and the pragmatic in the legal field only. Potentially, other fields that have found educational homes in professional doctoral programs within the university system, such as medicine, dentistry, pharmacy, and optometry, face a similar tension between the academic and the pragmatic. For instance, future research might consider how physicians rhetorically have constructed the medical professor persona through medical writings. If other fields face tensions like the tension that law has faced at least since it assumed a place within the university system, approaches like invitational rhetoric and cooperative rhetoric may have helpful implications for other fields besides law. In short, much worthy future research could stem from this present study.

In conclusion, the voices of the many lawyers whose rhetoric received consideration in this study have illustrated how communication is not a perfect phenomenon—nor should communication be a perfect idea. As communication scholar John Durham Peters envisioned the concept, communication is "the project of reconciling self and other" (9). Communication usually involves two or more parties, the self and the other or others, and those parties often have differing views of the world. Since life is complex, thinking that better communicating "will solve the problems of communication" is misguided (Peters 9). Indeed, a standard of perfection is too high because humans "can never communicate like the angels" (Peters 29).

Nonetheless, human communicators do not have to be "lonely zombies searching for soul mates" (Peters 29), nor do they have to be overly zealous advocates unwilling to listen to each other. The prospect of imperfect communication, which often involves relying on "faith and risk" (Peters 30), is still a possibility. More specifically, alternative approaches to communication, such as cooperative rhetoric, are examples of this possibility. Part of cooperative rhetoric is invitational rhetoric, through which a communicator takes the risk that fellow communicators may decline an invitation. However, another aspect of invitational rhetoric is that a communicator takes the chance that fellow communicators may accept an invitation and that new relationships may develop. Viewpoints may be different, and even hard to understand, yet the opportunity for positive communication remains. This opportunity is an important promise of invitational rhetoric. Placed in conversation with a respectful version of Aristotelian rhetoric, invitational rhetoric can function within a dynamic dialectic that becomes cooperative rhetoric. Individuals can take the chance that cooperative rhetoric will open new doors to imperfect, but positive, communication. At a minimum, the persona of the law professor and the legal field may be healthier for the risk.

Works Cited in Conclusion

Borthwick, Robert J., and Jordan R. Schau. "Gatekeepers of the Profession: An Empirical Profile of the Nation's Law Professors." *University of Michigan Journal of Law Reform*, vol. 25, 1991, pp. 191–238.

McFarland, Douglas D. "Self-Images of Law Professors: Rethinking the Schism in Legal Education." *Journal of Legal Education*, vol. 35, 1985, pp. 232–60.

McFarland, Douglas Dale. *Self-Images of Law Professors: Rethinking Legal Education*. 1983. University of Minnesota, Ph.D. dissertation.

Ostrom, Jason. "The Competing Roles of Law Professors." *South Texas Law Review*, vol. 42, 2001, pp. 539–44.

Peters, John Durham. *Speaking into the Air: A History of the Idea of Communication*. U of Chicago P, 1999.

Works Cited in This Book

"ABA-Approved Law Schools." *American Bar Association Section of Legal Education and Admissions to the Bar*, www.americanbar.org/groups/legal_education/resources/aba_approved_law_schools/. Accessed 28 June 2023.

Abrams, Robert H. "Sing Muse: Legal Scholarship for New Law Teachers." *Journal of Legal Education*, vol. 37, 1987, pp. 1–13.

Aden, Roger C., et al. "Doubling Down: President Barack Obama's Doubled Persona after the Zimmerman Verdict." *Communication Studies*, vol. 67, 2016, pp. 605–22.

Ahmad, Nadia B. "'Blood, Sweat, Tears': A Muslim Woman Law Professor's View on Degenerative Racism, Misogyny, and (Internal) Islamophobia from Preeclampsia and Presumed Incompetent to Pandemic Tenure." *FIU Law Review*, vol. 16, 2021, pp. 13–74.

Ala-Kortesmaa, Sanna, and Pekka Isotalus. "Relational Tensions and Optimal Listening in the Communication Relationships of American and Finnish Legal Professionals." *Journal of Intercultural Communication Research*, vol. 43, 2014, pp. 173–93.

Alexander, Bryant Keith, and Michele Hammers. "An Invitation to Rhetoric: A Generative Dialogue on Performance, Possibility, and Feminist Potentialities in Invitational Rhetoric." *Cultural Studies ←→ Critical Methodologies*, vol. 19, 2019, pp. 5–14.

Alexander, Jay F. "Legal Careers in Eighteenth Century America." *Duquesne Law Review*, vol. 23, 1985, pp. 631–58.

Alfieri, Anthony V. "Against Practice." *Michigan Law Review*, vol. 107, 2009, pp. 1073–92.

Allen, Francis A. "The Prospects of University Law Training." *Journal of Legal Education*, vol. 29, 1978, pp. 127–38.

Ames, James Barr. "The Vocation of the Law Professor." *American Law Register*, vol. 48, 1900, pp. 129–46.

Amram, David Werner. "Law School Instruction in Practice." *American Law School Review*, vol. 3, 1914, pp. 439–49.

Archer, Dennis W., et al. *Report of the Task Force on the Financing of Legal Education. American Bar Association*, June 2015, www.americanbar.org/content/dam/aba/administrative/legal_education_and_admissions_to_the_bar/reports/2015_june_report_of_the_aba_task_force_on_the_financing_of_legal_education.pdf. Accessed 28 June 2023.

"Archive: 2000–2015 ABA End-of-Year Summaries—Applicants, Admitted Applicants & Applications." *Law School Admission Council*, www.lsac.org/archive-2000-2015-aba-end-year-summaries-applicants-admitted-applicants-applications. Accessed 28 June 2023.

Aristotle. *On Rhetoric: A Theory of Civic Discourse*. Translated by George A. Kennedy, Oxford UP, 1991.

Arnold, William E. "Debate and the Lawyer." *Journal of the American Forensic Association*, vol. 3, 1966, pp. 26–28.

Arriola, Elvia Rosales. "Amor y Esperanza: A Latina Lesbian Becomes a Law Professor." *Journal of Legal Education*, vol. 66, 2017, pp. 484–92.

Austin, Arthur D. "The Waste Land of Law School Fiction." *Duke Law Journal*, vol. 1989, 1989, pp. 495–509.

Baker v. Carr. 369 U.S. 186 (1962). *Library of Congress*, tile.loc.gov/storage-services/service/ll/usrep/usrep369/usrep369186/usrep369186.pdf. Accessed 28 June 2023.

Bard, Robert L. "Legal Scholarship and the Professional Responsibility of Law Professors." *Connecticut Law Review*, vol. 16, 1984, pp. 731–51.

Barnard, Raymond H. "A Non-Credit Course in Business and Professional Speaking." *Speech Teacher*, vol. 2, 1953, pp. 41–45.

Bartholomew, Mark. "Legal Separation: The Relationship between the Law School and the Central University in the Late Nineteenth Century." *Journal of Legal Education*, vol. 53, 2003, pp. 368–403.

Barzun, Charles L. "Jerome Frank and the Modern Mind." *Buffalo Law Review*, vol. 58, 2010, pp. 1127–74.

Bashman, Howard J. "The Battle over the Soul of Law Professor Blogs." *Washington University Law Review*, vol. 84, 2006, pp. 1257–61.

Bates, Sophia N., and Valerie Lynn Schrader. "Sharing 'The Music of My Soul': Invitational Rhetoric in the Musical *Memphis*." *Kentucky Journal of Communication*, vol. 40, 2021, pp. 45–62.

Becker, Susan J. "Advice for the New Law Professor: A View from the Trenches." *Journal of Legal Education*, vol. 42, 1992, pp. 432–46.

Berger, Todd A. "Three Generations and Two Tiers: How Participation in Law School Clinics and the Demand for 'Practice-Ready' Graduates Will Impact the Faculty Status of Clinical Law Professors." *Journal of Law and Policy*, vol. 43, 2013, pp. 129–55.

Bergin, Thomas F. "The Law Teacher: A Man Divided against Himself." *Virginia Law Review*, vol. 54, 1968, pp. 637–57.

Berman, Douglas A. "Scholarship in Action: The Power, Possibilities, and Pitfalls for Law Professor Blogs." *Washington University Law Review*, vol. 84, 2006, pp. 1043–60.

Bile, Jeffrey Thomas. "Communication, Advocacy, Argumentation, and Feminisms: Toward a Dialectical Partnership." *Speaker and Gavel*, vol. 32, 1995, pp. 55–70.

Binford, Warren. "How to Be the World's Best Law Professor." *Journal of Legal Education*, vol. 64, 2015, pp. 542–61.

Black, Edwin. "The Second Persona." *Quarterly Journal of Speech*, vol. 56, 1970, pp. 109–19.

Blackstone, William. "A Discourse on the Study of the Law." *The Gladsome Light of Jurisprudence: Learning the Law in England and the United States in the 18th and 19th Centuries*, edited by Michael H. Hoeflich, Greenwood Press, 1988, pp. 53–73.

Bone, Jennifer Emerling, et al. "Beyond Traditional Conceptualizations of Rhetoric: Invitational Rhetoric and a Move toward Civility." *Western Journal of Communication*, vol. 72, 2008, pp. 434–62.

Boon, Andrew, and Julian Webb. "Legal Education and Training in England and Wales: Back to the Future?" *Journal of Legal Education*, vol. 58, 2008, pp. 79–121.

Borthwick, Robert J., and Jordan R. Schau. "Gatekeepers of the Profession: An Empirical Profile of the Nation's Law Professors." *University of Michigan Journal of Law Reform*, vol. 25, 1991, pp. 191–238.

Bourne, Richard W. "The Coming Crash in Legal Education: How We Got Here, and Where We Go Now." *Creighton Law Review*, vol. 45, 2012, pp. 651–97.

Bovey, Wilfrid. "The Control Exercised by the Inns of Court over Admission to the Bar in England." *American Law School Review*, vol. 3, 1913, pp. 334–38.

Boyarin, Yishai. "Generating 'Win-Win' Results: Negotiating Contracts in the Drafting Process of the Uniform Collaborative Law Act." *Hofstra Law Review*, vol. 38, 2009, pp. 495–536.

Boyle, Robin A. "Employing Active-Learning Techniques and Metacognition in Law School: Shifting Energy from Professor to Student." *University of Detroit Mercy Law Review*, vol. 81, 2003, pp. 1–30.

Brennan, William J. "Constitutional Adjudication." *Notre Dame Lawyer*, vol. 40, 1965, pp. 559–69.

Breyer, Stephen G. "Response of Justice Stephen G. Breyer." *NYU Annual Survey of American Law*, vol. 64, 2008, pp. 33–35.

Britt, Elizabeth C. *Reimagining Advocacy: Rhetorical Education in the Legal Clinic*. Pennsylvania State UP, 2018.

Brockriede, Wayne. "Arguers as Lovers." *Philosophy and Rhetoric*, vol. 5, 1972, pp. 1–11.

Bronner, Ethan. "A Call for Drastic Changes in Educating New Lawyers." *The New York Times*, 10 Feb. 2013, www.nytimes.com/2013/02/11/us/lawyers-call-for-drastic-change-in-educating-new-lawyers.html. Accessed 28 June 2023.

---. "Law Schools' Applications Fall as Costs Rise and Jobs Are Cut." *The New York Times*, 30 Jan. 2013, www.nytimes.com/2013/01/31/education/law-schools-applications-fall-as-costs-rise-and-jobs-are-cut.html. Accessed 28 June 2023.

Brooks, Maegan Parker. "Oppositional Ethos: Fannie Lou Hamer and the Vernacular Persona." *Rhetoric & Public Affairs*, vol. 14, 2011, pp. 511–48.

Brown, Heidi K. "The Emotionally Intelligent Law Professor: A Lesson from *The Breakfast Club*." *University of Arkansas at Little Rock Law Review*, vol. 36, 2013, pp. 273–317.

Brown v. Board of Education. 347 U.S. 483 (1954). *Library of Congress*, tile.loc.gov/storage-services/service/ll/usrep/usrep347/usrep347483/usrep347483.pdf. Accessed 28 June 2023.

Bruner, M. Lane. "Producing Identities: Gender Problematization and Feminist Argumentation." *Argumentation and Advocacy*, vol. 32, 1996, pp. 185–98.

Burger, Warren E. "The Special Skills of Advocacy: Are Specialized Training and Certification of Advocates Essential to Our System of Justice?" *Fordham Law Review*, vol. 42, 1973, pp. 227–42.

Burr, Sherri L. "Reflections on a Scholarly Agenda for the Beginning Law Professor." *Saint Louis University Public Law Review*, vol. 10, 1991, pp. 155–59.

Byse, Clark. "Legal Scholarship, Legal Realism and the Law Teacher's Intellectual Schizophrenia." *Nova Law Review*, vol. 13, 1988, pp. 9–31.

Cali, Dennis D. "'Persona' in the 2012 Presidential Campaign." *Studies of Communication in the 2012 Presidential Campaign*, edited by Robert E. Denton, Lexington Books, 2014, pp. 41–70.

Campbell, Karlyn Kohrs. *Man Cannot Speak for Her: A Critical Study of Early Feminist Rhetoric*. Vol. 1, Praeger, 1989.

Campbell, Paul Newell. "The *Personae* of Scientific Discourse." *Quarterly Journal of Speech*, vol. 61, 1975, pp. 391–405.

Cantrall, Arch M. "Law Schools and the Layman: Is Legal Education Doing Its Job?" *American Bar Association Journal*, vol. 38, 1952, pp. 907–10, 972.

---. "Practical Skills Can and Must Be Taught in Law Schools." *Journal of Legal Education*, vol. 6, 1954, pp. 316–23.

Carlson, A. Cheree. "Creative Casuistry and Feminist Consciousness: The Rhetoric of Moral Reform." *Quarterly Journal of Speech*, vol. 78, 1992, pp. 16–32.

Case, David W. "A Pedagogical Rationale for the Law Professor as Moot Court Coach." *Mississippi Law Journal*, vol. 89, 2020, pp. 367–406.

Chamallas, Martha. "The Shadow of Professor Kingsfield: Contemporary Dilemmas Facing Women Law Professors." *William and Mary Journal of Women and the Law*, vol. 11, 2005, pp. 195–208.

Chase, Anthony. "The Birth of the Modern Law School." *American Journal of Legal History*, vol. 2, 1979, pp. 329–48.

---. "The Legal Scholar as Producer." *Nova Law Review*, vol. 13, 1988, pp. 57–67.

Chemerinsky, Erwin. "Why Not Clinical Education?" *Clinical Law Review*, vol. 16, 2009, pp. 35–41.

Cherry, Roger D. "Ethos versus Persona: Self-Representation in Written Discourse." *Written Communication*, vol. 15, 1998, pp. 384–410.

Chick, Daniel M. "Memorializing Senator McCain's 'Uncivil Tongue': Invitational Rhetoric and the Problem of Confrontation and Violence." *Southern Communication Journal*, vol. 86, 2021, pp. 320–34.

Christie, George C. "The Recruitment of Law Faculty." *Duke Law Journal*, vol. 1987, 1987, pp. 306–16.

Chroust, Anton-Hermann. *The Rise of the Legal Profession in America*. Vol. 2. U of Oklahoma P, 1965.

Church, Russell Taylor. "The Educational Value of Oral Communication Courses and Intercollegiate Forensics: An Opinion Survey of College Prelegal Advisors and Law School Deans." *Journal of the American Forensic Association*, vol. 12, 1975, pp. 49–55.

Clarke, Brian S. "Coming Out in the Classroom: Law Professors, Law Students and Depression." *Journal of Legal Education*, vol. 64, 2015, pp. 403–15.

Cloud, Dana L. "The Null Persona: Race and the Rhetoric of Silence in the Uprising of '34." *Rhetoric and Public Affairs*, vol. 2, 1999, pp. 177–209.

Cohen, Amy B. "The Dangers of the Ivory Tower: The Obligation of Law Professors to Engage in the Practice of Law." *Loyola Law Review*, vol. 50, 2004, pp. 623–73.

Coleman, Clare Keefe, and William Albertson. "Teaching International Law Students: A Collaboration between a Law Professor and an ESL Specialist." *Journal of Law & Education*, vol. 50, 2021, pp. 1–34.

"Collaborative Law Act." *Uniform Law Commission*, www.uniformlaws.org/committees/community-home?communitykey=fdd1de2f-baea-42d3-bc16-a33d74438eaf&tab=groupdetails. Accessed 28 June 2023.

Comes, Diana M. "Meet Me in the Middle: The Time Is Ripe for Tennessee to Adopt the Uniform Collaborative Law Act." *University of Memphis Law Review*, vol. 41, 2011, pp. 551–96.

Condit, Celeste M., and Melanie Williams. "Gender Differences and Argumentation: A Positional Account of the Reception of Genetics Arguments." *Speaker and Gavel*, vol. 32, 1995, pp. 1–12.

"Conference on Legal Education." *American Bar Association Journal*, vol. 7, 1921, pp. 637–38.

Cook, John. "Taking a Shot at the (Unmodified) Title: The Value of the Title 'Professor of Law' for Improving the Status of Legal Writing Faculty and ALWD/LWI Survey Trends." *The Journal of the Legal Writing Institute*, vol. 24, 2020, pp. 65–70.

Coquillette, Daniel R., and Bruce A. Kimball. *On the Battlefield of Merit: Harvard Law School, the First Century*. Harvard UP, 2015.

Corcos, Christine A. "Growing Up with Popular Culture in the Time of Title IX." *Louisiana Law Review*, vol. 83, 2022, pp. 59–128.

Costello, John L. "Another Visit to the Man Divided: A Justification for the Law Teacher's Schizophrenia." *Journal of Legal Education*, vol. 27, 1975, pp. 390–417.

Coyne, Randall T. "A Law Professor's Reflections on Representing Guantánamo Detainees." *Northeastern University Law Journal*, vol. 1, 2009, pp. 97–110.

Crabb, John H. "On Integrating Law with the Academic World." *Journal of Legal Education*, vol. 14, 1962, pp. 329–42.

Craig v. Boren. 429 U.S. 190 (1976). *Library of Congress*, tile.loc.gov /storage-services/service/ll/usrep/usrep429/usrep429190/usrep429190 .pdf. Accessed 28 June 2023.

Cramton, Roger C. "Demystifying Legal Scholarship." *Georgetown Law Journal*, vol. 75, 1986, pp. 1–17.

Crenshaw, Carrie. "The Arguer's Identity: A Feminist Perspective on the Practice of Argumentation Theory." *Speaker and Gavel*, vol. 32, 1995, pp. 13–25.

---. "The Normality of Man and Female Otherness: (Re)Producing Patriarchal Lines of Argument in the Law and the News." *Argumentation and Advocacy*, vol. 32, 1996, pp. 170–84.

Currie, Brainerd. "The Materials of Law Study." *Journal of Legal Education*, vol. 3, 1951, pp. 331–83.

Curtis, Diane. "Collaborative Law—Solving Disputes the Friendly Way." *California Bar Journal*, Jan. 2005, archive.calbar.ca.gov/archive/Archive.aspx?articleId=60136&categoryId=60037&month=1&year=2005. Accessed 28 June 2023.

Czubaroff, Jeanine. "Dialogue and the Prospect of Rhetoric." *The Review of Communication*, vol. 12, 2012, pp. 44–65.

---. "Justice and Argument: Toward Development of a Dialogical Argumentation Theory." *Argumentation and Advocacy*, vol. 44, 2007, pp. 18–35.

Daicoff, Susan. "Collaborative Law: A New Tool for the Lawyer's Toolkit." *University of Florida Journal of Law & Public Policy*, vol. 20, 2009, pp. 113–45.

D'Amato, Anthony. "The Decline and Fall of Law Teaching in the Age of Student Consumerism." *Journal of Legal Education*, vol. 37, 1987, pp. 461–94.

Daniels, Steven E., and Gregg B. Walker. *Working through Environmental Conflict: The Collaborative Learning Approach*. Praeger, 2001.

Darling-Hammond, Sean, and Kristen Holmquist. "Creating Wise Classrooms to Empower Diverse Law Students: Lessons in Pedagogy from Transformative Law Professors." *Berkeley La Raza Law Journal*, vol. 25, 2015, pp. 1–67.

Daughton, Suzanne, and Patrice M. Buzzanell. Foreword. *Inviting Understanding: A Portrait of Invitational Rhetoric*, edited by Sonja K. Foss and Cindy L. Griffin, Roman & Littlefield, 2020, pp. xiii–xvi.

Delgado, Richard, and Derrick Bell. "Minority Law Professors' Lives: The Bell-Delgado Survey." *Harvard Civil Rights-Civil Liberties Law Review*, vol. 24, 1989, pp. 349–75.

Deo, Meera E. "Trajectory of a Law Professor." *Michigan Journal of Race and Law*, vol. 20, 2015, pp. 441–84.

"Doceō." *Oxford Latin Dictionary*, edited by P. G. W. Glare, Oxford UP, 1982, p. 568.

"Doctor." *Follett World-Wide Latin Dictionary*, edited by Edwin B. Levine et al., Follett, 1967, p. 125.

"Doctor." *A Latin-English Dictionary*, edited by Charlton T. Lewis and Charles Short, 1879, Oxford UP, 1975, p. 605.

"Doctrīna." *A Latin-English Dictionary*, edited by Charlton T. Lewis and Charles Short, 1879, Oxford UP, 1975, p. 605.

"Doctrix." *A Latin-English Dictionary*, edited by Charlton T. Lewis and Charles Short, 1879, Oxford UP, 1975, p. 605.

Doss, Erin F. "Indie Dyers, Instagram, and the Visual Persona." *The Electronic Journal of Communication/La Revue Électronique de Communication*, vol. 29, 2019, www.cios.org/getfile/029126_EJC. Accessed 28 June 2023.

Doss, Erin F., and Robin E. Jensen. "Balancing Mystery and Identification: Dolores Huerta's Shifting Transcendent Persona." *Quarterly Journal of Speech*, vol. 99, 2013, pp. 481–506.

Downey, Sharon D. "Rhetoric as Balance: A Dialectical Feminist Perspective." *Women's Studies in Communication*, vol. 20, 1997, pp. 137–50.

Drachman, Virginia G. *Sisters in Law: Women Lawyers in Modern American History.* Harvard UP, 1998.

Durako, Jo Anne. "Second-Class Citizens in the Pink Ghetto: Gender Bias in Legal Writing." *Journal of Legal Education*, vol. 50, 2000, pp. 562–86.

EagleWoman, Angelique Townsend (Wambdi A. WasteWin). "Balancing between Two Worlds: A Dakota Woman's Reflections on Being a Law Professor." *Berkeley Journal of Gender, Law & Justice*, vol. 29, 2014, pp. 250–74.

Edwards, Harry T. "Another Look at Professor Rodell's *Goodbye to Law Reviews*." *Virginia Law Review*, vol. 100, 2014, pp. 1483–1511.

---. "The Growing Disjunction between Legal Education and the Legal Profession." *Michigan Law Review*, vol. 91, 1992, pp. 34–78.

---. "The Role of Legal Education in Shaping the Profession." *Journal of Legal Education*, vol. 38, 1988, pp. 285–93.

Ehninger, Douglas, and Wayne Brockriede. *Decision by Debate*. 2nd ed., Harper, 1978.

Elliott, Emory B. "*Persona* and Parody in Donne's *The Anniversaries*." *Quarterly Journal of Speech*, vol. 58, 1972, pp. 48–57.

Elshtain, Jean Bethke. "Feminism Discourse and Its Discontents: Language, Power, and Meaning." *Signs: Journal of Women in Culture and Society*, vol. 7, 1982, pp. 603–21.

Emery, Robert E. "Easing the Pain of Divorce for Children: Children's Voices, Causes of Conflict, and Mediation—Comments on Kelly's 'Resolving Child Custody Disputes.'" *Virginia Journal of Social Policy and the Law*, vol. 10, 2002, pp. 164–78.

Engle, Jill C. "Collaborative Law in Legal Education: No Time like the Present." *Yearbook on Arbitration and Mediation*, vol. 2, 2010, pp. 65–88.

Entin, Jonathan L. "The Law Professor as Advocate." *Case Western Reserve Law Review*, vol. 38, 1988, pp. 512–36.

Epstein, Sandra P. *Law at Berkeley: The History of Boalt Hall.* U of California, Institute of Governmental Studies P, 1997.

Faass, Irene P. "Shades of Gray: Alternative Metaphors for Argumentation." *Arguing Communication and Culture: Selected Papers from the Twelfth NCA/AFA Conference on Argumentation*, edited by Thomas Goodnight, National Communication Association, 2002, pp. 219–21.

Farley, Christine Haight. "Confronting Expectations: Women in the Legal Academy." *Yale Journal of Law and Feminism*, vol. 8, 1996, pp. 333–58.

Farrell, Kathleen, and David Hingstman. "Teaching Advanced Seminars in Legal and Business Argument: Sharpening the Critical Edge." *Argumentation and Advocacy*, vol. 36, 2000, pp. 151–60.

Fiero, J. Newton. "Teaching Law without Experience at the Bar." *American Law School Review*, vol. 3, 1914, pp. 558–60.

Finesilver, Sherman G. "The Tension between Practical and Theoretical Legal Education: A Judge's View of the Gap." *Brigham Young University Law Review*, vol. 1977, 1977, pp. 1061–71.

Fisher, Roger, et al. *Getting to Yes: Negotiating Agreement without Giving In*. 2nd ed., Penguin, 1991.

Fontana, David. "What Do Constitutional Law Professors Do?" *Wisconsin Law Review*, vol. 2020, 2020, pp. 317–41.

Foss, Karen A., and Sonja K. Foss. "Personal Experience as Evidence in Feminist Scholarship." *Western Journal of Communication*, vol. 58, 1994, pp. 39–43.

Foss, Sonja K., and Karen A. Foss. *Inviting Transformation: Presentational Speaking for a Changing World*. 2nd ed., Waveland, 2003.

Foss, Sonja K., and Cindy L. Griffin. "Beyond Persuasion: A Proposal for an Invitational Rhetoric." *Communication Monographs*, vol. 62, 1995, pp. 2–18.

Foss, Sonja K., and Cindy L. Griffin. "The Metatheoretical Foundations of Invitational Rhetoric: Axiological, Epistemological, and Ontological Explorations." *Inviting Understanding: A Portrait of Invitational Rhetoric*, edited by Sonja K. Foss and Cindy L. Griffin, Roman & Littlefield, 2020, pp. 59–73.

Foss, Sonja K., and Jeanine Warisse Turner. "Challenges to the Enactment of Invitational Rhetoric in the Age of Mobile Communication Technologies." *Inviting Understanding: A Portrait of Invitational Rhetoric*, edited by Sonja K. Foss and Cindy L. Griffin, Roman & Littlefield, 2020, pp. 157–79.

Fossum, Donna. "Law Professors: A Profile of the Teaching Branch of the Legal Profession." *American Bar Foundation Research Journal*, vol. 1980, 1980, pp. 501–54.

Frank, Jerome. "A Plea for Lawyer-Schools." *Yale Law Journal*, vol. 56, 1947, pp. 1303–44.

---. "Why Not a Clinical Lawyer-School?" *University of Pennsylvania Law Review*, vol. 81, 1933, pp. 907–23.

Frankfurter, Felix. "The Law and the Law Schools." *American Bar Association Journal*, vol. 1, 1915, pp. 532–40.

Friedman, Lawrence M. *A History of American Law*. Touchstone, 1973.

Fulkerson, Richard. "Transcending Our Conception of Argument in Light of Feminist Critiques." *Argumentation and Advocacy*, vol. 32, 1996, pp. 199–217.

Gajda, Amy. "The Law Professor as Legal Commentator." *The Journal of the Legal Writing Institute*, vol. 10, 2004, pp. 209–43.

Gearhart, Sally Miller. "The Womanization of Rhetoric." *Women's Studies International Quarterly*, vol. 2, 1979, pp. 195–201.

Gee, E. Gordon, and Donald W. Jackson. "Bridging the Gap: Legal Education and Lawyer Competency." *Brigham Young University Law Review*, vol. 1977, 1977, pp. 695–990.

Gibbons, Michelle G. "Persona 4.0." *Quarterly Journal of Speech*, vol. 107, 2021, pp. 49–72.

Gibson, Katie L., and Amy L. Heyse. "'The Difference between a Hockey Mom and a Pit Bull': Sarah Palin's Faux Maternal Persona and Performance of Hegemonic Masculinity at the 2008 Republican National Convention." *Communication Quarterly*, vol. 58, 2010, pp. 235–56.

Gilmore, Angela. "How Amendment 1 (North Carolina's Anti-Marriage Equality Constitutional Amendment) Helped Me Become a Better Law Professor." *Law & Sexuality*, vol. 22, 2013, pp. 91–101.

Gilmore, Eugene A. "Some Criticisms of Legal Education." *American Bar Association Journal*, vol. 7, 1921, pp. 227–30.

Golden, James L., et al. *The Rhetoric of Western Thought*. 6th ed., Kendall, 1997.

Goodman, Hayley R. "Divorcing Partners and Fighting Siblings: Using the Collaborative Law Model to Resolve Disputes in Family Businesses." *University of Miami Business Law Review*, vol. 30, 2021, pp. 1–28.

Goodnight, G. Thomas. "The Personal, Technical, and Public Spheres of Argument: A Speculative Inquiry into the Art of Public Deliberation." *Journal of the American Forensic Association*, vol. 18, 1982, pp. 214–27.

Gordon, Daniel. "Hiring Law Professors: Breaking the Back of an American Plutocratic Oligarchy." *Widener Law Journal*, vol. 19, 2009, pp. 137–58.

Greene, Susan. "Knitting 101: Why Law Professors Should Share Their Hobbies with Their Students." *Journal of Legal Education*, vol. 68, 2019, pp. 751–53.

Griffin, Cindy L. *Invitation to Public Speaking*. 2nd ed., Thomson Wadsworth, 2006.

Griswold, Erwin N. "English and American Legal Education." *Journal of Legal Education*, vol. 10, 1958, pp. 429–35.

Grutter v. Bollinger. 539 U.S. 306 (2003). *Library of Congress*, tile.loc.gov/storage-services/service/ll/usrep/usrep539/usrep539306/usrep539306.pdf. Accessed 28 June 2023.

Hacker, Kenneth L., et al. "Components of Candidate Images: Statistical Analysis of the Issue-Persona Dichotomy in the Presidential Campaign of 1996." *Communication Monographs*, vol. 67, 2000, pp. 227–38.

Hand, Learned. "Have the Bench and Bar Anything to Contribute to the Teaching of Law?" *Michigan Law Review*, vol. 24, 1926, pp. 466–82.

Hantzis, Catharine W. "Kingsfield and Kennedy: Reappraising the Male Models of Law School Teaching." *Journal of Legal Education*, vol. 38, 1988, pp. 155–64.

Henderson, William D., and Rachel M. Zahorsky. "The Law School Bubble: How Long Will It Last If Law Grads Can't Pay Bills?" *ABA Journal*, 1 Jan. 2012, www.abajournal.com/magazine/article/the_law_school_bubble_how_long_will_it_last_if_law_grads_cant_pay_bills. Accessed 28 June 2023.

Herman, Edward S., and Robert W. McChesney. *The Global Media: The New Missionaries of Corporate Capitalism*. Cassell, 1997.

Hernández, Tanya K. "Placing the Cart before the Horse: Publishing Scholarship before Entering the Legal Academy." *Michigan Journal of Race & Law*, vol. 7, 2002, pp. 517–22.

Hervey, John G. "The Juris Doctor Degree...An Inquiry into Some Reasons Advanced against Adoption." *The Student Lawyer Journal*, vol. 11, 1966, pp. 11–13, 28–31.

---. "Law School Graduates Should Receive 'Professional Doctorates'...Time for a Change from LL.B. to J.D. Degree." *The Student Lawyer Journal*, vol. 10, 1965, pp. 5–8, 27.

"Historians Discuss Reagan's Legacy." *PBS Newshour*, 7 June 2004, www.pbs.org/newshour/show/historians-discuss-reagans-legacy. Accessed 28 June 2023.

"Historical Data—LSAT Trends: Total LSATs Administered by Admin & Year." *Law School Admission Council*, report.lsac.org/TestTakers.aspx. Accessed 28 June 2023.

Hobbs, Jeffrey Dale, et al. "Intercollegiate Debate as Invitational Rhetoric: An Offering." *Contemporary Argumentation and Debate*, vol. 21, 2000, pp. 76–94.

Hoeflich, M. H. "The Craft of the Law: An Essay after Forty Years as a Law Teacher." *Kansas Law Review*, vol. 70, 2022, pp. 483–503.

---. "Plus Ça Change, Plus C'est la Même Chose: The Integration of Theory and Practice in Legal Education." *The History of Legal Education in the United States*, edited by Steve Sheppard, vol. 2, Salem Press, 1999, pp. 861–75.

Hoeflich, Michael H. Introduction. *The Gladsome Light of Jurisprudence: Learning the Law in England and the United States in the 18th and 19th Centuries*, edited by Hoeflich, Greenwood Press, 1988, pp. 1–14.

Hoffman, David A. "A Healing Approach to the Law: Collaborative Law Doesn't Have to Be an Oxymoron." *The Christian Science Monitor*, 9 Oct. 2007, www.csmonitor.com/2007/1009/p09s01-coop.html. Accessed 28 June 2023.

Hoffman, David A., and Andrew Schepard. "To Disclose or Not to Disclose? That Is the Question in Collaborative Law." *Family Court Review*, vol. 58, 2020, pp. 83–104.

Houck, Davis W., and Maegan Parker Brooks. "Fannie Lou Hamer, 'We're on Our Way' (September 1964)." *Voices of Democracy*, vol. 6, 2011, pp. 21–43.

Hricik, David, and Victoria S. Salzmann. "Why There Should Be Fewer Articles like This One: Law Professors Should Write More for Legal Decision-Makers and Less for Themselves." *Suffolk University Law Review*, vol. 38, 2005, pp. 761–87.

Hurst, James Willard. "Research Responsibilities of University Law Schools." *Journal of Legal Education*, vol. 10, 1957, pp. 147–61.

Hutchins, H. B. "The Law Teacher: His Functions and Responsibilities." *Columbia Law Review*, vol. 8, 1908, pp. 362–74.

Japp, Phyllis M. "Esther or Isaiah? The Abolitionist-Feminist Rhetoric of Angelina Grimké." *Quarterly Journal of Speech*, vol. 71, 1985, pp. 335–48.

Jarman, Jeffrey W., and Kelly M. McDonald. "Invitation Declined: A Response to Intercollegiate Debate as Invitational Rhetoric." *Arguing Communication and Culture: Selected Papers from the Twelfth NCA/AFA Conference on Argumentation*, edited by Thomas Goodnight, National Communication Association, 2002, pp. 205–11.

Jarvis, Robert M. "Why Law Professors Should Not Be Hessian-Trainers." *Nova Law Review*, vol. 13, 1988, pp. 69–78.

Jensen, Robin E., et al. "Theorizing the Transcendent Persona: Amelia Earhart's Vision in *The Fun of It*." *Communication Theory*, vol. 20, 2010, pp. 1–20.

Jerrim, John. "Family Background and Access to 'High Status' Universities." *Sutton Trust*, 13 Nov. 2013, www.suttontrust.com/our-research/family-background-access-high-status-universities/. Accessed 28 June 2023.

Jesson, Lucinda. "So You Want to Be a Law Professor." *Journal of Legal Education*, vol. 59, 2010, pp. 450–53.

Johnson, Alex M. "Think like a Lawyer, Work like a Machine: The Dissonance between Law School and Law Practice." *Southern California Law Review*, vol. 64, 1991, pp. 1231–60.

Johnson, Andre E. "The Prophetic Persona of James Cone and the Rhetorical Theology of Black Theology." *Black Theology: An International Journal*, vol. 8, 2010, pp. 266–85.

Johnson, Jenell, et al. "'Keep Talking, I Keep Changing My Mind': The Value of Invitational Rhetoric for Focus Group Research." *Western Journal of Communication*, vol. 85, 2021, pp. 381–99.

Johnson, William R. *Schooled Lawyers: A Study in the Clash of Professional Cultures*. New York UP, 1978.

Joy, Peter A., and Robert R. Kuehn. "The Evolution of ABA Standards for Clinical Faculty." *Tennessee Law Review*, vol. 75, 2008, pp. 183–232.

"Juris Doctor Information." *The Student Lawyer Journal*, vol. 12, 1967, p. 24.

Kales, Albert M. "Discussion: The Ultimate Function of the Teacher of Law." *American Law School Review*, vol. 3, 1911, pp. 9–11.

---. "Should the Law Teacher Practice Law?" *Harvard Law Review*, vol. 25, 1912, pp. 253–69.

Katz, Taylor. "The Second Persona and the Third Way: Danny Cortez's Ideological Rhetoric." *Western Journal of Communication*, vol. 87, 2023, pp. 432–50.

Kay, Herma Hill. *Paving the Way: The First American Women Law Professors*, edited by Patricia A. Cain, U of California P, 2021.

Kelly, Alfred H., et al. *The American Constitution: Its Origins and Development*. 7th ed., Norton, 1991. 2 vols.

Kelly, Joan B. "Psychological and Legal Interventions for Parents and Children in Custody and Access Disputes: Current Research and Practice." *Virginia Journal of Social Policy and the Law*, vol. 10, 2002, pp. 129–63.

Kelso, R. Randall, and Charles D. Kelso. *Studying Law: An Introduction*. West, 1984.

Kendall, Brenden E. "Personae and Natural Capitalism: Negotiating Politics and Constituencies in a Rhetoric of Sustainability." *Environmental Communication*, vol. 2, 2008, pp. 59–77.

Kent, James. "An Introductory Lecture to a Course of Law Lectures." *Columbia Law Review*, vol. 3, 1903, pp. 330–43.

Kimball, Bruce A. *The Inception of Modern Professional Education: C. C. Langdell, 1826–1906*. U of North Carolina P, 2009.

Kirkpatrick, Walter G. "Bolingbroke and the Opposition to Sir Robert Walpole: The Role of a Fictitious *Persona* in Creating an Audience." *Central States Speech Journal*, vol. 32, 1981, pp. 12–23.

Koegel, Otto E. "Speech and the Legal Profession." *Quarterly Journal of Speech*, vol. 37, 1951, pp. 471–72.

Kor, Ryan. "The Commenting Persona: Reception Theory and the Digital Rhetorical Audience." *Journal of Media Research*, vol. 11, 2018, pp. 55–70.

Kronman, Anthony T. "Foreword: Legal Scholarship and Moral Education." *Yale Law Journal*, vol. 90, 1981, pp. 955–69.

Kurland, Adam Harris. "Court's in Session: A Law Professor Returns to the Majestic Chaos of a Criminal Jury Trial." *Howard Law Journal*, vol. 52, 2009, pp. 357–73.

Kurtz, Jeffrey B. "Condemning Webster: Judgment and Audience in Emerson's 'Fugitive Slave Law.'" *Quarterly Journal of Speech*, vol. 87, 2001, pp. 278–90.

Lande, John. "Possibilities for Collaborative Law: Ethics and Practice of Lawyer Disqualification and Process Control in a New Model of Lawyering." *Ohio State Law Journal*, vol. 64, 2003, pp. 1315–84.

Langdell, C. C. "Teaching Law as a Science." *American Law Review*, vol. 21, 1887, pp. 123–25.

Lanzinger, Judith Ann. "Judges Teaching in Law School: Who, What, Where, and Why Not?" *Journal of Legal Education*, vol. 43, 1993, pp. 96–107.

Larson, Charles U. *Persuasion: Reception and Responsibility*. 7th ed., Wadsworth, 1995.

Lawprofblawg and Darren Bush. "LAW REVIEWS, CITATION COUNTS, and TWITTER (Oh my!): Behind the Curtains of the Law Professor's Search for Meaning." *Loyola University Chicago Law Journal*, vol. 50, 2018, pp. 327–64.

Lawrence, Windy Y. "A Crisis in Civil Rights Leadership: The Prophetic Persona in Lyndon B. Johnson's Howard University Address." *Texas Speech Communication Journal*, vol. 31, 2007, pp. 35–43.

Leff, Michael. "The Habitation of Rhetoric." *Argument and Critical Practices: Proceedings of the Fifth SCA/AFA Conference on Argumentation*, edited by Joseph W. Wenzel, Speech Communication Association, 1987, pp. 1–8.

Leflar, Robert A. "The Law Teacher's Place in the American Legal Profession." *Journal of the Society of Public Teachers of Law*, vol. 8, 1964, pp. 21–30.

Legally Blonde. Directed by Robert Luketic, performances by Reese Witherspoon, Luke Wilson, Selma Blair, Matthew Davis, Victor Garber, and Jennifer Coolidge, Metro-Goldwyn-Mayer Pictures, 2001.

Leleiko, Steven H. "Legal Education—Some Crucial Frontiers." *Journal of Legal Education*, vol. 23, 1971, pp. 502–27.

Levit, Nancy. "Scholarship Advice for New Law Professors in the Electronic Age." *Widener Law Journal*, vol. 16, 2007, pp. 947–82.

Levy, Leonard W. "Introduction: The Making of the Constitution, 1776–1789." *Essays on the Making of the Constitution*, edited by Levy, 7th ed., Oxford UP, 1987, pp. ix–xl.

Liemer, Susan P., and Hollee S. Temple. "Did Your Legal Writing Professor Go to Harvard? The Credentials of Legal Writing Faculty at Hiring Time." *University of Louisville Law Review*, vol. 46, 2008, pp. 383–436.

Litvak, Kate. "Blog as a Bugged Water Cooler." *Washington University Law Review*, vol. 84, 2006, pp. 1061–70.

Llewellyn, K. N. "On What Is Wrong with So-Called Legal Education." *Columbia Law Review*, vol. 35, 1935, pp. 651–78.

Longtin, Krista, and Kelsey Binion. "Creating Choice and Building Consensus: Invitational Rhetoric as a Strategy to Promote Vasectomies in the United States." *Rhetoric of Health & Medicine*, vol. 4, 2021, pp. 367–87.

Lozano-Reich, Nina M., and Dana L. Cloud. "The Uncivil Tongue: Invitational Rhetoric and the Problem of Inequality." *Western Journal of Communication*, vol. 73, 2009, pp. 220–26.

Macfarlane, Julie. "Experiences of Collaborative Law: Preliminary Results from the Collaborative Lawyering Research Project." *Journal of Dispute Resolution*, vol. 2004, 2004, pp. 179–227.

MacKinnon, Catherine A. "Feminism, Marxism, Method and the State: An Agenda for Theory." *Signs: Journal of Women in Culture and Society*, vol. 7, 1982, pp. 515–44.

Makau, Josina M. "A Conversation about Communication Ethics with Josina M. Makau." *Exploring Communication Ethics: Interviews with Influential Scholars in the Field*, edited by Pat Arneson, Peter Lang, 2007, pp. 69–87.

---. "Revisioning the Argumentation Course." *Women's Studies in Communication*, vol. 15, 1992, pp. 79–91.

Makau, Josina M., and Debian L. Marty. *Cooperative Argumentation: A Model for Deliberative Community*. Waveland, 2001.

Make, Jeremy, and Adam Lauver. "Increasing Trust and Vaccine Uptake: Offering Invitational Rhetoric as an Alternative to Persuasion in Pediatric Visits with Vaccine-Hesitant Parents (VHPs)." *Vaccine: X*, vol. 10, 2022, pp. 1–9.

Mallin, Irwin, and Karrin Vasby Anderson. "Inviting Constructive Argument." *Argumentation and Advocacy*, vol. 36, 2000, pp. 120–33.

Malone, Dumas. *The Story of the Declaration of Independence*. Oxford UP, 1954.

Manley, Stewart. "Degree (Un)Equivalencies: The Confounding Case of the Juris Doctor." *Journal of Legal Education*, vol. 68, 2019, pp. 392–415.

Markovic, Milan. "The Law Professor Pipeline." *Temple Law Review*, vol. 92, 2020, pp. 813–35.

Martin, Paul L. "Practical Legal Education." *American Law School Review*, vol. 3, 1913, pp. 237–40.

Matlon, Ronald J. "Bridging the Gap between Communication Education and Legal Education." *Communication Education*, vol. 31, 1982, pp. 39–53.

---. "Teaching Communication in the Legal Process." *Communication Education*, vol. 30, 1981, pp. 399–409.

Matthews, Donald R. *The Social Background of Political Decision-Makers*. Doubleday, 1954.

Maynard, Goldburn P. "Killing the Motivation of the Minority Law Professor." *Minnesota Law Review*, vol. 107, 2022, pp. 245–96.

McBath, James H. "Speech and the Legal Profession." *Speech Teacher*, vol. 10, 1961, pp. 44–47.

McCrary, Justin, et al. "The Ph.D. Rises in American Law Schools, 1960–2011: What Does It Mean for Legal Education?" *Journal of Legal Education*, vol. 65, 2016, pp. 543–79.

McDonald, Nicole D. "The Persona of the Humble Teacher: A Rhetorical Theory to Engage in Dialogue about Sexuality in the Church." *Journal of Communication and Religion*, vol. 45, 2022, pp. 86–96.

McDougall, Harold. "The Rebellious Law Professor: Combining Cause and Reflective Lawyering." *Journal of Legal Education*, vol. 65, 2015, pp. 326–51.

McFarland, Douglas D. "Self-Images of Law Professors: Rethinking the Schism in Legal Education." *Journal of Legal Education*, vol. 35, 1985, pp. 232–60.

---. "Students and Practicing Lawyers Identify the Ideal Law Professor." *Journal of Legal Education*, vol. 36, 1986, pp. 93–107.

McFarland, Douglas Dale. *Self-Images of Law Professors: Rethinking Legal Education*. 1983. University of Minnesota, Ph.D. dissertation.

McGovney, Dudley O. "The Function of the American University Law School." *American Law School Review*, vol. 3, 1911, pp. 17–19.

McPeak, Agnieszka. "The Internet Made Me Do It: Reconciling Social Media and Professional Norms for Lawyers, Judges, and Law Professors." *Idaho Law Review*, vol. 55, 2019, pp. 205–32.

Mehler, Irving M. "In Defense of Practitioners as Teachers." *Journal of Legal Education*, vol. 9, 1956, pp. 231–34.

Mertz, Elizabeth. *The Language of Law School: Learning to "Think like a Lawyer."* Oxford UP, 2007.

Meyerson, Michael I. "Law School Culture and the Lost Art of Collaboration: Why Don't Law Professors Play Well with Others?" *Nebraska Law Review*, vol. 93, 2015, pp. 547–91.

Minei, Elizabeth M., et al. "Modern Day Digital Pen Pals: A Semester-Long Collaborative Online International Learning (COIL) Project." *Communication Teacher*, vol. 35, 2021, pp. 336–44.

"Minnesota Adopts J.D. Degree." *The Student Lawyer Journal*, vol. 12, 1967, p. 24.

Mitchell, Gordon R., et al. "The Debate Authors Working Group Model for Collaborative Knowledge Production in Forensics Scholarship." *Argumentation and Advocacy*, vol. 47, 2010, pp. 1–24.

Moliterno, James E. "Exporting American Legal Education." *Journal of Legal Education*, vol. 58, 2008, pp. 274–89.

Monk, Linda R. *The Words We Live By: Your Annotated Guide to the Constitution*. Hyperion, 2003.

Morris, Charles E. "Pink Herring & the Fourth Persona: J. Edgar Hoover's Sex Crime Panic." *Quarterly Journal of Speech*, vol. 88, 2002, pp. 228–44.

Moses, Marlene Eskind, and Manuel Benjamin Russ. "A Paradigm Shift to Collaborative Law." *Tennessee Bar Journal*, vol. 55, 2019, pp. 23–25.

Newton, Brent E. "The Ninety-Five Theses: Systemic Reforms of American Legal Education and Licensure." *South Carolina Law Review*, vol. 64, 2012, pp. 55–141.

---. "Preaching What They Don't Practice: Why Law Faculties' Preoccupation with Impractical Scholarship and Devaluation of Practical Competencies Obstruct Reform in the Legal Academy." *South Carolina Law Review*, vol. 62, 2010, pp. 105–56.

New York Times Co. v. Sullivan. 376 U.S. 254 (1964). *Library of Congress*, tile.loc.gov/storage-services/service/ll/usrep/usrep376/usrep376254/usrep376254.pdf. Accessed 28 June 2023.

O'Connell, Johannah. "Don't Settle for 'the Devil You Know': The Benefits of Using Collaborative Law rather than Litigation to Resolve Employment Disputes." *Indiana Law Review*, vol. 49, 2016, pp. 533–53.

Ofulue, Nneka Ifeoma. "President Clinton and the White House Prayer Breakfast." *Journal of Communication and Religion*, vol. 25, 2002, pp. 49–63.

Orbe, Mark P., and Gabrielle L. Orbe. "Progressive Political Leadership through an Orientation of Invitational Rhetoric: An Analysis of the Twittersphere of 'The Squad.'" *Journal of Contemporary Rhetoric*, vol. 12, 2022, pp. 17–33.

Organ, Jerome M. "Legal Education and the Legal Profession: Convergence or Divergence?" *Ohio Northern University Law Review*, vol. 38, 2012, pp. 885–909.

Orschel, Albert K. "Is Legal Education Doing Its Job? Brief of *Amicus Curiae*." *American Bar Association Journal*, vol. 40, 1954, pp. 121–24, 166–69.

Ostrom, Jason. "The Competing Roles of Law Professors." *South Texas Law Review*, vol. 42, 2001, pp. 539–44.

Palazzolo, Joe. "Law Grads Face Brutal Job Market." *The Wall Street Journal*, 25 June 2012, www.wsj.com/articles/SB10001424052702304458604577486623469958142. Accessed 28 June 2023.

Palczewski, Catherine Helen. "Argument in an Off Key: Playing with the Productive Limits of Argument." *Arguing Communication and Culture: Selected Papers from the Twelfth NCA/AFA Conference on Argumentation*, edited by Thomas Goodnight, National Communication Association, 2002, pp. 1–23.

---. "Special Issue: Argumentation and Feminisms." *Argumentation and Advocacy*, vol. 32, 1996, pp. 161–69.

Paliewicz, Nicholas S. "Industrial Pioneerism in the Beehive State: Rio Tinto and the Corporate Persona." *Western Journal of Communication*, vol. 86, 2022, pp. 60–82.

The Paper Chase. Directed by James Bridges, performances by Timothy Bottoms, Lindsay Wagner, and John Houseman, 20th Century Fox, 1973.

Papke, David Ray. "Crusading Hero, Devoted Teacher, and Sympathetic Failure: The Self-Image of the Law Professor in Hollywood Cinema and in Real Life, Too." *Vermont Law Review*, vol. 28, 2004, pp. 957–73.

Pariera, Katrina L., and Jeanine W. Turner. "Invitational Rhetoric between Parents and Adolescents: Strategies for Successful Communication." *Journal of Family Communication*, vol. 20, 2020, pp. 175–88.

Pasley, Robert S. "The Position of the Law School in the University." *Catholic University Law Review*, vol. 16, 1966, pp. 34–52.

Pauley, John L. "Reshaping Public Persona and the Prophetic *Ethos*: Louis Farrakhan at the Million Man March." *Western Journal of Communication*, vol. 62, 1998, pp. 512–36.

Pedrioli, Carlo A. "Judicial Neutrality Awash with Ideology: Justice Scalia, Sexual Orientation, and Rhetorical Personae." *Texas Journal on Civil Liberties & Civil Rights*, vol. 21, 2016, pp. 183–217.

---. "A New Image in the Looking Glass: Faculty Mentoring, Invitational Rhetoric, and the Second-Class Status of Women in U.S. Academia." *Hastings Women's Law Journal*, vol. 15, 2004, pp. 185–215.

---. "Pope Francis, Poverty, and the Third Persona." *Iowa Journal of Gender, Race & Justice*, vol. 21, 2018, pp. 367–93.

Persky, Anna Stolley. "Law School? Bag It, Bloggers Say." *ABA Journal*, 1 Feb. 2011, www.abajournal.com/magazine/article/law_school_bag_it_bloggers_say. Accessed 28 June 2023.

Peters, John Durham. *Speaking into the Air: A History of the Idea of Communication.* U of Chicago P, 1999.

Pickering, Barbara A. "Women's Voices as Evidence: Personal Testimony in Pro-Choice Films." *Argumentation and Advocacy*, vol. 40, 2003, pp. 1–22.

Posner, Richard A. "The Present Situation in Legal Scholarship." *Yale Law Journal*, vol. 90, 1981, pp. 1113–30.

Pound, Roscoe. "The Achievement of the American Law School." *Dicta*, vol. 38, 1961, pp. 269–75.

---. "Some Comments on Law Teachers and Law Teaching." *Journal of Legal Education*, vol. 3, 1951, pp. 519–32.

Power, Garrett. "In Defense of the J.D." *Journal of Legal Education*, vol. 20, 1967, pp. 67–70.

Presser, Stephen B. *Law Professors: Three Centuries of Shaping American Law.* West Academic, 2017.

Prosser, William L. "Advice to the Lovelorn." *Journal of Legal Education*, vol. 3, 1951, pp. 505–14.

Re, Edward D. "Law Office Sabbaticals for Law Professors." *Journal of Legal Education*, vol. 45, 1995, pp. 95–98.

Reardon, Sean F., et al. "Race, Income, and Enrollment Patterns in Highly Selective Colleges, 1982–2004." *Stanford University Center for Education Policy Analysis*, 3 Aug. 2012, cepa.stanford.edu/sites/default/files/race%20income%20%26%20selective%20college%20enrollment%20august%203%202012.pdf. Accessed 28 June 2023.

Redding, Richard E. "'Where Did You Go to Law School?' Gatekeeping for the Professoriate and Its Implications for Legal Education." *Journal of Legal Education*, vol. 53, 2003, pp. 594–614.

Rehnquist, William H. "The Legal Profession Today." *Indiana Law Journal*, vol. 62, 1987, pp. 151–57.

Reimann, Mathias. "A Career in Itself: The German Professoriate as a Model for American Legal Academica." *The Reception of Continental Ideas in the Common Law World: 1820–1920*, edited by Reimann, Duncker & Humblot, 1993, pp. 165–202.

---. "Nineteenth Century German Legal Science." *Boston College Law Review*, vol. 31, 1990, pp. 837–97.

Reuschlein, Harold Gill. "Law Professor—Post-War." *Minnesota Law Review*, vol. 30, 1946, pp. 68–77.

Reynolds, Douglas C., and Doris F. Tennant. "Collaborative Law—An Emerging Practice." *Boston Bar Journal*, vol. 45, Nov.–Dec. 2001, pp. 12–13, 27–29.

Richards, H. S. "Discussion: The Ultimate Function of the Teacher of Law." *American Law School Review*, vol. 3, 1911, pp. 8–9.

Rieke, Richard D., et al. *Argumentation and Critical Decision Making*. 6th ed., Pearson, 2005.

Rieke, Richard Davis. *Rhetorical Theory in American Legal Practice*. 1964. Ohio State University, Ph.D. dissertation.

Roberts, John. "A Conversation with Chief Justice Roberts." Interview by J. Harvie Wilkinson. *C-SPAN*, 25 June 2011, www.c-span.org/video/?300203-1/conversation-chief-justice-roberts. Accessed 28 June 2023.

Robinson, Nick. "The Decline of the Lawyer-Politician." *Buffalo Law Review*, vol. 65, 2017, pp. 657–737.

Rodell, Fred. "Goodbye to Law Reviews." *Virginia Law Review*, vol. 23, 1936, pp. 38–45.

Rohr, Marc. "A Law School for the Consumer." *Nova Law Review*, vol. 13, 1988, pp. 101–05.

Rossiter, Clinton. *1787: The Grand Convention*. Macmillan, 1966.

Rubin, Edward L. "Law and and the Methodology of Law." *Wisconsin Law Review*, vol. 1997, 1997, pp. 521–65.

Ruhl, J. B., et al. "Total Scholarly Impact: Law Professor Citations in Non-Law Journals." *Journal of Legal Education*, vol. 69, 2020, pp. 782–815.

Rutledge, Njeri Mathis. "Walking the Tightrope: Reflections of a Black Female Law Professor." *Campbell Law Review*, vol. 43, 2021, pp. 233–41.

Schlegel, John Henry. "Between the Harvard Founders and the American Legal Realists: The Professionalization of the American Law Professor." *Journal of Legal Education*, vol. 35, 1985, pp. 311–25.

Schoenfeld, Marcus. "J.D. or LL.B. as the Basic Law Degree?" *Cleveland-Marshall Law Review*, vol. 12, 1963, pp. 573–79.

Schultheis, Emily. "*Sitzfleisch*: The German Concept to Get More Work Done." *BBC*, 4 Sept. 2018, www.bbc.com/worklife/article/20180903-to-have-sitzfleisch---its-a-professional-compliment. Accessed 28 June 2023.

Schuwerk, Robert P. "The Law Professor as Fiduciary: What Duties Do We Owe to Our Students." *South Texas Law Review*, vol. 45, 2004, pp. 753–813.

Schwab, William H. "Collaborative Lawyering: A Closer Look at an Emerging Practice." *Pepperdine Dispute Resolution Law Journal*, vol. 4, 2004, pp. 351–99.

Scott, A. O. "A Rich Ditz Has Both Brains and the Last Laugh." *The New York Times*, 13 July 2001, www.nytimes.com/2001/07/13/movies/film-review-a-rich-ditz-has-both-brains-and-the-last-laugh.html. Accessed 28 June 2023.

"SCU School of Law Offers Exciting New Course." *Santa Clara University School of Law*, 25 Feb. 2003, law.scu.edu/news/scu-school-of-law-offers-exciting-new-course/. Accessed 28 June 2023.

Secunda, Paul M. "Tales of a Law Professor Lateral Nothing." *University of Memphis Law Review*, vol. 39, 2008, pp. 125–51.

Segal, David. "What They Don't Teach Law Students: Lawyering." *The New York Times*, 19 Nov. 2011, www.nytimes.com/2011/11/20/business/after-law-school-associates-learn-to-be-lawyers.html. Accessed 28 June 2023.

Segall, Eric J., and Adam Feldman. "The Elite Teaching the Elite: Who Gets Hired by the Top Law Schools?" *Journal of Legal Education*, vol. 68, 2019, pp. 614–22.

Seligman, Joel. *The High Citadel: The Influence of Harvard Law School.* Houghton, 1978.

Sheppard, Steve. "An Introductory History of Law in the Lecture Hall." *The History of Legal Education in the United States*, edited by Sheppard, vol. 1, Salem Press, 1999, pp. 7–71.

Silverman, Hugh W. "The Practitioner as a Law Teacher." *Journal of Legal Education*, vol. 23, 1971, pp. 424–39.

Sloan, Thomas O. "The Persona as Rhetor: An Interpretation of Donne's *Satyre III*." *Quarterly Journal of Speech*, vol. 51, 1965, pp. 14–27.

Smith, Craig R. "The Persona of Jesus in the Gospel according to St. Matthew." *Journal of Communication and Religion*, vol. 14, 1991, pp. 57–69.

Smith, George P. "Much Ado about Nothing—The J.D. Movement." *The Student Lawyer Journal*, vol. 11, 1966, pp. 8–10, 26–27.

Smith, Nanci A. "Divorce with Dignity: Using the Collaborative Law Approach to Achieve Procedural, Substantive and Psychological Satisfaction." *Vermont Bar Journal*, vol. 42, spr. 2016, pp. 24–26.

Smith, Ralph. "The Teaching of Public Speaking in Law Schools." *Quarterly Journal of Speech Education*, vol. 11, 1925, pp. 54–57.

Snow, C. P. *The Two Cultures and the Scientific Revolution*. Cambridge UP, 1959.

Solum, Lawrence B. "Blogging and the Transformation of Legal Scholarship." *Washington University Law Review*, vol. 84, 2006, pp. 1071–88.

Stein, Jay W. "The Juris Doctor." *Journal of Legal Education*, vol. 15, 1963, pp. 315–20.

Stevens, Robert. "American Legal Scholarship: Structural Constraints and Intellectual Conceptualism." *Journal of Legal Education*, vol. 33, 1983, pp. 442–48.

---. *Law School: Legal Education in America from the 1850s to the 1980s*. U of North Carolina P, 1983.

---. "Legal Education: The Challenge of the Past." *New York Law School Law Review*, vol. 30, 1985, pp. 475–90.

Stone, Harlan F. "The Function of the American University Law School." *American Law School Review*, vol. 3, 1911, pp. 11–17.

---. "The Future of Legal Education." *American Bar Association Journal*, vol. 10, 1924, pp. 233–35.

---. "The Importance of Actual Experience at the Bar as a Preparation for Teaching Law." *American Law School Review*, vol. 3, 1912, pp. 205–11.

Strickland, Elizabeth K. "Putting 'Counselor' Back in the Lawyer's Job Description: Why More States Should Adopt Collaborative Law Statutes." *North Carolina Law Review*, vol. 84, 2006, pp. 979–1012.

"The Study of Legal Education." *American Law School Review*, vol. 3, 1914, pp. 450–54.

Sullivan, William M., et al. *Educating Lawyers: Preparation for the Profession of Law.* Carnegie Foundation for the Advancement of Teaching, 2007.

Swiencicki, Jill. "Rhetorics of Invitation and Refusal in Terry Tempest Williams's *The Open Space of Democracy*." *Women's Studies in Communication*, vol. 38, 2015, pp. 151–66.

Swygert, Michael I. "Striving to Make Great Lawyers—Citizenship and Moral Responsibility: A Jurisprudence for Law Teaching." *Boston College Law Review*, vol. 30, 1989, pp. 803–20.

Swygert, Michael I., and Jon W. Bruce. "The Historical Origins, Founding, and Early Development of Student-Edited Law Reviews." *Hastings Law Journal*, vol. 36, 1985, pp. 739–91.

Taft, William Howard. "Legal Education and the University Law School." *Minnesota Law Review*, vol. 10, 1926, pp. 554–56.

Tamanaha, Brian Z. *Failing Law Schools*. U of Chicago P, 2012.

Tamer, Christine, and Melissa Shultz. "The Adaptable Law Professor: Ten Tips for Keeping the Magic of an Oral Argument Competition Alive on Zoom." *Syllabus*, vol. 52, 2021, qa.americanbar.org/groups/legal_education/publications/syllabus_home/volume-52-2020-2021/syllabus-winter-2021-52-2/adaptable-law-professor. Accessed 28 June 2023.

Tesler, Pauline H. "Collaborative Family Law." *Pepperdine Dispute Resolution Law Journal*, vol. 4, 2004, pp. 317–36.

---. "Collaborative Law: A New Paradigm for Divorce Lawyers." *Psychology, Public Policy and Law*, vol. 5, 1999, pp. 967–1000.

Thayer, Ezra Ripley. "Note." *Harvard Law Review*, vol. 25, 1912, pp. 269–73.

Thayer, James Bradley. "The Teaching of English Law at Universities." *Harvard Law Review*, vol. 9, 1895, pp. 169–84.

Tindall, Harry L., and Jennie R. Smith. "The Uniform Collaborative Law Act as a Teaching Tool." *Hofstra Law Review*, vol. 38, 2009, pp. 685–98.

Tocqueville, Alexis de. *Democracy in America*. Translated by George Lawrence and edited by J. P. Mayer, HarperCollins, 2000.

Tolman, Elizabeth G. "Observing Cell Phone Use and Enhancing Collaborative Learning Using a Wiki." *Communication Teacher*, vol. 27, 2013, pp. 16–20.

Towers, Walter K. "A Student's Opinion of Practical Law School Instruction." *American Law School Review*, vol. 2, 1911, pp. 556–58.

Traynor, Roger J. "To the Right Honorable Law Reviews." *UCLA Law Review*, vol. 10, 1962, pp. 3–10.

Turner, Jeanine Warisse, and Sonja K. Foss. "Options for the Construction of Attentional Social Presence in a Digitally Enhanced Multicommunicative Environment." *Communication Theory*, vol. 28, 2018, pp. 22–45.

Turner, Paaige K., and Patricia Ryden. "How George Bush Silenced Anita Hill: A Derridian View of the Third Persona in Public Argument." *Argumentation and Advocacy*, vol. 37, 2000, pp. 86–97.

Turow, Scott. "Law School v. Reality." *The New York Times Magazine*, 18 Sept. 1988, www.nytimes.com/1988/09/18/magazine/law-school-v-reality.html. Accessed 28 June 2023.

"2014 Law Graduate Employment Data." *American Bar Association Section of Legal Education and Admissions to the Bar*, 28 Apr. 2015, www.americanbar.org/content/dam/aba/administrative/legal_education_and_admissions_to_the_bar/statistics/2014_law_graduate_employment_data_042915.authcheckdam.pdf. Accessed 28 June 2023.

Ulen, Thomas S. "The Unexpected Guest: Law and Economics, Law and Other Cognate Disciplines, and the Future of Legal Scholarship." *Chicago-Kent Law Review*, vol. 79, 2004, pp. 403–29.

Underwood, Willard A. "A Survey of Lawyers' Training in and Attitudes toward Speech in Illinois." *Journal of the American Forensic Association*, vol. 6, 1969, pp. 108–10.

U.S. Const. art. II, § 1, cl. 1. *Constitution Annotated*, constitution.congress.gov/browse/article-2/section-1/. Accessed 28 June 2023.

Vance, William R. "The Ultimate Function of the Teacher of Law." *American Law School Review*, vol. 3, 1911, pp. 2–8.

Van Zile, Philip T. "Practice Work in the Law Colleges." *American Law School Review*, vol. 2, 1907, pp. 71–76.

Veysey, Laurence R. *The Emergence of the American University*. U of Chicago P, 1965.

Voegele, Gary L., et al. "Collaborative Law: A Useful Tool for the Family Law Practitioner to Promote Better Outcomes." *William Mitchell Law Review*, vol. 33, 2007, pp. 971–1027.

Waisanen, Don J., and Amy B. Becker. "The Problem with Being Joe Biden: Political Comedy and Circulating Personae." *Critical Studies in Media Communication*, vol. 32, 2015, pp. 256–71.

Wald, Eli. "A Thought Experiment about the Academic 'Billable' Hour or Law Professors' Work Habits." *Marquette Law Review*, vol. 101, 2018, pp. 991–1018.

Wald, Patricia M. "Teaching the Trade: An Appellate Judge's View of Practice-Oriented Legal Education." *Journal of Legal Education*, vol. 36, 1986, pp. 35–44.

Walker, Gregg B., and Steven E. Daniels. "Dialogue and Deliberation in Environmental Conflict: Enacting Civic Science." *Environmental Communication Yearbook*, edited by Susan L. Senecah, Lawrence Erlbaum, 2004, pp. 135–52.

Wander, Philip. "The Third Persona: An Ideological Turn in Rhetorical Theory." *Central States Speech Journal*, vol. 35, 1984, pp. 197–216.

Ware, B. L., and Wil A. Linkugel. "The Rhetorical *Persona*: Marcus Garvey as Black Moses." *Communication Monographs*, vol. 49, 1982, pp. 50–62.

Warkentine, Edith R. "Kingsfield Doesn't Teach My Contracts Class: Using Contracts to Teach Contracts." *Journal of Legal Education*, vol. 50, 2000, pp. 112–33.

Warren, Charles. *A History of the American Bar*. Little, Brown, 1911.

Waxman, Seth P. "Rebuilding Bridges: The Bar, the Bench, and the Academy." *University of Pennsylvania Law Review*, vol. 150, 2002, pp. 1905–13.

Weaver, Richard M. *The Ethics of Rhetoric*. Henry Regnery, 1953.

Webb, Stu. "Collaborative Law Introduction." *Pepperdine Dispute Resolution Law Journal*, vol. 4, 2004, p. 315.

Wei, Fang-Yi Flora. "Creating a Collaborative 'Hot Clock': Using Smart Phones to Motivate Students' Learning in News Interviewing and Reporting." *Communication Teacher*, vol. 30, 2016, pp. 11–16.

Weisbrod, Carol. "Brahmin Connections: A Note on the Vocation of the Law Professor." *Connecticut Law Review*, vol. 52, 2021, pp. 1653–82.

Wellington, Harry H. "Challenges to Legal Education: The 'Two Cultures' Phenomenon." *Journal of Legal Education*, vol. 37, 1987, pp. 327–30.

Wheaton, Carl C. "Law Teaching and Pragmatism." *Georgetown Law Journal*, vol. 25, 1937, pp. 338–50.

Williams, Donald E. "Group Discussion and Argumentation in Legal Education." *Quarterly Journal of Speech*, vol. 41, 1955, pp. 397–402.

Woodyard, Kerith M. "Competition and Control: The Open Hand of Dialogue in a Closed-Fist Tradition." *The Forensic of Pi Kappa Delta*, vol. 87, 2002, pp. 13–24.

---. "Depatriarchalizing in Rhetorical Theory: Toward a Feminist Prophetic Tradition." *Ohio Communication Journal*, vol. 48, 2010, pp. 27–42.

---. "'If by Martyrdom I Can Advance My Race One Step, I Am Ready for It': Prophetic *Ethos* and the Reception of Elizabeth Cady Stanton's *The Woman's Bible*." *Journal of Communication and Religion*, vol. 31, 2008, pp. 272–326.

Zarefsky, David. "Future Directions in Argumentation Theory and Practice." *Perspectives on Argumentation: Essays in Honor of Wayne Brockriede*, edited by Robert Trapp and Janice Schuetz, Waveland, 1990, pp. 287–97.

Zietlow, Rebecca E. "Writing Scholarship While You Practice Law." *Michigan Journal of Race & Law*, vol. 7, 2002, pp. 511–16.

Zimmerman, Emily. "Should Law Professors Have a Continuing Practice Experience (CPE) Requirement?" *Northeastern University Law Journal*, vol. 6, 2013, pp. 131–87.

Zulick, Margaret D. "The Agon of Jeremiah: On the Dialogic Invention of Prophetic Ethos." *Quarterly Journal of Speech*, vol. 78, 1992, pp. 125–48.

Index

E

F